# American
# Costume Jewelry

## Art & Industry, 1935-1950

## N-Z

Roberto Brunialti
&
Carla Ginelli Brunialti

Schiffer Publishing Ltd

4880 Lower Valley Road  Atglen, Pennsylvania 19310

# CREDITS

Photographs: Douglas Congdon-Martin.
English translation (revised by the author): Globostudio Como.
Posters Reproductions courtesy of: URL and Northwestern University Library, Curtis Publications Inc., USA Navy Archives.

Copyright © 2008 by Roberto Brunialti
Library of Congress Control Number: 2008926126

Designed by John P. Cheek
Cover design by Bruce Waters
Type set in Tiffany Lt BT/Souvenir Lt BT

ISBN: 978-0-7643-2983-8

Printed in China

Schiffer Books are available at special discounts for bulk purchases for sales promotions or premiums. Special editions, including personalized covers, corporate imprints, and excerpts can be created in large quantities for special needs. For more information contact the publisher:

Published by Schiffer Publishing Ltd.
4880 Lower Valley Road
Atglen, PA 19310
Phone: (610) 593-1777; Fax: (610) 593-2002
E-mail: Info@schifferbooks.com

For the largest selection of fine reference books on this and related subjects, please visit our web site at
**www.schifferbooks.com**
We are always looking for people to write books on new and related subjects. If you have an idea for a book please contact us at the above address.

This book may be purchased from the publisher.
Include $3.95 for shipping.
Please try your bookstore first.
You may write for a free catalog.

In Europe, Schiffer books are distributed by
Bushwood Books
6 Marksbury Ave.
Kew Gardens
Surrey TW9 4JF England
Phone: 44 (0) 20 8392-8585; Fax: 44 (0) 20 8392-9876
E-mail: info@bushwoodbooks.co.uk
Website: www.bushwoodbooks.co.uk
Free postage in the U.K., Europe; air mail at cost.

# CONTENTS
## Volume 2

# ABBREVIATIONS

AC = Accessocraft
AM = Albert Manufacturing
An = Anthony
B = Boucher
C = Coro
Ch = Chanel
BB = Bates & Bacon
Ca = Castlecliff
CLV = Calvaire
DJ = Dujay
DR = De Rosa
E= Eisenberg
EL = Elzac
ES = Ernest Steiner
FB = Fred A. Block
H = Hobé
HA = Hess – Appel
HC = Hattie Carnegie
J = Joseff
JB = Jelly Bellies
Kr = Kreisler
LG = Leo Glass
M = Mazer
MH = Miriam Haskell
Mo = Mosell
Mrl = Marleen
Mrs = Marslieu
NB = Natacha Brooks
NLUM = Nat Levy – Urie Mandle

P = Pennino
PAC = Patriotic Accessocraft
PB = Patriotic Boucher
PC = Patriotic Coro
PCar = Patriotic Cartier
PCh = Patriotic Chanel
PGP = Patriotic Goldstein – Poland
PLG = Patriotic Leo Glass
PR = Patriotic Réja
PRW = Patriotic Rice-Weiner
PSi = Patriotic Silson
PSt = Patriotic Staret
PT = Patriotic Trifari
PU = Patriotic Unsigned
PWL = Patriotic Walter Lampl
R = Réja
Rb = Rebajes
Re = Reinad
RW = Rice-Weiner
S = Sandor
Si = Silson
St = Staret
Sch = Schiaparelli
T = Trifari
U = Unsigned
UM = Urie Mandle
Unc = Uncas
WL = Walter Lampl

# MANUFACTURERS

## NORMA JEWELRY, CORP.

*See JB139.*

## PENNINO

Oreste Pennino was born in Naples in 1888. He was his father Pasquale's child by his first marriage. His father's second marriage to Giuseppina Vergati produced four more children: Maria, Anselmo (later called Frank), Gennaro (called Jack), and Carmela. In 1904 Pasquale Pennino with his sixteen year old son Oreste emigrated to New York on the Vincenzo Florio ship, arriving in the States on 14th November. The profession indicated by both on the immigration form was goldsmith. Father and son settled in Brooklyn, with Pasquale's brother-in-law, Domenico Migliaro, at 604 Hicks Street. Then, after a while, they moved to 211 Hamilton Avenue. In 1908 Pasquale's second wife and four children also emigrated to America on The Cedric ship. On 17th May 1908, a few weeks after the arrival of the family, Pasquale died and Oreste, aged twenty, had to take on the role of father to his younger siblings. In 1927 Oreste, by then an American citizen, founded the Oreste Pennino company which, when his two brothers Anselmo and Gennaro joined the company (1930?), was renamed Pennino Brothers, with offices in New York, at 38 West 48th Street. Practically at the same time as the company was established, a trademark with the nine Zodiac signs (Sagittarius, Virgo, Aquarius, Taurus, Libra, Cancer, Gemini, Capricorn and Scorpio) was registered. On 14th August 1928 Pennino patented two designs: a brooch with the Libra sign (des. pat. n. 73,039) and a bracelet with the Virgo sign (des. pat. n. 73,040), respectively. *WWD*, on 8th August 1931, reported that the Pennino Bros. had presented a 14/k gold brooch collection entirely made by hand in the "French Colonial" style, that had become fashionable on the wake of an exhibition with this theme held in Paris that year. A line of rings completed the collection. There is, unfortunately, no trace of this or any other collections up to 1939 on the antique market.

On 23rd May 1939, Pennino patented a novelty brooch made of rhodium-plated metal with red and green enamel details, rhinestones and baguettes of a pre-Disney Pinocchio inspired by illustrations in Collodi's book (P1.); it was one of very few figurative subjects made by Pennino. A fourth patent obtained on 20th February 1940 was for the design of a tree with a rhinestone-studded trunk and round pearl blossoms on the branches (P2.). Although Pennino's sterling production was rather plentiful, having started during wartime, (at the end of 1942), no patent was submitted by Pennino between 1940 and 1946, therefore any unpatented pieces can be attributed with good approximation to that period.

On 12th February 1946, designs of two sterling brooches with floral motifs were patented (P8. and P9.) and on 26th February a "jewelry finding" reproducing the motif of one of the two brooches was also patented (des. pat. n. 143,988). Then, in 1947, a shining sun made of sterling or gold-plated metal was patented, followed, in 1948, by a sterling tree with rhinestone-studded trunk and red rhinestone flowers (which were also reproduced in other brooches made in the same year), "Sunburst" and "Tree," respectively (P5. e P3.). In 1948 another tree similar to the 1940 design (des. pat. n. 149,833 of 1st June 1948) and a sterling brooch with a watch (des. pat. n. 151,529) were patented.

*WWD*, April 11, 1947: "Curved, radiating spray" by Pennino Brothers.

**Sparkling Sprays For Glamor**

X222

The last six Pennino patents are designs of watches with sterling bracelets and rhinestone and baguette details (11th January 1949 from des.pat. n. 152,352 to des. pat. n. 152,357). This line was advertised with the slogan "The Pennino Look," in "Jewelers' Circular Keystone," October 1948.

Oreste Pennino is the only known designer for this company.

All items are marked "Pennino" in small block letters with the addition, whenever it was the case, of "Sterling." In the period herein reviewed the trademark had not been registered.

Production continued throughout the early 1950s and was always characterized by good quality items made of rhodium or gold-plated metal with stones and rhinestones.

In 1964 the Pennino Brothers company was quoted on the stock market and the three brothers were its major shareholders. However, they no longer worked for the company, which a few years later ceased business.

In spite of its excellent design and manufacturing quality, costume jewelry designed by Pennino was somehow repetitive with its mainly floral or plant motifs and constant tendency to imitate precious jewels in the so-called "real look" style.

P1. "Pinocchio," Pennino 1939****
Manufacturer Pennino Bros.
Designer Oreste Pennino.
Patent n° 114,905 Oreste Pennino, New York, 23rd May 1939, filed on 1st April 1939.

P2. "Apple Tree," Pennino 1940****
Manufacturer Pennino Bros.
Designer Oreste Pennino.
Patent n° 119,091 Oreste Pennino, New York, 20th February 1940, filed on 17th January 1940.

Rhodium and gold plated metal pin clip of Collodi's Pinocchio, wearing green enamel clothes with red enamel trimmings, black enamel shoes, long socks with baguettes and rhinestone pavé beret with black enamel accents for his hair, eyes and the joints of his hinged limbs. 6x4cm.
Marked Des. Pat. 114905.
The subject was inspired by traditional Pinocchio iconography, the puppet character in Carlo Lorenzini's (known as Collodi) book of 1883, which at the time was well-known and much loved in Italy, but was not so famous in the States. It was only in 1940, after Walt Disney made the famous cartoon movie of the same name, that the story and the characters in the book became famous abroad. In the movie version however, the imagery of the story was completely altered. Except for the Zodiac signs of 1928, this is the first and only patent issued to Pennino for a design of a human subject.

Rhodium plated metal brooch with rhinestones and grey pearl essence, depicting an apple tree. 4.5x5.8cm.
Marked Pennino.
The patent refers to a pin clip and has an additional downward facing branch on the right. This model was manufactured both in a larger pin clip version, and in a smaller brooch version.

P3. "Tree," Pennino 1948\*\*\*\*
Manufacturer Pennino Bros.
Designer Oreste Pennino.
Patent n° 149,832 Oreste Pennino,
New York, 1st June 1948, filed
on 24th April 1947.

Rhodium plated sterling brooch/pendant of a tree in bloom with rhinestone pavé trunk and branch, and flowers made of four small red stones with central rhinestone. 4.5x5.5cm.
Marked Pennino Sterling Des. Pat. Pend.
These flowers, made of four stones with a central rhinestone, are typical of Pennino pieces of this period and thus allow for the dating of the items in which they featured.

P4. "Sunburst," Pennino 1947\*\*\*
Manufacturer Pennino Bros.
Designer Oreste Pennino.
Not patented.

WWD, *October 31, 1947: "Sunburst Watch" by Pennino.*

Gold-plated sterling brooch with white baguettes, citrine stones and rhinestones, depicting a beaming sun. Diameter 4.5cm.
Marked Pennino Sterling.
See P6. for the spiral version of this brooch and relative references.

P5. "Sunburst," Pennino 1947\*\*\*
Manufacturer Pennino Bros.
Designer Oreste Pennino.
Patent n° 147,762 Oreste Pennino, New York,
28th October 1947, filed on 18th July 1946.

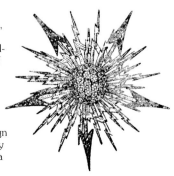

Gold-plated metal brooch/pendant of a beaming sun with a cluster of blue stones in the center and a double row of arrow-shaped rays with rhinestones. Diameter 6.5cm.
Marked Pennino.
The design was patented in 1947, however the application, and therefore production, date from 1946. In the spring of 1946 the industry met with and complained of serious difficulties in purchasing sterling, which accounts for the presence of metal and sterling jewels. The center of the various "cluster" models, i.e. a central convex mound of stones, is a trademark feature of Pennino products.
The "Sunburst" motif became popular between 1945 and 1946 following a design by the Duke of Verdura for a platinum and diamond jewel selling for $13,500. This design proved to be inspirational and various versions were made by Sandor, Trifari, Coro, Reinad, Réja, Nettie Rosenstein, Donna (David Grad) and others.

P6. "Sunburst," Pennino 1947****
Manufacturer Pennino Bros.
Designer Oreste Pennino.
Not patented.
   Gold-plated sterling brooch, pink stones, white baguettes and rhinestones, in the shape of a sunburst. 7x4.5cm.
   Marked Pennino Sterling.
   The same design was produced without the spirals both with center stones and a watch in the centre. This last one was reproduced in *WWD*, 31st October 1947 as "Sunburst Watch," and was specified as a lapel watch.

P7. "Bulrush Set," Pennino 1947**
Manufacturer Pennino Bros.
Designer Oreste Pennino.
Not patented.
   Set made up of gold-plated sterling brooch and earrings with blue faceted stone pavé, depicting a bulrush. Brooch: 7.5x9.6cm; clip earrings: 2.5cm.
   Brooch marked Pennino Sterling. Earrings marked Pennino Sterling Pat. Pend.
   The Pat. Pend. mark on the earring clips refers to the clip mechanism.

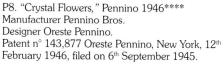

   Gold-plated sterling brooch, sky blue crystal and rhinestones, depicting a bunch of flowers. 6.2x7cm.
   Marked Pennino Sterling.
   Both the brooch and the design of the single flower are patented. (Des. 143,988, 26th February 1946, "Jewelry Finding for a pin or similar article").

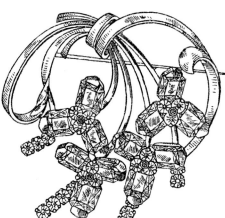

P8. "Crystal Flowers," Pennino 1946****
Manufacturer Pennino Bros.
Designer Oreste Pennino.
Patent n° 143,877 Oreste Pennino, New York, 12th February 1946, filed on 6th September 1945.

P9. "Blue Flowers," Pennino 1946****
Manufacturer Pennino Bros.
Designer Oreste Pennino.
Patent n° 143,878 Oreste Pennino, New York, 12th February 1946, filed on 6th September 1945.

   Gold-plated sterling brooch, blue stones and rhinestones, depicting flowers with a bow ribbon. 7.5x6.5cm.
   Marked Pennino Sterling.

PENNINO

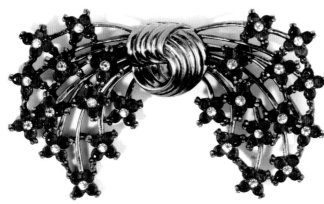

P10. "Bow," Pennino 1947****
Manufacturer Pennino Bros.
Designer Oreste Pennino.
Not patented.
　Gold-plated sterling brooch of a bowknot with two bunches of branches with flowers made of four small red stones with central rhinestone. 5x8.8cm.
　Marked Pennino Sterling "3".
　This item features the same flowers as those used for the "Tree" (P3.) and therefore probably belongs to the same collection.

# PROVIDENCE JEWELERS INC.

U4. "Cleopatra," Unsigned 1946*****
Manufacturer Providence Jewelers Inc.

U3. "Ibis," Unsigned 1946****
Manufacturer Providence Jewelers Inc.
　Gold-plated sterling brooch with black enamel and rhinestones, of an ibis perched on a lotus flower. 6.5x4cm.
　Marked Sterling.
　This item is part of the "Cleopatra jewelry" line made by Providence Jewelers Inc. for the launch of the movie "Caesar and Cleopatra" (U4.). The brooch featured in *WWD*, 13th September 1946, together with matching earrings.

*WWD*, September 13, 1946. "Cleopatra" and "Ibis," by Providence Jewelry, Inc.

　Gold-plated and rhodium-plated sterling brooch, red and black enamel, pearls and rhinestones, depicting a Cleopatra who resembles Vivian Leigh. 7.5x4cm.
　Marked Sterling.
　The brooch featured in *WWD*, 13th September 1946, which reported that: "In conjunction with the forth coming première of "Cesar and Cleopatra," the much-heralded motion picture, Providence Jewelers, Inc., have produced a complete line consisting of 15 items all of which are either a replica of jewelry worn by Vivian Leigh or are significant of some scenes in the motion picture. The "Head" is an authentic reproduction of Miss Leigh as Cleopatra in full headdress." The motion picture Cesar and Cleopatra of 1946, taken from the comedy of the same name by George Bernard Shaw, was directed by Gabriel Pascal and starred Claude Rains, Vivian Leigh and Stewart Granger.

## Caesar and Cleopatra Inspire Jewelry

### Motion Picture Inspires Egyptian Designed Jewelry In Heraldic Theme

# REBAJES

On 10th July 1953 *WWD* dedicated a long article accompanied by photographs to Francisco Rebajes and his "Success Saga," which was a typical story of the American dream come true.

Francisco Torres Rebajes was born in Puerta Plata, in the Dominican Republic, on 6th February 1906. His parents, Antonio Torres Ros and Francisca Rebajes de Torres were Spaniards who had emigrated from Majorca to the New World.

His father was a shoemaker who had his own workshop, where Francisco grew up honing his manual skills by using his father's tools. After a brief school education, for which he showed little interest, in 1923 at the age of sixteen,

*WWD*, July 10, 1953: Françisco Rebajes.

he emigrated to the United States where he did all sorts of odd jobs including that of assistant waiter.

Having remained jobless during the Great Depression, Rebajes literally lived on the streets until 1932, when, at a Greenwich Village party he met and soon after married Pauline Schwartz. In his days on the streets of New York, Rebajes used to collect cans and metal scraps from which he made animal figures. His first creation, according to *WWD*, was of a tin horse.

In 1931 when the first Washington Square art exhibition was announced, Francisco decided to display his animals which, neatly arranged on an iron table, captured the attention of Juliana Force, director of the Whitney Museum. Force asked him to bring his creations to the museum at the end of the exhibition and offered to purchase all ten items on display for a total of $30.

With this money Rebajes rented a shed in Greenwich Village at 182½ W, 4th Street. Here he began his commercial activity, designing and manufacturing metal by hand and, later on, copper animals and objects, including costume jewelry. His success was shown by the opening, on 19th December 1941, of a showroom at 377 Fifth Avenue designed by José Fernandez. At the same time production was moved to a larger workshop at 17th Street West, where forty people worked, later growing to sixty.

Rebajes personally designed all his items, including, in addition to costume jewelry, ashtrays, plates, ornamental wall plaques, and knick-knacks. The most used

material was copper, but he also made some silver pieces, especially during the war, when copper was reserved for war production.

Rebajes, with the help of his wife Pauline who was in charge of administration, was in charge of the company until the beginning of the 1960s, when he sold the firm to his production manager, Otto Bade, and retired to Torremolinos in Spain, where he lived and designed until his death in the spring of 1990.

Francisco Rebajes was a talented and creative designer and his copper and silver jewelry with its animal and ethnic, abstract, geometric and stylized subjects, figures prominently in the history of American costume jewelry.

No design by Rebajes was ever patented.

The jewelry is marked R≡baj≡∞, with the typical stylized E and S.

Rb1. "Lobster," Rebajes 1941-42*****
Manufacturer Rebajes Metal Art Craftsmen.
Designer Francisco Rebajes.
   Copper brooch of a lobster with mobile head, shell, tail and claws. 10.7x3.6cm.
   Marked REbajE∞.
   The Lobster was on sale for $4.95 plus taxes.

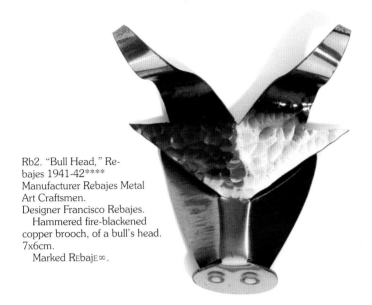

Rb2. "Bull Head," Rebajes 1941-42**** Manufacturer Rebajes Metal Art Craftsmen.
Designer Francisco Rebajes.
    Hammered fire-blackened copper brooch, of a bull's head. 7x6cm.
    Marked REbajE∞.

Rb4. "Pekinese," Rebajes 1941-42**** Manufacturer Rebajes Metal Art Craftsmen.
Designer Francisco Rebajes.
    Copper brooch of a Pekinese dog. 8x4.9cm
    Marked REbajE∞

Rb5. "Butterfly," Rebajes 1941-42***** Manufacturer Rebajes Metal Art Craftsmen.
Designer Francisco Rebajes.

Rb3. "Curved Antelope," Rebajes 1941-42***** Manufacturer Rebajes Metal Art Craftsmen.
Designer Francisco Rebajes.
    Copper brooch of an antelope head. 9x3.3cm.
    Marked REbajE∞.
        The brooch was on sale for $4.95 plus taxes.

*Vogue*, May 15, 1943: "Flight of Fancy" by Rebajes.

    Hand-wrought copper brooch of a butterfly. 6.5x5.5cm.
    Marked Original Hand Wrought Design REbajE∞.
    The sterling version of this brooch featured, together with matching earrings, in *Vogue*, 15th May 1943. The brooch was on sale for $5.50 (earrings $2.75), taxes included.

**Flight of Fancy...** In distinguished handwrought jewel-pieces of sterling silver. Rich Spanish artistry by the one and only Rebajes. Butterfly Pin . . . $5.50 Earrings . . . . $2.75 Including tax and postage. Mail orders invited

**Rebaje**
**METAL ART CRAFTSMEN**
**377 FIFTH AVENUE, NEW YORK**

Rb6. *"Coiled Wire Bracelets,"* Rebajes
1941-42****
Manufacturer Rebajes Metal Art Craftsmen.
Designer Francisco Rebajes.
   Pair of copper cuff bracelets anodized on the
inside and fire-blackened on the outside, with
attached coiled copper wire. Width: 5.5cm.
   Marked REBAJE∞.

Rb7. *"Theatrical Masks Set,"* Rebajes 1941-42****
Manufacturer Rebajes Metal Art Craftsmen.
Designer Francisco Rebajes.

*Vogue*, May 1, 1945: "Theatrical Masks" by Rebajes.

   Set made up of two copper brooches and a cuff bracelet,
depicting comedy and tragedy masks. Brooches: comedy:
5.2x5cm; tragedy: 4.9x4.2cm; bracelet width: 6cm.
   Marked REBAJE∞.
   "Theatrical Masks" is the original name of the set and featured in a *Vogue* advertisement on 1st May 1945. The set advertised in Vogue was the sterling version of the set. The brooches
were on sale for $5 each, the earrings for $5, taxes included.

Rb8. "Tribal Masks Bracelet," Rebajes 1941-42****
Manufacturer Rebajes Metal Art Craftsmen.
Designer Francisco Rebajes.
    Fire-blackened copper link bracelet with tribal masks in relief. 18x3.2cm.
    Marked REbajE∞.

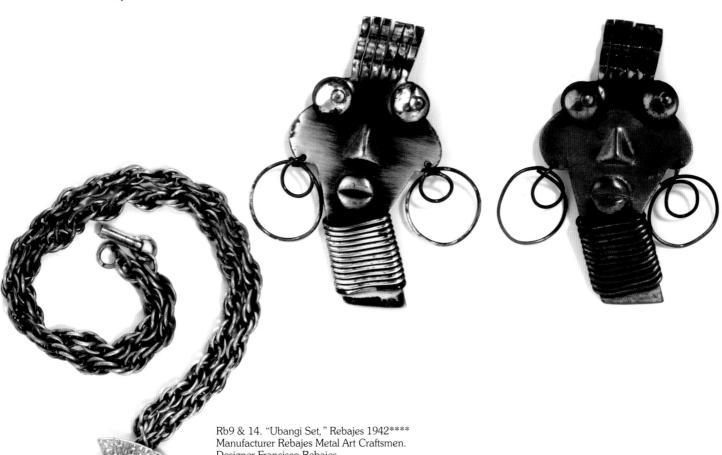

Rb9 & 14. "Ubangi Set," Rebajes 1942****
Manufacturer Rebajes Metal Art Craftsmen.
Designer Francisco Rebajes.
    Set made up of two brooches; a copper and a silver plate one, and of a silver plate necklace with pendant, depicting the heads of "Ubangi" women seen from the front and in profile (necklace). Brooches: 7.5x4.3cm; necklace pendant: 7.6x3.8cm.
    Marked REbajE∞.
    African motifs were very popular at the beginning of 1940s thanks to the Broadway revues and the musical movie of the time; and many manufacturers included these subjects in their jewelry collections (see Coro, Réja).
    The Ubangi was one of Rebajes' greatest successes and was mentioned in *WWD*, 27th February 1942, as being part of the items on display in the new Fifth Avenue store. The article stated that the jewelry would continue to be made of copper until this metal went out of stock (it was the beginning of metal rationing for war production) then it would be made of silver. The brooches were sold at $2.95 plus taxes.
    The whole set has been dated from 1942 based on the *WWD* article in which it was mentioned, however these items remained in production throughout the following years, until the first half of 1950s.

*Vogue*, December 1, 1942: "The Kiss" by Rebajes.

Copper brooch of the heads of a man and a woman kissing. 6x4.5cm. Marked REbajE∞.
A link bracelet with the kissing heads in the middle was also made. Four versions of the subject were made of: copper, sterling, copper and silver plate and silver plate.
The sterling version appeared in *Vogue*, 1st December 1942, together with the bracelet. The brooch was on sale for $7.50, the bracelet for $15, taxes included.

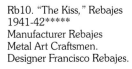

Rb10. "The Kiss," Rebajes
1941-42*****
Manufacturer Rebajes
Metal Art Craftsmen.
Designer Francisco Rebajes.

Rb11. "Dove Pendant," Rebajes
1941-42***
   Manufacturer Rebajes Metal Art
Craftsmen.
   Designer Francisco Rebajes.
   Hammered copper necklace pendant of a dove in flight.
6.8x3.5cm.
   Marked REbajE∞.

Rb12. "Man on Donkey,"
Rebajes 1941-42***
Manufacturer Rebajes Metal Art
Craftsmen.
Designer Francisco Rebajes.
   Copper brooch of a Mexican on a donkey. 5.4x4.2cm.
   Marked REbajE∞.
   The brooch was on sale for $2.95 plus taxes.

Rb13. "Mayan Goddess Pendant Necklace," Rebajes
1941-42****
Manufacturer Rebajes Metal Art Craftsmen.
Designer Francisco Rebajes.
   Copper necklace with pendant, of a Mayan goddess.
Pendant 7.5x5.8cm.
   Marked REbajE∞.
   "Mayan Goddess" was also the name given to an identical brooch pictured in an undated Rebajes catalog.

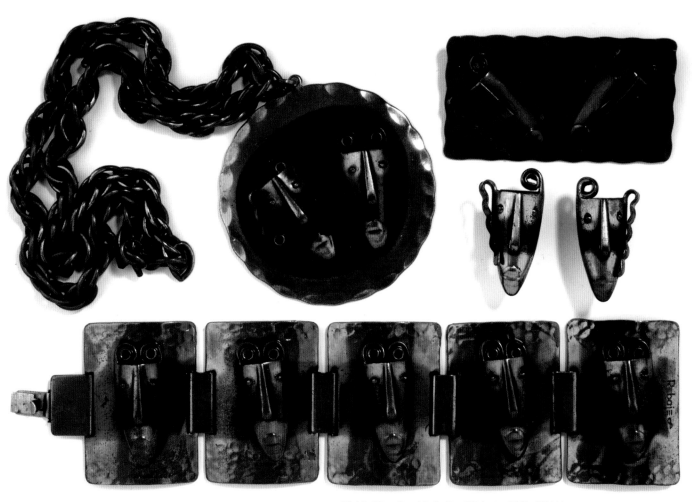

Rb15. "Brazilian Masks Set," Rebajes 1941-42****
Manufacturer Rebajes Metal Art Craftsmen.
Designer Francisco Rebajes.
    Set made up of copper necklace with pendant, link bracelet, barrette brooch
and earrings with a motif of Brazilian tribal masks. The necklace pendant, the
bracelet and the earrings feature fire-blackened masks. Pendant diameter: 6cm;
brooch 6.5x3.3cm; bracelet 18x4.5cm; earrings 3.4cm.
    Marked REbajE∞. The earrings are unmarked.

Rb16. "Grecian Head Set," Rebajes 1941-42****
Manufacturer Rebajes Metal Art Craftsmen.
Designer Francisco Rebajes.
    Set made up of hammered and engraved copper necklace with pendant, depicting the head of a Greek athlete
wearing a laurel wreath, and of screwback dangle earrings of the same subject. Pendant: 6cm diameter; earrings 4.3cm.
    Marked REbajE∞.

Rb17. "Leaves Set," Rebajes 1941-42***
Manufacturer Rebajes Metal Art Craftsmen.
Designer Francisco Rebajes.
   Set made up of lariat style copper
necklace with leaf-shaped finals, copper
cuff bracelet anodized on the inside with a
leaf motif, leaf-shaped screwback copper
earrings. Necklace total length: 47cm;
bracelet width: 3.2cm; earrings 4cm.
   Marked Rᴇʙᴀjᴇ∞. The earrings are
unmarked.

Rb18. "Kinetic Face Pendant Necklace," Rebajes 1941-42***
Manufacturer Rebajes Art Metal Craftsmen.
Designer Francisco Rebajes.
   Copper necklace with pendant, depicting an abstract-style face, with mobile forehead, nose and mouth. Pendant 7x4.5cm.
   Marked Rebaje∞.

Rb19. "Ethnic Pendant Necklace," Rebajes 1941-42***
Manufacturer Rebajes Metal Art Craftsmen.
Designer Francisco Rebajes.
   Copper necklace with pendant of an exotic face. 6x3.5cm.
   Marked Rebaje∞.

# RÉJA

Solomon Finkelstein began to work, probably in 1932, with Sol Finkelstein Co., New York, first at 990 Sixth Avenue, then at 55 West 47th Street. The company manufactured rhinestone jewelry and ornaments for wholesale distribution and therefore did not advertise. For this reason it is not known what items belonged to its production, or what trademark it used.

In 1939 Finkelstein decided to manufacture jewelry for the retail trade too and changed the name of the company to Déja Costume Jewelry, Inc., with a show-room in New York, 366 Fifth Avenue, and its plant at 47 West 47th Street.

Du Jay, Inc., summoned Déja, Inc. to appear before the Supreme Court of New York requesting that it changed its name, on the grounds that it was too similar to Du Jay. On 10th October 1940 Du Jay, Inc. obtained an injunction prohibiting Déja from using this name or any other name that was similar to Du Jay, Inc., in connection with the production and sale of novelty costume jewelry, as of 1st April 1941.

As early as the 17th January 1941, with an announcement in *WWD*, Déja announced its change of name to Réja, Inc., with no change in address. In March of the same year, however, the showroom was moved to 377 Fifth Avenue. The choice of the name Réja was apparently dictated by practical reasons, since the mark Réja could be stamped over the Déja mark, thus saving the items already manufactured with that mark (R3.).

**ANNOUNCEMENT**

Deja Costume Jewelry incorporated.

Changes its Name to

**Réja**

INDIVIDUALIZED   JEWELRY

WE look forward, with expectation that your most valued patronage of the past be sustained and that continued relationships and progress be our mutual goal...

**REJA INC.**

366 Fifth Ave., New York

Déja Costume Jewelry, Inc. did not advertise much in *Women's Wear Daily* – only a brief item appeared with its name and address and the words "Individualized Costume Jewelry" – and in February 1939 the paper dedicated a report to the company's first collection, complete with a reproduction of the designs of a brooch and a bracelet. The trademarks used for the stamping of the items were Déja, Déja Reg., Déja Original, and Déja Fleurs, registered on behalf of Déja Inc. The few known Déja items – the company only managed to present four collections – are made of white or gold-plated metal, sometimes with enamel accents, which were not very heavy, and were of floral or figurative subjects and date from 1939 and 1940. Déja was also the owner of a patent for a brooch of a heart holding a torch, called "carry the torch." The patent was assigned to Noel Meadow and Sidney Herbert on 21st May 1940 with No. 120,626, in response to the application filed on 2nd April 1940.

The company operated under the name of Réja from January 1941 to 4th December 1953, when it announced its bankruptcy (*WWD*, 4th December 1953). Its President at the time was still Solomon Finkelstein, while the company address was 143 West 20th Street.

The company had been in trouble for some time and in fact Réja's production from 1948 onwards had grown much worse. An attempt to salvage the company was made in June 1953, when Réja Jewelry signed a commercial agreement with Heller-Deltah Co., Inc., 411 Fifth Avenue, New York. With a notice in *WWD*, 5th June 1953, Heller-Deltah announced that "Now Heller-Deltah will sell and advertise Réja Jewelry with the famous name La Tausca." Unfortunately this attempt proved unsuccessful.

Heller-Deltah, established in 1904 in New York as L. Heller & Son, Inc., specialized in the manufacture of jewelry with pearls with the trademark La Tausca. Heller-Deltah also went bankrupt in 1956 and the La Tausca division was purchased by D'Arlan Jewelry Co., Inc.

The first collection (*WWD*, 28th March 1941) included a series of gold and silver-plated brooches with enamel accents and plant, floral and figurative subjects, called "King Arthur's Knights" (see description of series R8.).

Réja advertised in *Women's Wear Daily* with its name and address and the slogan "Individualized Costume Jewelry." The daily often presented its collections with articles and jewel designs that nowadays are a precious source of information for the dating and attribution of jewelry items. In February 1946 the company began to advertise in *Vogue* and *Harper's Bazaar*, i.e. nationwide and in style, with full page color advertisements. The first advertisement appeared in *Harper's Bazaar* in 1946 and featured three items of the "Africana" series, a line of four brooches with matching earrings, made of sterling and black enamel, of African masks called: "Ubangi," "Congo Belle," "Nubian Head" and "Witch Doctor" (R33., R34., R35., R36.).

*Harper's Bazaar,* February 1946: Africana by Réja.

The company – which had a very individual character, and despite its small size was very successful, as demonstrated by the attention it received from the press – manufactured limited quantities of items for the medium-upper market segment. Production was characterized by great emphasis on design, which was always original and of undisputed artistic value.

Most designs were created by Solomon Finkelstein who patented only four of them; three brooches of the "Africana" series in 1946 and the "Jack in the Box" (R39.) of 1947 (with patent application submitted in 1946) belonging to the "Rose Opal" (registered trademark) line, which was characterized by the light, openwork structure of the sterling and by the use of pink cabochons. In 1949 (*WWD*, 27th July 1949) Joseph C. Klafter designed a collection, of which nothing else is known.

Réja followed normal market practice by presenting two collections a year, a spring and a fall collection, which included several themes and lines. Each line or item was given a name inspired by the theme. Figurative subjects featured prominently: fantasy or anthropomorphic animals, masks, special objects, fairy tale figures, and characters from folklore. Réja

was renown for its masks and in its 1945-46 production made great use of large colored oval stones, or faceted drop-shaped stones, for the body of animals, or as the central piece of the design as in "Man from Mars" (R25.) or "Atomic Bomb" (PR40.). These stones were made by a specialized firm, the Oval Manufacturing Co., New York, 64 W. 36th St., which, in a series of advertisements in the *Jewelers' Circular Keystone* (April, July, September 1945) advertised its production and showed its applications in some Réja items.

One of the most beautiful collections was the spring collection of 1946 – presented in *Women's Wear Daily* in January – which included, in addition to the "Africana" series: "Punchinello" (R30.), the "Chinese Mandarin" (R29.), the "Court Jester" (R31.), brooches shaped like golden hands and feet, and a pair of fish. The collection also featured some vegetable subjects, including shiny enamel tomatoes and beetroots ("Hucksters"), the "Modern Heirloom" series characterized by a fretwork manufacture resembling lace, the "Via Lattea (Milky Way)" series with rhinestone spirals, and "Alba" (Dawn), a brooch representing the sun with a golden cupola with rhinestone-studded rays and little birds flying towards the sun. The fall collection was equally extraordinary, featuring, among other pieces, a "Medusa" (R26.), a "Good Fairy" (R32.), and the "Rose Opal" line.

For the spring of 1947 Sol Finkelstein designed the "Gardenesque" line (R40., R41., R42., R43.), Chinese-inspired brooches shaped like flower vases made of gold-plated sterling, blue sapphire, or China red stones, or moonstones and colored enamel that expressed well his taste for miniature. For the fall collection of the same year he designed the "Dancing Women" brooches of ballet dancers with rhinestone-studded gowns and hair and faces made of colored stones, and "Exclamation Point," a brooch shaped like an exclamation mark with a large pearl on top, rhinestones, and large alexandrites. Use of sterling started in the middle of 1942 and continued until about 1947. Afterwards the "real look" prevailed, which had a simple repetitive style and used poorer materials. Production comprised the entire range of jewelry. Nowadays, however, practically only the brooches remain, sometimes with matching earrings and only rarely necklaces and bracelets.

The trademarks stamped on the jewelry were: REJA, registered in 1941, written in small, thin, sometimes barely legible block letters. In 1941 the letters REG. were added to the trademark and also the trademark REJA INC. appeared, however only on metal products.

Réja also registered a few trademarks such as "Rose Opal," "Artistry in Jewelry," and "Pinch Pin."

R1. "Indian Mask," Déja 1939-40***
Manufacturer Déja, Inc.
Designer Solomon Finkelstein.
Not patented.
    Brooch, rhodium-plated at the back and
gold-plated at the front, of an Indian head
with turban and loop earrings. With red
and white enamel. 5x4.7cm.
    Marked Déja Original.
    All items marked Déja can be dated from
1939-40, when the company was using this
trademark.

R2. "Cambodian Dancers," Déja 1939****
Manufacturer Déja Costume Jewelry, Inc.
Designer Solomon Finkelstein.
Not patented.
    Pair of gold-plated pin clips with pink, red and black
enamel, of a couple of Cambodian dancers. 6.5x2cm.
    Marked Déja Reg.
    Reg. stands for registered and, as in the case of the
first items marked Réja, refers to the registration date of
the trademark, which, in Déja's case, was 1939.

R3. "Blue Carnation," Déja-Réja 1941****
Manufacturer Réja, Inc.
Designer Solomon Finkelstein.
Not patented.
    Rhodium-plated metal brooch, blue and white enamel, pearl in the
center, rhinestones, in the shape of a carnation. 9x6.8cm.
    Marked Déja-Réja.
    Owing to Dujay having successfully sued the company for brand name
similarity, Déja had to change its name to Réja. The change should have
taken place from 1st April 1941, however, as early as 17th January 1941
Déja announced in *WWD* its change of name to Réja Inc. The choice of the
new name Réja was probably due to the fact that the "D" of Déja could easily
be re-engraved as "R" without too much difficulty and the company could therefore still sell the goods that had already been manufactured under the name Déja.
    This brooch actually has both names engraved on it: with a poorly corrected
Déja on the stem, and Réja on a petal. This allows for a precise dating of the
brooch.

R4. "Flower," Déja 1939-40***
Manufacturer Déja Costume Jewelry, Inc.
Designer Solomon Finkelstein.
Not patented.
    Gold-plated metal brooch with red and white rhine-
stones, in the shape of a flower. 8.5x4.8cm.
    Marked Déja.

R5. "Raspberries," Réja 1941***
Manufacturer Réja, Inc.
Designer Solomon Finkelstein.
Not patented.
    Gold-plated metal brooch, red, green and black enamel, rhinestones, in the shape of raspberries. 6.2x5.7cm.
    Marked Réja Reg.
    Series "King Arthur's Knights" (R8.)

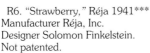

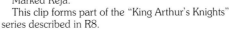

R6. "Strawberry," Réja 1941***
Manufacturer Réja, Inc.
Designer Solomon Finkelstein.
Not patented.
    White metal brooch, red, yellow and green enamel, rhinestones, in the shape of a strawberry. 6x6cm.
    Marked Réja Reg.
    Series "King Arthur's Knights" (R8.)

R7. "Tomato," Réja 1941***
Manufacturer Réja, Inc.
Designer Solomon Finkelstein.
Not patented.
    Gold-plated metal pin clip, red and green enamel, rhinestones, in the shape of a tomato. 5x5.3cm.
    Marked Réja.
    This clip forms part of the "King Arthur's Knights" series described in R8.

R8. "Totem Pole," Réja 1941****
Manufacturer Réja, Inc.
Designer Solomon Finkelstein.
Not patented.
    Gold-plated metal brooch, red, black and sky blue enamel, colored rhinestones, depicting a totem pole. 10.5x2.5cm.
    Marked Réja Reg.
    The "Totem Pole" is part of the first collection of items manufactured by Réja after its name change. The collection was featured in *WWD*, 28th March 1941, which described it as being: "A lapel series called "King Arthur's Knights" and executed in antique-finished gold or silver metal with tiny rhinestones is a new jewelry group at Réja Costume Jewelry, a firm which formerly traded as Déja and is now in new quarters at 377 Fifth Avenue. Biggest promotional group here in enameled metal jewelry is a collection of vegetables, fruit and nuts to supplement a variety of flower pieces. Nicely designed and colored, the pieces include decorative stalks of celery, bunches of scallions, strawberries, a cucumber studded with tiny green stones and a pea pod with pearls for peas. There are little vegetable earrings to match and charm bracelets dangling miniatures. In addition to the flower spray group, there is a line of dogs of all breeds, in enamel and rhinestones, and others of flying seagulls and tropical fish.
    An Indian item is a long, brightly colored totem pole pin with matching earrings".
    The mark "Reg," that appears on only some of the items in this first series, stands for "registered" and demonstrates that the company had registered the new name.

R9. "Sunflower," Réja 1943***
Manufacturer Réja, Inc.
Designer Solomon Finkelstein.
Not patented.
   Gold-plated sterling brooch shaped like a sunflower with large round blue crystal in the center and rhinestone studded petals and leaves. 6.5x4.5cm.
   Marked Réja Sterling.
   A picture published in *WWD*, 17th September 1943, shows that for its fall collection of that year, Réja had made floral brooches with the same characteristics as this item, i.e. with a large central stone, surrounded by small white stones and gold-plated sterling leaves that were small in comparison with the flower.

R10. "Bowknot," Réja 1944***
Manufacturer Réja, Inc.
Designer Solomon Finkelstein.
Not patented.
   Pink gold-plated brooch shaped like a cockade with large round topaz at the center and rhinestones on the edges. 8x5.5cm.
   Marked Réja Sterling.

R11. "Flamingo," Réja 1945**
Manufacturer Réja, Inc.
Designer Solomon Finkelstein.
Not patented.
   Gold-plated sterling brooch of the profile of a resting flamingo with a raised leg. Its body is made of a large drop-shaped amethyst violet stone, and its wings are sprinkled with rhinestones. 7x3.5cm.
   Marked Réja Sterling.

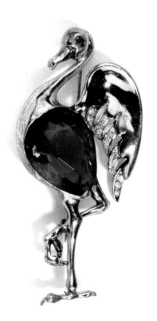

R12. "Turtle Set," Réja 1943***
Manufacturer Réja, Inc.
Designer Solomon Finkelstein.
Not patented.

*WWD*, September 17, 1943. "Turtle" by Reja.

   Set made up of gold-plated sterling brooch and screwback earrings with rhinestones, depicting a turtle. Brooch 6.5x3.5cm; earrings 3.2cm.
   The brooch is marked Réja Sterling while the earrings are just marked sterling.
   Only the brooch design was featured in *WWD*, 17th September 1943. A sterling copy of this item also exists from the same period, made by Alpha Craft, Inc of New York.

R13. "Monster Flower," Réja, 1941****
Manufacturer Réja, Inc.
Designer Solomon Finkelstein.
Not patented.
    Large brooch, rhodium-plated at the back and gold-plated at the front, of a "serpent's tongue," i.e. a type of fern, the inside of which resembles a snake's tongue. The inside of the leaves is made of rhinestone pavé. 13x6.5cm.
    Marked Réja.

R14. "Big Arrow," Réja 1945***
Manufacturer Réja, Inc.
Designer Solomon Finkelstein.
Not patented.
    Gold-plated sterling brooch of an arrow with two large ruby red, drop-shaped crystals on the arrow point and tail, and rhinestone-studded shaft. 8.3x3.5cm.
    Marked Réja Sterling.
    Matching earrings with the same design in miniature also exist.

R15. "Arrow," Réja 1943**
Manufacturer Réja, Inc.
Designer Solomon Finkelstein.
Not patented.

*WWD, February 24, 1943: "Arrow" and "Gazelle" (R17) by Reja.*

    Rhodium-plated sterling brooch of an arrow with five red carrè cut crystals at the center and rhinestones on the tail. 6.5x2.3cm.
    Marked Réja Sterling.
    The design, complete with matching earrings, was presented by *Women's Wear Daily* on 24th February 1943 and the description indicates that the use of red rectangular stones was chosen to emphasize the stone brightness.
    There is also another version of this brooch with the same design but made of different materials (gold-plated metal), and with a different weight (it was lighter). This other version is unmarked and cannot be attributed to Réja. It is an imitation of the original item, dating from the same period.

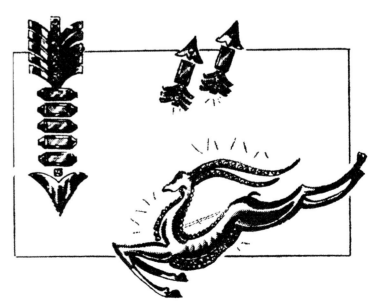

R16. "Duck," Réja 1945\*\*\*
Manufacturer Réja, Inc.
Designer Solomon Finkelstein.
Not patented.
    Gold-plated sterling brooch and earrings, with oval faceted citrine stone and rhinestones. The design is of a duck. Brooch 5x5.5cm, earrings 1.8x1cm.
    The brooch is marked Réja Sterling, the earrings just Sterling.
    This set belongs to a series of items of animal subjects characterized by the presence of a large drop-shaped faceted oval stone for the body. This kind of stones, with this peculiar cut, is common to items made in 1945 - early 1946, and confirms the practice of purchasing large quantities of stones to be used according to the models available, for a certain period of time, until the company ran out of stock. These stones were made by a specialized company, the Oval Manufacturing Co. of New York (64 West 36th Street) that advertised in the "Jewelers' Circular Keystone" by presenting Réja jewelry featuring its stones ("JCK," April, July and September 1945). Other animals of the same series are: "Flamingo" (R11.), "Fly" (R18.), "Geese" (R19.), "Lyre Bird" (R20.), "Peacock" (R22.), eagle, owl, butterfly, salamander, frog, partridge, crab, camel, giraffe, deer, fish, parrot.

R17. "Gazelle," Réja 1943\*\*\*
Manufacturer Réja, Inc.
Designer Solomon Finkelstein.
Not patented.
    Gold-plated sterling brooch with rhinestones, depicting a running gazelle with an elongated profile, emphasized by a line of rhinestones on its horns. 10x4.5cm.
    Marked Réja Sterling.
    This design was presented together with the "Arrow" (R15.) by *WWD* on 24th February 1943 with a description of the item.

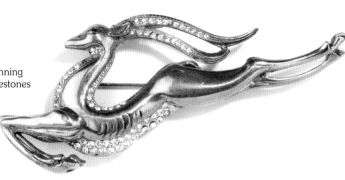

R18. "Fly," Réja 1945\*\*\*
Manufacturer Réja, Inc.
Designer Solomon Finkelstein.
Not patented.
    Gold-plated sterling brooch, multi-faceted sky blue oval stone and rhinestones, in the shape of a fly. 4.5x4.5cm.
    Marked Réja Sterling.

R19. "Geese," Réja 1945\*\*\*
Manufacturer Réja, Inc.
Designer Solomon Finkelstein.
Not patented.
    Matching gold-plated sterling brooches of two geese with a drop shaped green crystal for the body. The female has a rhinestone studded hat and is holding an umbrella; the male is wearing a tailcoat with a rhinestone studded collar and hat, and is holding a cane. Female 6.5x3.5cm; male 6x3.2cm.
    The male is marked Réja Sterling. The female just Sterling.
    There is also another version of these brooches with blue crystals. This design was rather common on the market. Brooches sold in pairs are usually marked with one having the complete trademark, and the other marked only with Sterling, which makes it sometimes difficult to identify a single brooch whose design is not known. A single brooch of such a perfect and obviously complementary pair as this, has a lower value on the collector's market.

R20. "Lyre Bird," Réja 1945****
Manufacturer Réja, Inc.
Designer Solomon Finkelstein.
Not patented.

*WWD*, July 13, 1945: "Lyre Bird" by Réja.

Gold-plated sterling brooch of a lyre bird with a drop-shaped green crystal for the body and wings and a tail ornamented with rhinestones and red stones. 6.5x6.5cm.
Marked Réja Sterling.
The brooch appeared with this name in *WWD*, 13th July 1945.

R21. "Phœnix," Réja 1945***
Manufacturer Réja, Inc.
Designer Solomon Finkelstein.
Not patented.
Gold-plated sterling brooch, with small red stones and rhinestones, of a phoenix perched on a branch, seen from the front, with spread wings and a long straight tail. 7.5x9cm.
Marked Réja Sterling.
The phoenix is a mythical bird which is the size of an eagle and has red and golden wings. According to legend, every five hundred years, the phoenix spontaneously burns till it is no more than ashes and from these ashes it is born again. In ancient Egypt it was considered a sacred bird, and was believed to inhabit the deserts of Ethiopia and Arabia. With the advent of Christianity, the myth became a symbol of the Resurrection.

*WWD*, June 23, 1944: "Peacock" by Réja.

Set made up of pink gold-plated sterling brooch and earrings, of a peacock, with faux amethyst at the center of its body and rhinestone sprinkled wings, breast and head. The screwback earrings have the same design, only in a smaller version. Brooch 8.5x7cm; earrings 3.5cm.
Brooch marked Réja Sterling. Earrings marked Sterling.
The set design appeared in *WWD* on 23rd June 1944 with the name of "Peacock". Apparently Réja made rather spare use of pink gold for the gilding of its jewelry and mainly in 1944.

R22. "Peacock Set," Réja 1944****
Manufacturer Réja, Inc.
Designer Solomon Finkelstein.
Not patented.

R23. "Hand Set," Réja 1949-50***
Manufacturer Réja, Inc.
Designer Solomon Finkelstein.
Not patented.
    Set made up of rhodium- and gold-plated metal
brooch and earrings, depicting a gloved hand holding a
rhinestone and baguette fountain. The glove has a puffed
cuff ornamented with red stones. The clip earrings are of a
gloved hand. Brooch 6x3cm; earrings 2.5cm.
    Brooch marked Réja. The earrings are unmarked.

R24. "Necklace," Réja 1949**
Manufacturer Réja Inc.
    Rhodium and gold-plated metal
necklace with rhinestones, with a snake
chain and central "lace" fretwork motif.
Central motif 14x1.5cm.
    Marked Réja Inc.

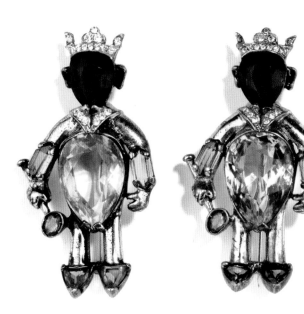

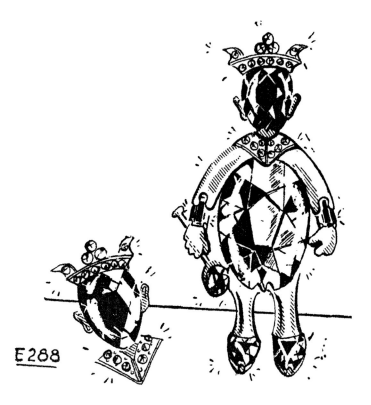

R25. "Men from Mars," Réja 1945\*\*\*\*
Manufacturer Réja, Inc.
Designer Solomon Finkelstein.
Not patented.

*WWD*, March 2, 1945: "Man from Mars" by Réja.

Pair of gold-plated brooches of "Martians". The body is made of a large drop-shaped blue stone, the face of a drop-shaped ruby red stone, the feet are made of a large triangular blue stone, the arms and shaft of citrine stones, and the headdress of rhinestones. The two brooches have slightly different sizes: 7.5cm and 7x4cm.
Marked Réja Sterling.
The name and design of the brooches, complete with matching clip earrings that reproduce only the head of the Martian, are mentioned in *WWD*, 2nd March 1945, which remarks on the unusual subject and on the fantastic color combination of the stones. The subject is defined by the name given to it by *WWD*, though, actually, the figures are strangely regal looking, as hinted at by their headdresses which resemble royal crowns and by the shaft which is very much like a scepter. It is possible that, as shown by the design reproduced in *WWD*, the brooches were not conceived of as a pair, and their remarkable size and identical design seem to suggest this. However, if this were the case, the different markings used would be difficult to explain. In effect one brooch bears the complete trademark– Réja Sterling – whereas the other is simply marked sterling, as was common for pairs of brooches.

E288

R26. "Medusa Set," Réja 1946\*\*\*\*\*
Manufacturer Réja, Inc.
Designer Solomon Finkelstein.
Not patented.

Set made up of rhodium and gold-plated sterling brooch and earrings, depicting a Medusa head with a face of gold-plated sterling and rhodium-plated sterling hair with rhinestone pavé. The clip earrings reproduce the same design, only in a smaller version. Brooch 6.3x6cm; earrings 3cm.
The brooch is marked Réja Sterling. The earrings are marked Réja Sterling Pat. Pend.
This item was described as "extraordinary" by *WWD*, 21st June 1946, which mentions it with its original name among the new items. The presented version is the original one, with a black enamel face. The design is unpatented and the Pat. Pend. mark on the earring clips refers to the clip mechanism.
The fine and elaborate workmanship of this item, especially of the fretwork headdress with rhinestone pavé, is similar to that of the "Good Fairy" (R32.), which belongs to the same collection.

R27. "Balinese Masks," Réja 1945****
Manufacturer Réja, Inc.
Designer Solomon Finkelstein.
Not patented.

A Balinese mask shows the delicately angular face of a man. The headdress is of colored stones and rhinestones, and simulated emeralds are used for the eyes. A curved molded look is typical of all of Reja's cast merchandise. Matching earrings are tiny replicas of the pin.

WWD, July 13, 1945: "Balinese Mask" by Réja.

Pair of gold-plated sterling brooches of Balinese or Javanese masks with strongly marked features, emphasized by colored enamel accents, wearing tiaras ornamented with colored stones, and with black enamel hair and carved eyes and mouth. King 7.3x4cm; Queen 5.8x4.5cm.
    Marked Réja Sterling.
    Both brooches are marked. The male mask was called "Balinese Mask" by WWD, which reproduced this design in its 13th July 1945 issue. The brooches were conceived of as a pair, since there is a male and female version of the same subject, however they are not complementary and are therefore valuable also as single brooches.

R28. "Oriental Mask," Réja 1945****
Manufacturer Réja, Inc.
Designer Solomon Finkelstein.
Not patented.
    Gold-plated sterling pin clip of the head of an oriental dignitary with rhinestone studded, grooved beret, carved eyes with small red stones, carved mouth with red enamel accents, thin black enamel mustache, and rhinestone studded collar. 6x3.5cm.
    Marked Réja Sterling.

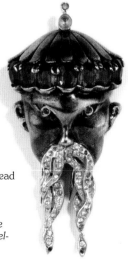

R29. "Chinese Mandarin," Réja 1946****
Manufacturer Réja, Inc.
Designer Solomon Finkelstein.
Not patented.
    Gold-plated sterling pin clip, pink stones and rhinestones, of the head of a Chinese Mandarin, with long whiskers. 6.8x3.5cm.
    Marked Réja Sterling.
    Matching earrings also exist.
    The item was mentioned in WWD, January 11th 1946, as "Chinese Mandarin with long rhinestone whiskers" and was advertised in Jewelers' Circular Keystone, March 1946.

R30. "Punchinello," Réja
1946****
Manufacturer Réja, Inc.
  Designer Solomon Finkel-
    stein.
  Not patented.

*Harper's Bazaar,* March 1946: "Punchinello" by Réja.

Gold-plated sterling pin clip of the mask of Punchinello, with wide red enamel mouth, eyes made of red marquise-cut stones, thick black enamel eyebrows, rhinestone sprinkled cheeks and rhinestones under its eyes, large ears, and lateral tufts of hair. 5.5x5cm.
  Marked Réja Sterling.
  Matching clip earrings with the same design, only in a smaller version, also exist.
  "Punchinello" is the original name of this set of a pin clip and earrings, which was presented in *Women's Wear Daily,* 11th January 1946, and also appeared in an advertisement published in *Harper's Bazaar,* March 1946. The subject differs from the usual Punchinello image and appears more similar to the male grimacing and grotesque masks typical of Phoenician art in the VI-V century b.C. Or, more simply, Finkelstein might have been inspired by the mask worn by Punchinello in some theater pieces which actually featured tufts of hair at the sides of his otherwise bald head and a wide mouth.

R31. "Court Jester," Réja 1945****
Manufacturer Réja Inc.
Designer Solomon Finkelstein.
Not patented.
  Set made up of gold-plated sterling brooch and screwback earrings, with red enameled mouth, green and pink stones and rhinestones, depicting the head of a jester on a stilt. Brooch 9x3cm; earrings 2x2cm.
  Brooch marked Réja Sterling; earrings marked Sterling.
  The name "Court Jester" was used in an article that appeared in *WWD,* 10th August 1945, in which Réja's fall 1945 collection was praised thus: "particularly striking are the court jesters on long, thin stilts. According to the manufacturer of the brooches – of which there were two versions; a front and a profile view – they should be worn together". The jesters were mentioned again in *WWD,* 11th January 1946, together with the spring collection which also included, among others, the "Africana" series.

R32. "Good Fairy," Réja 1946*****
Manufacturer Réja, Inc.
Designer Solomon Finkelstein.
Not patented.

WWD, October 4, 1946: "Good Fairy" by Réja.

Rhodium-plated sterling brooch with rhinestone pavé, of a fairy, with rhinestone-studded, fretwork wings and black enamel border. 9.5x5.7cm.
Marked Réja Sterling.
The "Good Fairy," which is the brooch's original name, was presented by WWD, 21st June 1946, and the design was reproduced in the issue of 4th October 1946. It is a true copy of a Van Cleef & Arpels model called "Wings of Victory," which was advertised in Vogue, 1st December 1944, and in Harper's Bazaar, December 1944. This subject also inspired Brody Designs, Inc., which, in 1945 (WWD, 27th April) made a gold-plated sterling brooch, with lucite and rhinestones, of a fairy with lucite wings (JB149.)

**Delicate star by Reja, Inc., combines pale Alexandrite stone with rhinestone melees, while ethereal "Good Fairy" lends a holiday spirit to those customers who want jewelry with the real look. Paved rhinestone body on rhodium base is set off with gold tipped wings.**

R33. "Africana": "Witch Doctor," Réja 1946****
Manufacturer Réja, Inc.
Designer Solomon Finkelstein.
Patent n° 144,774 Solomon Finkelstein, New York, May 21st 1946, filed December 7th 1945.

Set made up of gold-plated sterling pin clip and earrings, red stones and rhinestones, depicting a witch doctor's head, wearing a turban ornamented with a central red crystal and rhinestones. His eyes and earrings are made of rhinestones. The shape of his eyes and the rhinestones representing the pupils aim to convey the impression of a hypnotic stare. Pin clip 6.5x4cm; earrings 2.5cm.
Pin clip marked Réja Sterling. Earrings marked Réja Sterling Pat. Pend.
The patent was issued for the brooch. The Pat. Pend. mark on the earring clips refers to the clip mechanism.
In another version of this design, the face is black enamel. The name mentioned by WWD, 11th January 1946 and published in Harper's Bazaar, February 1946, is the original one.

R34. "Africana": "Nubian Head," Réja 1946****
Manufacturer Réja, Inc.
Designer Solomon Finkelstein.
Patent n° 144,773 Solomon Finkelstein, New York,
21st May 1946, filed on 7th December 1945.

Set made up of gold-plated sterling brooch and clip earrings, with black enamel and rhinestones, depicting a Nubian head with a traditional headdress which is kept in place by golden rings and terminates in a rhinestone-ornamented tuft of hair, and a long rhinestone necklace. Brooch 5x7cm; earrings 2.8cm.
Brooch marked Réja Sterling. Earrings marked Sterling Pat. 1967965.
The patent number marked on the earring clips refers to the mechanism and was assigned to Eugene Morehouse and Melvin W. Moore, Providence, R.I., on 24th July 1934, filed on 30th March 1934, for B.A. Ballou & Co., Inc., Rhode Island. Ballou was an important Providence company, which had been established in 1876 by Barton A. Ballou, and produced gold and gold-plated jewelry and jewelry components. This is further evidence that the mechanisms, due to their function, remained in use for a long time – and are therefore of little use in dating items. These mechanisms were mostly patented on behalf of companies specializing in the production of jewelry components, which they then supplied to jewelry manufacturers. The marked component could be purchased by any costume jewelry manufacturer that assembled it in its jewelry and, for this reason, it is possible to find the same mechanism in use by different companies during the same period. This same model of earring clips was used by Coro for its "Hoots" earrings, in the metal version datable from 1947 (C94.) and for the "Cuban Dancer" earrings by Grayce Norato (U25.).
There is also a version of this brooch without enamel, where the face is made of gold-plated sterling. The name used is the same as the original name and the item was mentioned in *WWD*, 11th January 1946, and photographed for an advertisement in *Harper's Bazaar*, February 1946.
Nubia is a region in north-east Africa, between Egypt and Sudan, which includes the Nile valley. From pre-historical times it was linked to Egypt by political and commercial relations as well as religious and cultural traditions.

R35. "Africana": "Congo Belle," Réja 1946****
Manufacturer Réja, Inc.
Designer Solomon Finkelstein.
Not patented.
Gold-plated sterling pin clip, with black and red enamel and rhinestones, depicting the head of a woman from the Sara tribe, with a black enamel face, large red enamel lips, typical spiral gold-plated sterling headdress with rhinestones at the top and at the end of the fringe on the forehead, collar made of stacked gold-plated sterling rings and black enamel. 5.5x4.5cm.
Marked Réja Sterling.
The name is original and the item was mentioned in *WWD*, 11th January 1946.
Strangely enough, the design was not patented and the brooch was not photographed for the advertising campaign made for the launch of the line.
The design was inspired by the face of a Sara woman, a tribe in French equatorial Africa, which lives on the banks of the Bahr Sara, a tributary of the Shari. The Sara people has a total population of about one million.

Before the advent of Islam, which imposed the use of large cotton robes, the Sara tribe used to wear only short hip wraps. They often shaved their heads completely and the women liked to shave their heads in special ways, in order to create fancy patterns. Scar tattoos were also much appreciated. Women sometimes wore large lip plates, mainly double plates, called *sundu* in their language, the function of which was to elongate their lips to their maximum extent, even reaching down to their breasts. The name "femmes a plateau," created during the colonial period, comes from this practice. The Sara women also wore several brass thread jewelry around their ankles and in their ears, bead necklaces and brass and copper bangles.

Set made up of gold-plated sterling pin clip and earrings with black and red enamel, depicting an Ubangi head wearing an elaborate headdress with engraved gold-plated feathers and, in the middle, six opalescent blue cabochons (only one cabochon in the earrings), red enamel lips and pupils, eyes with small rhinestones, double loop earrings (only in the pin clip), high collar made of stacked rings. Pin clip 7x6cm; earrings 2cm.

Pin clip marked Réja Sterling. Earrings marked Sterling Pat. Pend. The Pat. Pend. mark refers to the clip mechanism.

The series "Africana by Réja" was presented in an article which appeared in *WWD*, 11th January 1946, which stated that the series was made up of four models, called: "Ubangi," "Nubian Head," "Witch Doctor" and "Congo Belle," respectively. It is interesting to note that the subjects were inspired by ethnic and cultural subjects from equatorial and north-eastern Africa and were designed with accuracy, denoting a certain knowledge of the subject, possibly derived from an exhibition or fashion based on African motifs and colors. Three of these brooches – "Ubangi," "Witch Doctor" and "Nubian Head" – were patented and appeared in an advertisement in *Harper's Bazaar*, February 1946, with the trademark "Africana by Réja". The fourth was not patented and did not appear anywhere else.

"Ubangi" was only made in this version with black enamel and is the most beautiful of the series, and also the largest and most accurate both in terms of materials and workmanship. Ubangi is the name of the inhabitants of Ubangi Shari, a French colony in equatorial Africa, which became independent in 1958 and renamed itself the Central African Republic.

R36. "Africana": "Ubangi," Réja 1946*****
Manufacturer Réja, Inc.
Designer Solomon Finkelstein.
Patent n° 144,772 Solomon Finkelstein, New York, 21st May 1946, filed on 7th December 1945.

R37. "Sea Horses," Réja 1946*****
Manufacturer Réja Inc.
Designer Solomon Finkelstein.
Not Patented.

Pair of gold-plated sterling brooches with moonstone cabochons and rhinestones, depicting two facing sea horses. Both 6.5x2.8cm.

Marked Réja Sterling.

Moonstone cabochons are a trademark feature in 1946 Réja collections. The position of the brooches suggests that they were meant to be worn together.

R38. "Jack in the Box," Réja 1946*****
Manufacturer Réja, Inc.
Designer Solomon Finkelstein.
Patent n° 146,764 Solomon Finkelstein, New York, 13th May 1947, filed on 29th May 1946.

Gold-plated sterling brooch of a "Jack in the Box" – a puppet on a spring jammed in a box, from which it would pop out, as soon as the lid was opened – with a collar made of five pink opal cabochons, rhinestone pavé on its gloves and hat, rhinestones on the spring loops and the box, and rhinestone accents its on eyes and mouth. 7x6cm.

Marked Réja Sterling.

Matching earrings for this brooch also exist and reproduce the design of the puppet head in miniature. The design dated from 26th May 1946, but the patent was only issued in May 1947. Whilst patents were usually issued just a few months after the filing of the application, in 1946 there were long delays, as long as one year, probably due to the reorganization of the patent office.

This jewelry item belongs to the "Rose Opal" line mentioned in a *WWD* article, 21st June 1946, which emphasized the fact that it was the first time after the war that pink opals were used by Réja in brooches, bracelets and necklaces with a fan motif of tiny rhinestones, yellow gold lace details and sterling with anti-rust finish. The name is the original one. "Hobby Horse" (R39.) also belonged to the same high-price line. The set – brooch and earrings – appeared in a *Vogue* advertisement, 15th August 1946, also with the name "Jack in the Box".

In spite of the design patent, a non-identical copy of the "Jack in the Box" was made by Harves Jewelry, a company based in New York, in 303 Fifth Avenue, which advertised it in *Women's Wear Daily*, 23rd February 1947, with the same name. The Harves copy was made of gold-plated metal with coral colored stones as well as in silver-plated metal with turquoise stones and was a chatelaine, which was a fashionable type of brooch at the time. The brooch was joined by a thin chain to another smaller brooch which represented the Jack's head. These items were on sale for: $24 the chatelaine, $18 the brooch, $12 the earrings and $12 the scatter pin (these being the prices per dozen pieces). Though nowadays easily distinguishable from the original by differences in design and materials, the low-priced copies were at the time a disaster for Réja, since the great diffusion of the subject, risked ruining the market for the high-price originals, which lost their early appeal. On the other hand, this subject was rather frequently used, an example being the "Jack in the Box" brooch by Alfred Philippe, designed in 1941 (T110.) and mentioned as a reference item in Finkelstein's patent.

R39 "Hobby Horse," Réja 1946****
Manufacturer Réja, Inc.
Designer Solomon Finkelstein.
  Not patented.
    Gold-plated sterling brooch, with rhinestone pavé and pink opal cabochon, of a hobby horse, with a rhinestone studded body, a red stone for its eye, and a base ornamented with six pink opals and small rhinestones. 5.5x5.5cm.
    Marked Réja Sterling.
  This item, which was a part of the "Rose Opal" line, was mentioned with this name, so it can be assumed to be its original name, by *WWD*, 21st June 1946. With the brooches of this "Rose Opal" line, Réja began to follow the new trend of making smaller and lighter models. Apparently, the brooches of children's toys were must-have items in the spring of 1946. Adolph Katz, for example, patented the design of a brooch of a rocking horse for Coro (Des. n° 146,576 of 8th April 1947, filed on 8th February 1946) with rhinestones, baguettes and enamel and a brooch of a wheel with a horse's head (Des. n° 146,575 of 8th April 1947, filed on 2nd February 1946). This confirms the fact that there was a general trend of several designers working on the same successful subjects.

R40. "Gardenesque Flower Vase," Réja 1947****

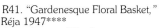
poised in the poetry of jewels...

*Vogue*, February 15, 1947: "Gardenesque" by Réja.

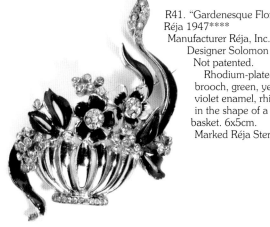

R41. "Gardenesque Floral Basket," Réja 1947****
Manufacturer Réja, Inc.
  Designer Solomon Finkelstein.
  Not patented.
    Rhodium-plated sterling brooch, green, yellow and violet enamel, rhinestones, in the shape of a floral basket. 6x5cm.
    Marked Réja Sterling.

Manufacturer Réja, Inc.
Designer Solomon Finkelstein.
Not patented.
Gold and rhodium-plated sterling brooch, black and green enamel, pink and blue stones, moonstone, pearls and rhinestones, in the shape of a vase of flowers. 8.5x4.5cm.
  Marked Réja Sterling.
  The "Gardenesque" collection was featured in *WWD*, 7th and 21st February 1947: "Réja, Inc., features the exotic gardenesque series of Chinese inspired enamel and stone set lapel pins. Group of three pins going down in size, suggest a flower tipped vase, a floral basket, a plant and a weeping willow tree". In an advertisement in *Vogue*, 15th February 1947, the plant (R43.), vase and floral basket (R41.) were all featured. There were also matching earrings, which reproduced these subjects in miniature.

R42. "Gardenesque ," Réja 1947***
Manufacturer Réja, Inc.
Designer Solomon Finkelstein.
Not patented.
    Rhodium and gold-plated sterling brooch, with green enamel and small white and pink opals, of a miniature plant, like a bonsai, in a pot. 6x6cm.
    Marked Réja Sterling.

R43. "Gardenesque Chinese Plant," Réja 1947****
Manufacturer Réja Inc.
Designer Solomon Finkelstein.
Not patented.
    Set made up of a brooch and clip earrings made of gold and rhodium-plated sterling, moonstones, red and blue stones and rhinestones, depicting a blooming plant in a flower pot. Plant 7x6.2cm; earrings 2.4x1.5cm.
    The brooch is marked Réja Sterling; the earrings Réja Sterling PAT. PEND. The patent pending mark refers to the patent of the clip mechanism which Réja also used in other earrings of the same period.
    The brooch appeared under its original name of "Chinese Plant" together with its matching earrings, in *WWD*, 7<sup>th</sup> March 1947 and in an advertisement published in *Vogue*, 15<sup>th</sup> February 1947.

# RICE-WEINER

    The name Rice-Weiner does not mean much even to experts, but in the period under review, Rice-Weiner was an important firm, which, particularly in the years between 1938 and 1950 manufactured premium jewelry, which was famous for the quality of its design, materials, and manufacture.

    The firm, which was founded in 1911 with the name of New England Glass Work, almost immediately registered the trademarks Jeray Jewelry and American Beauty Pearls.

    In January 1938 it changed its name to Rice-Weiner & Co., with offices and showroom in New York, 366 Fifth Avenue and a plant in Providence, R.I., first at 150, and later at 95 Chestnut Street. Successively it acquired another showroom in Chicago, at 36 So. State Street, and a third one in Los Angeles, at 607 So Hill Street. From 1936 to December 1948 the most representative figure of the company was Louis E. Hirsch, the general sales manager, who was later replaced by Martin Lasher.

*WWD*, February 19, 1937: New England Glass Work Jewelry. The company became Rice-Weiner in 1938.

£ 151

The first design patented on behalf of Rice-Weiner by Louis C. Mark of Providence, the firm's head designer, was an American eagle in fighting stance, dated 13th August 1940 (PRW21.). In September 1940, Mark designed a brooch and two necklaces with a plant motif (vine leaves and grapes), two necklaces, and a bracelet with large faceted stones. In September of the following year Mark designed and partly patented brooches, necklaces, bracelets, and earrings inspired, according to *Women's Wear Daily* of 7th July 1941, by Byzantine, Moorish, and Persian motifs (the latter bear the trademark PERSIAN CRAFT accompanied by signs that could be Persian alphabet letters), as well as Etruscan (the trademark Etrusceana probably refers to this), Maya (trademark Athennic Arts), and Chinese motifs. The latter include a brooch of a water bearer (RW11.). Since all these items bear neither the name Rice-Weiner, nor a patent number, the only way to trace their designer or manufacturer is by comparing them with the few patented designs, fourteen in all, of the period between 13th August 1940 and 23rd September 1941.

The importance of Rice-Weiner can only be appreciated in full when one considers that it was this firm that promoted and produced jewelry designed by McClelland Barclay bearing the artist's signature. Moreover, Rice-Weiner manufactured the jewelry marked "Thief of Bagdad Korda" and "Alexander Korda." The former was inspired by the film *The Thief of Bagdad,* 1940, a very successful production, which was awarded an Oscar for best colors. The latter was inspired by *The Jungle Book*, 1942, from the book of the same name by Rudyard Kipling. The first film mentioned was produced by Alexander Korda and directed by Ludwig Berger (and others), while the second film was produced by Alexander and directed by his brother, Zoltan Korda.

Sir Alexander Korda (1893-1956). Hungarian born filmmaker who succeeded as a producer in England.

The company's collaboration with McClelland Barclay began in the second half of 1938 and was documented in *Women's Wear Daily* which, on 5th July 1938, reported that the famous artist was about to deliver a collection of 150 models for Rice-Weiner. This collaboration continued until Barclay's death in 1943.

In 1939 Barclay designed a gold-plated jewelry collection with rhinestones and stones. An example of the collection is the "V Shaped" (RW16.) necklace. *WWD* also made mention of the 1940 and 1941 fall collections and, since the two printed articles describe most circulating items designed and signed by McClelland Barclay, the content of these articles deserves to be reported in full. The jewelry designed for the fall 1940 collection included a series of items featuring maple leaves, and, in particular, a small rhinestone-studded leaf laid on a larger gold-plated one. These leaves were used as clasps for a gold-plated flexible necklace and a bracelet. The necklace could be adjusted to the required length by means of a gliding closure (RW13.). Another group of jewelry items was called "Autumn Foliage" and featured combined gold, copper and silver elements, with different leaf designs. A third group featured crystal baguettes with fake stones mounted on smooth and glossy metal with yellow gold finish. The various possibilities offered by curved and contoured lines was explored to the full extent with these designs.

The designs dating from the fall of 1941 included silver-plated metal wings laid over larger gold-plated metal wings (PRW22.), large, smooth and polished metal bangles with relief designs which were replicated in the medallions of necklaces or on large brooches and clips. There were motifs inspired by wheat and leaves with rhinestone-studded veins. A last group of items, called "Moderne" (RW17.) combined leaves and flowers ornamented with fake stones and rhinestone scrolls.

Finally, during the second half of 1942 or at the beginning of 1943, McClelland Barclay, despite being deployed at the front, managed to design more sterling jewelry for Rice-Weiner. Among these items there was a brooch of a Mexican woman's head (RW18.) and brooches representing ethnic heads and busts, animals, objects etc.

The items were mainly made of brass-like gold-plated metal with geometric lines that produced a "sculpture-like" effect. Frequently two components made of different metals were assembled together to emphasize the juxtaposition of colors and stones. Figurative subjects were less frequent.

McClelland Barclay was born in St. Louis, Illinois, on 9th May 1893. He went to college in St. Louis and Washington and studied at the Corcoran School of Art in Washington, the Art Students' League in New York and the Art Institute in Chicago. He was also

*New York Herald Tribune,* July 25, 1943. Lieut. Comdr. McClelland Barclay.

awarded a scholarship for life by the St. Louis Museum of Fine Arts. He left St. Louis at sixteen years of age, lived in Chicago during the First World War and later moved to New York. He began his career in 1912 as an advertising designer, but soon made a name for himself as a sculptor and portrait painter. In 1917 he was awarded first prize for a recruitment poster ("Fill the Breach" © 30th June 1917) by the Conference Committee on National Preparedness. During the next three years, he was awarded prizes for two posters called "The Human Cross" and "At the Front of the Front." He was the creator of the "Fisher Body Girl" and designed covers for *The Ladies Home Journal, The Pictorial Review, The Country Gentleman, Cosmopolitan,* the *Saturday Evening Post,* and other magazines. In addition to jewelry for Rice-Weiner, he designed other items including lamps, ashtrays, bookends, vases, bureau items, boxes, cigarette cases etc. He also made sculptures. Barclay obtained the copyright in his name on some of these works such as the sculptures "Ecstasy" © 2nd June 1931, "Dog" and "Seal" © 21st June 1932.

McClelland Barclay Art Products, Inc., was based in New York, with offices at 305 East 45th Street, and its trademark was registered on 29th November 1938. The company's work was to promote the marketing of these items and, in general, Barclay's work as an illustrator. It started business in 1937 as documented by advertisements published in the *Jewelers' Circular Keystone* between February and November 1937.

Barclay was also the author of some remarkable pictures and drawings.

In October 1940 he was appointed lieutenant-commander in the reserve troops of the United States Navy, in which he had voluntarily enrolled in order to assist in the recruitment program by designing several posters.

At the beginning of the war he was called to active service by the Navy Recruiting Service and, in the meantime, made a series of portraits of the Commanders of the American Army and Navy. He belonged to the first unit of the War Art Corps which had traveled to Australia where, two months before his death, he started on a portrait of General Douglas MacArthur. Since the General was too busy to pose for the painting, he lent his jacket and famous braided beret to a model, while Barclay had to make do with a picture of the General to paint a likeness of MacArthur's face. A few days before 24th July 1943 a telegram from the United States Navy informed Barclay's brother Hamilton that lieutenant-commander McClelland Barclay had been declared missing in action, date and place unknown, probably in Australia or New Guinea. He had just turned fifty.

As already mentioned, Rice-Weiner made jewels inspired by Alexander Korda's movies, *The Thief of Bagdad,* in 1940 and *The Jungle Book,* in 1942. Legend has it that Alexander Korda asked for a series of items

resembling the characters, animals and objects used in the film to be given as gifts to the film crew. More prosaically, Rice-Weiner obtained from United Artists the exclusive copyright and, in order to protect it, he marked the items "Thief of Bagdad Korda ©" and "Alexander Korda ©."

*WWD,* August 23, 1940: advertisement by Rice-Weiner and Bud Fox Enterprises.

The jewelry subjects designed were not exactly identical to those of the movie, but were freely inspired by Arab or jungle themes.

The signs that appear before and after the trademark "Thief of Bagdad Korda©" are not, as is commonly believed, the figures 113 and 61, but letters from the Arabic alphabet, something like ﻟﻟﺟﺛ and ﻊﺟ. Whether they are correct or a fantasy creation is not known. The designs were probably by Louis C. Mark.

The jewelry inspired by *The Jungle Book* was called "Jungle Jewelry" and was presented with this name exclusively at the Arnold Constable stores in January 1942. Sabou "the elephant boy" (from a 1937 movie by Korda of the same name) who played the role of Mowgli in *The Jungle Book* and the little thief Abu in *The Thief of Bagdad,* also came to the presentation.

Sir Alexander Korda, who was born in Hungary in 1893 and died in London in 1956, was the producer and director of many famous films including, in addition to the two mentioned above: *The Private Life of Henry VIII,* 1933, *The Four Feathers,* 1939, (after which a "Four Feathers" brooch was designed and manufactured by Silson) and *That Hamilton Woman,* 1941 (Natasha Brooks designed jewelry and accessories inspired by the film for Albert Manufacturing).

Rice-Weiner's products in the following years never again reached the same high standards as the products described and actually showed some signs of decline.

In 1946 Barclay Jewelry, Inc. was created as a result of a split in the company. The new company was set up by Alvin and Robert Rice together with head designer Louis C. Mark and other partners. Following the split the company assets were divided: the Providence plant at 150 Chestnut Street, went to Barclay, and Rice-Weiner moved to No. 95 in the same street.

The name Barclay was chosen in remembrance of the glorious products designed by McClelland Barclay, as is confirmed by the trademark (a palette with the Barclay logo and the words "Art in Jewelry") and by the mark impressed on the jewelry, which are very similar to the artist's signature. Moreover, the products of the firm's early years closely resembles McClelland's. This comes as no surprise, since in both cases production was under the supervision of Louis Mark.

The split weakened Rice-Weiner which tried to regain its position by using the trademarks Jeray and American Beauty Pearls and by hiring new designers, including Natacha Brooks (see monograph) to design its collections.

In 1949 under a new sales manager, Martin Lasher, an attempt was made to revive the old successful policy of making products inspired by the cinema, by purchasing from Paramount Pictures Corporation the copyright for the production of so-called "Minoic" jewelry inspired by Cecil B. De Mille's movie *Samson and Delilah* starring Hedy Lamarr and Victor Mature.

In 1950 another important designer, Norman Bel Geddes (reference is made to this designer in the section on Trifari) designed the fall collection for Rice-Weiner called "Flow Motion," which was made up of necklaces, bracelets, brooches and earrings. In Bel Geddes's words, as reported in an article in *WWD* of 16th June 1950 for the presentation of the collection at the Hotel Pierre in New York, the name stemmed from his conviction that jewelry should follow the body's movements and the way clothes fall. Hence, the choice of "Flow Motion."

The shapes of these items were not completely modern. Many had an antique quality, particularly those made of pearls and golden spirals, modernized by a contemporary construction and a modification of the models. The collection also had a fantasy element, especially the "gadget pins" which included, among others, small poodles, cats' heads with iridescent eyes, and devils' heads with rolling eyes.

The items designed by Bel Geddes, like those designed by McClelland Barclay, were marked with the designer's name, i.e. Bel Geddes, as in the case of a brooch of a snail reproduced in Gordon's *Twentieth Century Costume Jewelry*, p. 183, and *Design by Bel Geddes*.

In 1950, Betty Betz, a famous columnist and author of children's books, was asked to design for Rice-Weiner a special line of costume jewelry for teenagers. These items were marked with the designer's name, i.e. Betty Betz.

Unfortunately these initiatives did not meet with success and, on 1st January 1951, Rice-Weiner ceased its retailing business in order to concentrate entirely on wholesale. This new commercial policy meant an inevitable loss of identity and uniqueness in Rice-Weiner's production with the natural result that its products were no longer of interest to collectors.

RW1. "Crystal Gazer," Thief of Bagdad Korda 1940**** Manufacturer Rice-Weiner & Co., Providence, Rhode Island.

**Jewelry Reflecting the Persian Influences—**

The crescent necklace is one of a series of Persian jewelry in antique silver or gold and enamel cloisonne, featured by Rice-Weiner & Co. The crescent, symbol of the East, hangs from the chains to give a one-sided effect.

The pin at right, representing the Crystal Gazer, is from the "Thief of Bagdad" series advanced here, and is in antique silver. The crystal ball is a sphere, not flat. Both designs are copyrighted.

*WWD*, August 9, 1940.

Gold-plated metal brooch, with enamel and Lucite, of a seated fortune teller gazing into a crystal ball. The figure is wearing an enamel robe and a turban in different shades of beige and brown, with a blue bib and stars and a crescent moon on the turban. The fortune teller's bearded face and hands are made of dark pink, black and red enamel. The crystal ball is made of a large spinning citrine Lucite ball. 6.5x4.8cm.

Marked ﺝ ﺝ ﺝ ∃ Thief of Bagdad Korda ©∈ ſ. The signs that precede and follow the mark are not, as is often stated, the figures 113 and 61, but real or imitation Arab letters. In this case the © (copyright) indicated that Rice Weiner held an exclusive reproduction right on movie designs or designs inspired by the movie, which were copyrighted.

In fact in 1940 Rice-Weiner purchased from United Artists the exclusive right to reproduce jewelry inspired by the movie "The Thief of Bagdad," produced by Alexander Korda and directed by Ludwig Berger, Michael Powell, Tim Whelan and, though unmentioned, Zoltan Korda (*WWD*, 23rd August 1940, joint communiqué issued by Rice-Weiner and United Artists). The series included brooches, bracelets, necklaces, rings and earrings that variously used the characters and objects portrayed in the film, or generically oriental motifs: scimitars, stars and crescent moons, Ali Baba and his marauders (who did not actually appear in the film), as bracelet charms, a camel rider on camel back, the genie, the pink elephant, Ali Baba on his flying carpet, Sinbad the sailor and his crew (who again, did not appear in the movie) and many more. The "Crystal Gazer" featured in *WWD*, 9th August 1940, and in *Glamour*, December 1940, where its readers were informed that this item, which was part of the "American Beauty Fashion" by Rice-Weiner, was on sale for $ 1 at Lord & Taylor's of New York.

It is a possibility that the designs for this jewelry, like those of the successive "Jungle Jewelry" line, were made by Louis C. Mark, who was the company's head designer at that time.

RW2. "Silver Maid," Thief of Bagdad Korda 1940***
Manufacturer Rice-Weiner & Co., Providence, Rhode
Island.
    White metal brooch, blue and pink enamel, of a
seated woman. 5x4.2cm.
    Marked ♩ ♩ ∃ Thief of Bagdad Korda ©∈ ∫
    The design is reminiscent of the "Silver
Maid," the mechanical toy with which Jafar
killed the princess' father.

RW3. "Riding Guard," Thief of Bagdad Korda 1940****
Manufacturer Rice-Weiner & Co., Providence, Rhode
Island.
    White metal brooch of a galloping horseman with
a whip. 5.5x6.5cm.
    Marked ♩ ♩ ∃ Thief of Bagdad Korda ©∈ ∫
    This item could have been inspired by the guards
on horseback who, in the film, make their way through
the crowd, for the princess' arrival.
    The fact that there is an identical enameled piece marked
Staret (St10.) demonstrates that Rice-Weiner also worked for
Staret.

RW4. "Ship," Thief of Bagdad Korda 1940***
Manufacturer Rice-Weiner & Co., Providence, Rhode
Island
    White metal brooch of a ship. 5.5x5.5cm.
    Marked ♩ ♩ ∃ Thief of Bagdad Korda ©∈ ∫
    The piece is reminiscent of the ship of Jafar the
usurper.

RW5. "Jungle Jewelry Panther", Alexander Korda
1942***
    Manufacturer Rice-Weiner & Co., Providence,
    Rhode Island.
    White metal brooch, turquoise and blue
    cabochons, of a panther on two elephant tusks
    made from synthetic ivory. 4x6cm.
    Marked © Alexander Korda.

RW6. "Jungle Jewelry Orchid," Alexander Korda
1942****
Manufacturer Rice-Weiner & Co., Providence, Rhode
Island.
    Gold-plated metal brooch, blue and green enamel,
rhinestones, of an orchid. 7x5.5cm.
Marked © Alexander Korda.

RW7. "Jungle Jewelry Mask," Alexander Korda 1942****
Manufacturer Rice-Weiner & Co., Providence, Rhode Island.
Gold-plated metal brooch, black enamel and turquoise,
of a tribal mask with elephant-tusk headgear made of
synthetic ivory, nose ring and long metal dangling earrings
with red stones. 9x6cm.
Marked © Alexander Korda.

RW8. "Jungle Jewelry Head," Alexander Korda 1942*****
Manufacturer Rice-Weiner & Co., Providence, Rhode Island.
Gold-plated metal and black enamel pin clip of a Moor head
with an elaborate headdress with turquoises and ruby cabochons, with a faux ivory elephant tusk. In one ear the
Moor is wearing a long earring in the shape of a coiled
snake with a dangling faux ivory bead. 9.8x4cm.
Marked © Alexander Korda.
In 1942, after the huge success of the jewelry inspired by the "Thief of Bagdad," Rice-Weiner acquired
from United Artists, the exclusive right to manufacture
jewelry inspired by the movie "The Jungle Book,"
from Kipling's novel, even before the film reached
the cinema. This movie was produced by Alexander
Korda, directed by his brother Zoltan, and starred
the same actor, Sabu, who played the part of Abu in
the "Thief of Bagdad," in the role of Mowgli. This collection was called "Jungle Jewelry" and was exclusively
presented in New York by the Arnold Constable stores,
and was a huge commercial success. Among the most successful pieces, *WWD*, 30th January 1942, mentioned the brooch here
reproduced and a necklace, with matching earrings, the pendants
of which depicted elephant heads and tusks. The necklace and earrings featured in the "Ladies Home Journal," March 1942.

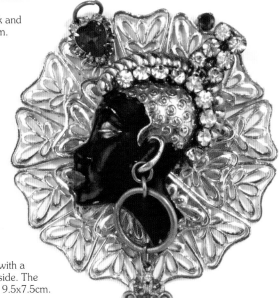

RW9. "Jungle Jewelry Drummer," Alexander Korda
1942****
Manufacturer Rice-Weiner & Co., Providence, Rhode
Island.
Gold-plated metal brooch, black, pink and
blue enamel, of a drummer. 4.5x6cm.
Marked ©Alexander Korda.

RW10. "Jungle Jewelry Head Locket," Rice-Weiner
1942****
Manufacturer Rice-Weiner & Co., Providence, Rhode
Island.
Gold-plated metal locket, red stones and rhinestones, with a
female head in black and red enamel and rhinestones inside. The
female is wearing a large dangling earring with a cameo. 9.5x7.5cm.
Unmarked.
This piece was undoubtedly made by Rice-Weiner due to the fact that the
head is identical to the "Jungle Jewelry Head" (RW8.).

RW11. "Chinese Water Boy," Rice-Weiner 1941\*\*\*
Manufacturer Rice-Weiner & Co., Providence, Rhode Island.
Designer Louis C. Mark.
Patent n° 129,573 Louis. C. Mark, Providence, R.I., 16th
September 1941, filed on 2nd August 1941.

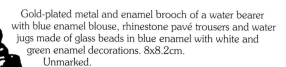

Gold-plated metal and enamel brooch of a water bearer
with blue enamel blouse, rhinestone pavé trousers and water
jugs made of glass beads in blue enamel with white and
green enamel decorations. 8x8.2cm.
Unmarked.
This design was inspired by a precious jewel created
by Trabert & Hoeffer for Mauboussin in the same
period, which had gold, rubies, sapphires, peridots and
diamonds.
The Trabert & Hoeffer model inspired other, more
or less identical imitations, some of which were marked
Sterling and Mexico Sterling.

RW12. "Horses Bracelet," McClelland Barclay 1938\*\*\*\*
Manufacturer Rice-Weiner & Co., Providence, Rhode Island.
Designer McClelland Barclay.
Sterling bracelets with four links depicting a horse with a tree in the background, joined by
smaller links with leaf motif. Length 18cm, width 2.3cm.
The first collection designed by McClelland Barclay for Rice-Weiner in 1938 included a series
of sterling jewelry and was presented in September of the same year by B. Altman & Co.

RW13. "Maple Leaf Set," McClelland Barclay 1940****
Manufacturer Rice-Weiner & Co., Providence, Rhode Island.
Designer McClelland Barclay.
   Set made up of gold-plated metal necklace, brooch and bracelet with rhinestones and double maple leaves; a larger gold-plated metal one and a smaller one with rhinestone pavé, on top. The bracelet has a hinged-link chain with a hidden clasp.
   The necklace has a double-link snake chain, with frontal clasp and three adjustable leaves.
   Necklace middle leaf 6x6cm.
   Brooch 7x7.3cm. Bracelet length 17.5cm, width 4.5cm.
   Marked McClelland Barclay on a rectangular plaque.
   Tamara de Lempicka wore this brooch in a picture reproduced in Gioia Mori's book, *Tamara de Lempicka, Parigi 1920-1938* (Giunti, 1994).
   Jewelry designed by McClelland Barclay for the 1940 collection included, in addition to the "Maple Leaf," another line with leaf motifs, called "Autumn Foliage" (*WWD*, 17th July 1940).

**Opposite page:**
RW14. "Raised Style," McClelland Barclay 1941****
Manufacturer Rice-Weiner & Co., Providence, Rhode Island.
Designer McClelland Barclay.

A line which was part of the fall 1941 collection, and was featured in *Women's Wear Daily* (7th July 1941), including a description of the items, which featured relief motifs of rhinestones and colored stones. The items had no names. This theme was used for a wide array of jewelry – necklaces, chains with pendants, hinged-link bracelet, bangles, square and rectangular brooches– in several stone color variants.

Inspiration for this line of jewelry came from Art Déco.

1) Gold-plated metal square brooch with rhinestones and sapphires. A relief geometrical motif of rhinestone pavé with sapphire inserts, placed on top of a sculpted frame. 5x5.3cm.

2) Gold-plated metal brooch and bangle set. The rectangular brooch features a sculpted frame and a rhinestone pavé relief overlay with emerald inserts. 3.3x6.5cm. The same motif is applied to the bangle. Width 2.5cm.

3) Chain with gold-plated metal, rhinestone and amethyst pendant. The round sculpted medallion features a geometrical overlay motif with rhinestone pavé and amethyst inserts. Medallion diameter: 5.9cm.

4) Two gold-plated bracelets with rectangular hinged links and "bridge" overlay motif with rhinestones and rubies in one version, and amethysts in another. Length 17cm, width 2.2cm. The bracelets can be matched to all the items in this series.

All items are marked McClelland Barclay on a rectangular plaque.

**Interior:**
RW15. "Raised Style Necklace," McClelland Barclay 1941****
Manufacturer Rice-Weiner & Co., Providence, Rhode Island
Designer McClelland Barclay.

Gold-plated metal necklace, red stones and rhinestones. 3x16cm, central motif.

Marked Barclay on a rectangular plate.

This mark should not be confused with that of Barclay Jewelry, Inc., because it reproduced part of McClelland's unmistakable signature.

**Exterior:**
RW16. "V Shaped Necklace," McClelland Barclay 1939****
Manufacturer Rice-Weiner & Co., Providence, Rhode Island.
Designer McClelland Barclay.

*Glamour*, December 1939.

Gold-plated metal necklace with a V-shaped central section, featuring relief motifs with rhinestone pavé and ruby inserts. Central motif 16cm.

Marked McClelland Barclay on a rectangular plaque.

A picture of this item appeared in *Glamour*, December 1939.

RW17. "Moderne Pin," McClelland Barclay 1941***
Manufacturer Rice-Weiner & Co., Providence, Rhode Island.
Designer McClelland Barclay.
   Rhodium plated metal brooch, with rhinestone pavé and blue marquise-cut sapphires with a circular spiraling line. 6.5x6cm.
   Marked McClelland Barclay.
   In the fall of 1941 (WWD, 7th July), McClelland Barclay designed a collection focused on four themes: "Wings" characterized by overlaid-silver plated metal wings (PRW22.); "Wheat" with wheat inspired motifs; "Moderne" with leaf and flower motifs, stone inserts and rhinestone spirals; whilst the fourth group, which was described without making a mention of its name, was characterized by relief motifs ("raised style"). This brooch, due to its characteristics, almost certainly belongs to the "Moderne" group.

RW18. "Mexican Head," McClelland Barclay 1942-43****
Manufacturer Rice-Weiner & Co., Providence, Rhode Island.
Designer McClelland Barclay.
   Pink gold-plated sterling brooch of a Mexican woman's head with large earrings and a sombrero. 6x7cm.
Marked McClelland Barclay Sterling.
   In the fall of 1942 or at the beginning of 1943, McClelland Barclay, who had already been deployed at the front, designed a sterling jewelry series manufactured by Rice-Weiner, which included the "Mexican Head".

# NETTIE ROSENSTEIN

Nettie Rosenstein, whose real name was Henrietta Rosencrans, was born in Austria in 1890 and, at two years of age emigrated with her family to the United States. She began to work as a milliner with her sisters and, in 1921, thanks to her skill as a designer, set up her own company which employed fifty seamstresses. In spite of her success, she decided to retire in 1927. Two years later she started working again as a designer for Corbett & Cie and, in the same year, re-opened her own *maison de couture* with the name of Nettie Rosenstein Gowns Inc. Within a few years the company became very successful.

In May 1942 Rosenstein began manufacturing costume jewelry through the Nettie Rosenstein Accessories Corporation with offices in New York, at 680 Fifth Avenue. The first collection, which as with practically all the successive collections, was designed by Rosenstein; it was presented in the issue of WWD of 17th July 1942. The collection included the usual array of metal and sterling brooches, clips, earrings, necklaces and bracelets. One of the most remarkable items made was a brooch and earrings set of a bunch of flowers. The flowers were made of cut emerald with leaves and stems in gold plated sterling and the brooch

was six inches long. Another extraordinary item was a sterling blue and black enamel brooch with earrings, of a rooster.

From this time onwards, she produced collections on a regular basis. Her production was always outstanding in terms of design and manufacture. Among Rosenstein items worthy of mention is her 1945 version of the "Sunburst" motif made popular by the precious jewelry with that name designed by the Duke of Verdura. In 1946, she made an extraordinary series of large sterling brooches of old pipes. In 1947 she made necklaces, bracelets and earrings with vegetation motifs, especially of leaves, with or without stones, and with coats of arms motifs, as in the "Court Order" series, inspired by the emblems of the Scottish and British nobility.

The jewelry of this period was large-sized and mainly made of gold-plated sterling. Typical items of this period were the large and heavy cuff bracelets that covered the wrist and hand, which were meant to be worn on both wrists. This jewelry was designed to harmonize with the fashion of the time and, in particular, with the clothes designed by Nettie Rosenstein.

Nettie Rosenstein

uses one of her favorite fabrics—pure
silk Canton crepe—for a deep-sleeved black dress.

*Town & Country,* April 1946: Nettie Rosenstein's dress and jewelry.

NR1. "Frog," Nettie Rosenstein 1944***
Manufacturer Nettie Rosenstein Accessories, Corp., New York.
Designer Nettie Rosenstein.
   Gold-plated sterling and rhinestone brooch of a frog.
4.5x5.8cm.
   Marked Nettie Rosenstein Sterling.
   According to *WWD,* 14 July 1944, Nettie Rosenstein's fall
1944 collection included animal brooches in sets of three, of
decreasing size, to be worn together. Sometimes the brooches
were joined together by a chain.

The use of sterling continued throughout the first
half of the 1950s and some remarkable specimens were
created. The 1949 and 1950 collections were designed
in collaboration with a designer called Sol Klein.

In 1961 Nettie Rosenstein abandoned the clothes-
making part of her business, and focused on manufacturing accessories, including costume jewelry. The Nettie
Rosenstein Accessories Corporation was documented
until 1985, when it had its offices at 220 East 23rd Street,
New York, and was staffed by twenty to fifty employees.
Its founder, however, had retired at the end of the 1960s
and had died in 1980 at ninety years of age.

None of Nettie Rosenstein's jewelry designs was
patented (unlike her clothes designs) and all items are
marked Nettie Rosenstein inscribed in a rectangular plate
with the addition, whenever it was the case, of the usual
sterling mark.

NR2. "Open Work Cuff Bracelet," Nettie Rosenstein 1947***
Manufacturer Nettie Rosenstein Accessories, Corp., New York.
Designer Nettie Rosenstein.
   Wide and heavy cuff bracelet made of openwork, gold-
plated sterling, with leaf motif. Width: 8.5cm.
   Marked Nettie Rosenstein Sterling.

NR3. "Elephant," Nettie Rosenstein 1944***
Manufacturer Nettie Rosenstein Accessories Corp., New York.
Designer Nettie Rosenstein.
    Pink gold-plated sterling pin clip of an elephant with a saddle cloth in
relief and ornamented with green rhinestones and pink enamel. 4.5x6.5cm.
    Marked Nettie Rosenstein Sterling "2".
    The trademark graphics are the same as the designer's signature, while
the number is the reference number of the stone setter.

NR4. "Swallow," Nettie Rosenstein 1947**
Manufacturer Nettie Rosenstein Accessories, Corp., New York.
Designer Nettie Rosenstein.
    Gold-plated sterling hat pin, with
faceted pink opal and rhinestones,
depicting a flying swallow. 5x5cm.
    Marked Nettie Rosenstein Sterling.
    According to *WWD*, 24 January 1947,
Nettie Rosenstein's spring 1947 collection included brooches of birds in
flight, to be worn on hats and dresses.
A characteristic common to all these
items was the use of Mexican
opals.

NR5. "Ma-
ple Leaves
Necklace,"
Nettie Rosen-
stein 1947***
Manufacturer
Nettie Rosenstein
Accessories Corp.,
New York.
Designer Nettie Rosen-
stein.
    Heavy gold-plated sterling necklace
with hinged links shaped like maple leaves in decreasing
sizes. The necklace has a hidden clasp worn at the front. Length
42.5cm, middle leaf: 5x6.5cm.
    Marked Nettie Rosenstein Sterling.
    This item belonged to the tailored line of the fall 1947
collection (*WWD*, 27 June 1947) which further developed the
theme of the spring collection, centered on sculpted oak
and maple leaves for necklaces with an airy design in
spite of the actual considerable weight of sterling.

NR6. "Chinese Couple," Nettie Rosenstein 1943****
Manufacturer Nettie Rosenstein Accessories Corp., New York.
Designer Nettie Rosenstein.
    Pair of pin clips made of gold-plated sterling and colored enamel, depicting a
Chinese couple wearing ancient Mandarin costumes. The man is seated, the woman is
standing and facing the man. Man: 5.8x3.5cm, woman: 7x3.5cm.
    Marked Nettie Rosenstein on a rectangular plaque, Sterling mark on the pin.
    According to *WWD*, 18 June 1943, Nettie Rosenstein's fall collection included Chi-
nese inspired subjects made of gold-plated sterling and enamel.

# SANDOR

The company was founded in 1938 by Sandor Goldberger, initially as a sole proprietorship, and was incorporated in 1943. Its offices and showroom were in New York, at 22 West 38th Street. In 1948 the plant and showroom were moved to 7 West 36th Street.

At the beginning of 1939 the company registered the trademark REGIMENTAL CRESTS for a collection of large brooches, lockets, and bracelets with the emblems of several regiments of the United States army, including the 3rd Field Artillery regiment and the 15th Infantry regiment. This was an early "military" or "patriotic" series inspired by the winds of war that were blowing all over Europe and Asia, with America caught between isolationist and the interventist factions. The enamels and stones of the emblems were in the national red, white and blue colors.

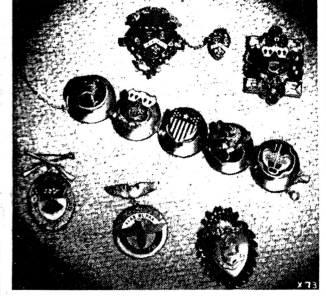

**Regimental Crests Inspire New "Military" Jewelry**

The war abroad is stimulating fashion interest in military themes, not only in Paris, but here as well. Thus we see a red-white-and-blue color scheme important for resort wear, new handbags taking their shapes from canteens and gas masks, coats and suits adopting military details of cut.

A new style source for costume jewelry has been utilized in the pieces shown above — regimental crests said to be taken from actual United States military units. The enameled crests are mounted in big pins, lockets, bracelets, many of them surrounded by brilliant red, white and blue stones, as the two brooches at the top carrying insignia of the third Field Artillery and 15th Infantry. The massive bracelet at center uses, among others, Air Service crests. This collection is from Sandor Goldberger.

*WWD*, February 10, 1939: Regimental Crests by Sandor Goldberger.

variety of materials and stones. These features crop up in other 1939 items, such as a necklace with large, pink "bubble" pearls, alternated with golden cellophane "passementary" beads, threaded onto a pink string, featured in *Women's Wear Daily*, 22nd December, and a necklace and bracelet set with ice-cube like stones, which was featured in *Vogue*, 1st December.

From 1939 onwards, *WWD* regularly featured Sandor Goldberger's collections, often with pictures of his designs.

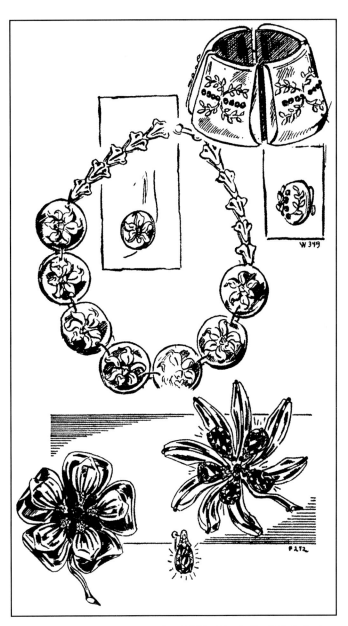

*WWD*, November 29, 1940 (above) and *WWD*, March 21, 1941 (below): Lucite Jewelry by Sandor Goldberger.

These items displayed all the typical characteristics which remained a constant in all of Sandor Goldberger's products who also was the designer: large dimensions, unusual subjects, sometimes ahead of his time, great

In 1940 Sandor was among the first jewelers to make significant use of Lucite in items which looked heavy but were actually light, thanks to the plastic material used. This was sometimes assembled to thin gold-plated metal supports, studded with stones and light enameled engravings with classic and modern designs. Lucite was regularly used by Sandor throughout the first half of the 1940s in "convertible" bangles and necklaces, i.e. items that could be transformed into single or double pieces, and in large brooches, with floral, vegetation, and figurative subjects. Subjects used were often of animal and human figures, such as the so-called "Balinese" heads (S1., S3., S4.) of 1942, made of black or white enameled metal with Lucite banana-leaf headdresses. The Sandor collections also included some more formal – albeit unconventional – items, such as necklaces with jet beads combined with crystals, or necklaces of gold-plated metal foxtail chains and red glass beads.

From the end of 1942 and throughout the war years, Sandor, like other costume jewelry manufacturers, replaced all metal alloys with sterling. Among the most significant Sandor items created during this time were, in 1943, a large brooch of a butterfly with pearly wings and a body made of stones imported from France, and, in 1944, an extraordinary brooch inspired by Chinese motifs, shaped like a square with a rhinestone and green stone studded frame. The same stones were used for an inlay square at the center of the brooch. Wartime production probably also included sterling and enamel brooches of a basket or vase of flowers (S6.), often paired with matching earrings. In 1945 Sandor was among the first to present a costume jewelry version of the "Sunburst" brooch (S5.). Inspired by a piece of jewelry of the same subject made of diamonds and platinum designed by the Duke of Verdura, it was an instant best-seller.

After the war, Sandor quickly replaced sterling with metals and plastic materials ornamented with stones to make designs of jewelry which had an immediate impact, this was especially the case with his necklaces made of synthetic coral and ceramic. Enamel, frequently in a matte version, was a constant in Sandor's collections and it continued to be used thereafter, and as late as 1950, with the creation of a brooch with matching earrings of a metal and red enamel tulip.

The company, whose earliest jewelry is rarely found on the market today, ceased to exist in the 1970s.

As shown by the almost identical nature of items marked Sandor, Sandor Goldberger also designed and manufactured jewelry for Fred A. Block.

The Sandor company designer was Sandor Goldberger who only patented one design. From the very start of his career, for about twenty years, he collaborated with Beatrice Grace McGowan, a designer of Portuguese origin, who had grown up in British Guyana.

The marks stamped on the jewelry were: at the beginning (1939-40) "Sandor Goldberger" in italics, then "SANDOR" in block letters, then, from 1954 onwards, "SANDOR©."

S1. "Balinese Head," Sandor 1942*****
Manufacturer Sandor Goldberger, New York.
Designer Sandor Goldberger.
　Gold-plated metal pin clip, white enamel, red cabochons and Lucite, depicting a head with an elaborate lucite hairstyle. 10x6.5cm.
　Marked Sandor.
　In the spring of 1942 Sandor returned to a theme that had already been used in the preceding season, defined by *WWD*, 8th February 1942, as "Balinese Heads". These are metal brooches with an enamel finish, which portray some heads with headdresses of banana leaves made of lucite.

S2. "Butterfly," Sandor 1941***
Manufacturer Sandor Goldberger, New York.
Designer Sandor Goldberger.
　Gold-plated metal brooch of a butterfly in flight, seen in profile. Its body is made of a large imitation topaz stone, its head of a green stone and its wings are rhinestone pavé. 5.5x6cm.
　Marked Sandor.
　*WWD*, on 17th October 1941, mentioned that Sandor items of the fall collections included designs of insects with large colored stones.

S4. "Balinese Head," Sandor 1942*****
Manufacturer Sandor Goldberger, New York.
Designer Sandor Goldberger.
Gold-plated metal and lucite pin clip, of a head with an elaborate lucite banana-tree leaf headdress. 5.2x8.2cm
Marked Sandor.

S5. "Sunburst," Sandor 1945****
Manufacturer Sandor Goldberger, New York
Designer Sandor Goldberger.

S3. "Balinese Head," Sandor 1942*****
Manufacturer Sandor Goldberger, New York.
Designer Sandor Goldberger.
Gold-plated metal brooch, with black and gold enamel and lucite, depicting a Balinese mask with a black enamel face, gold enamel mouth, eyes, eyebrows and forehead lines. It had a large and elaborate headdress made of three contoured lucite banana-tree leaves. 8.5x4.7cm.
Marked Sandor.

*WWD*, February 9, 1945: "Sunburst" brooch and earrings by Sandor.

Gold-plated sterling brooch with rhinestones in the shape of a sunburst. 6.5x6.5cm.
Marked Sandor Sterling.
The "Sunburst" was taken from a design created by the Duke of Verdura for a precious piece of jewelry (reproduced in *Fortune*, December 1946) which launched this fashion in costume jewelry. Many of the most important manufacturers made sunbursts.
This item confirms, once again, that Sandor designed and manufactured jewelry for Fred A. Block since a nearly identical piece by Fred A. Block featured in an advertisement in *Vogue*, 1st December 1946.

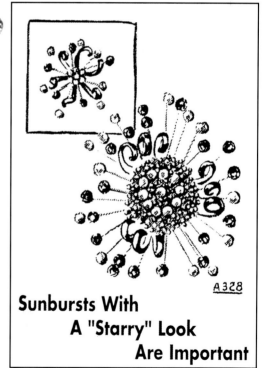

A328

## Sunbursts With A "Starry" Look Are Important

S6. "Flower Pot," Sandor 1943****
Manufacturer Sandor Goldberger, New York.
Designer Sandor Goldberger.
Gold-plated sterling brooch with matte white and green enamel and multicolor faceted stones, depicting a pot of flowers. The flowerpot is studded with bright blue baguettes and has green enamel borders, the flower petals are made of red, blue, green, pink and yellow marquise-cut stones and rhinestones around a small white enamel flower with a small blue stone at the center. There is a thin hook on the back of the brooch giving the wearer the possibility of pinning the brooch to her clothes in two points. 7.5x7.2cm.
Marked Sandor Sterling.
*Women's Wear Daily*, 24th July 1942, stated that Sandor's fall collection, made of gold-plated sterling, featured floral and vegetable motifs. The fact that a design from the spring 1943 collection featured a floral motif very similar to that of the "Flower Pot" allows for accurate dating of this item.

# H. M. SCHRAGER & CO., INC.

U5. "The Glorious Butterfly," Unsigned 1942\*\*\*\*
Manufacturer H.M. Schrager & Co., Inc.

"A Thing of Beauty Is a Joy Forever!"

"The Glorious Butterfly"—Shown nearly actual size this life-like butterfly pin is entirely of finest cut imported color stones set in a background of scintillating rhinestones—truly in spring motif to enhance milady's new ensemble. To retail at $5.95.

**H. M. Schrager & Co., Inc.**
303 5th Ave., New York City — 36 S. State St., Chicago
See Our Entire Line—Chicago Gift Show, Palmer House, Room 685

"Jewelers' Circular Keystone," January 1942: "The Glorious Butterfly" by Schrager

White metal brooch, faceted violet, blue, green, red and yellow crystals, rhinestones, in the shape of a butterfly. 8x10cm.
Unmarked.
The item was published in an advertisement by Schrager & Co. in *The Jewelers' Circular Keystone*, January 1942, and was on sale for $5,95. The advertisement stated that the stones used were imported and not synthetic.
The brooch also exists with the mark Staret which is confirmation of the fact that Schrager & Co. also designed and produced for Staret. The stones of the butterfly are identical to those of the "Lyon Mask" by Staret (St6.).
Schrager & Co. was founded in 1925 (*WWD*, 9th March 1943) and had its head office in New York, 305 Fifth Avenue, and an office in Chicago, 36 South State Street. In Chicago the company also had a gift store at Palmer House.

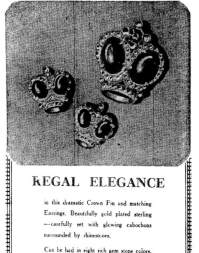

## REGAL ELEGANCE

in this dramatic Crown Pin and matching Earrings. Beautifully gold plated sterling —carefully set with glowing cabochons surrounded by rhinestones.

Can be had in eight rich gem stone colors.

**"OUR SECOND DECADE OF SERVICE".**

Pin to retail at $19.50
Pair of earrings to retail at $19.50
Small pin to retail at $10.00

*WWD*, March 9, 1945: "Regal Elegance" by Schrager.

Gold-plated sterling chatelaine joining two brooches shaped like a large (king) and a small (queen) crown with green cabochons and rhinestones. 4.3x4cm (King); 2.2x2.2cm (Queen).
The King Crown with matching earrings was reproduced in a Schrager advertisement in *WWD*, 9th March 1945. The slogan used was "Regal Elegance." The set was available in eight different stone colors and its sale price was $ 19.50 for the King Crown, $ 19.50 for the earrings, and $ 10 for the Queen Crown.

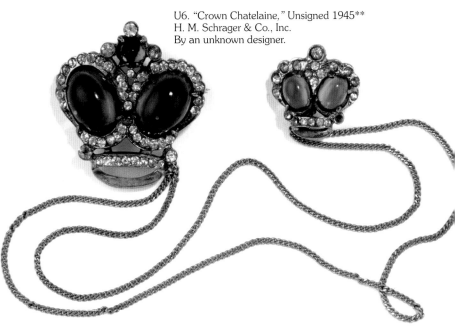

U6. "Crown Chatelaine," Unsigned 1945\*\*
H. M. Schrager & Co., Inc.
By an unknown designer.

# SILSON

Silson Inc. of New York was probably founded in 1937 by two brothers; Victor and Jack Silberfeld, who were probably of Australian origin and later becoming British citizens, changing their name to Silson. There are patents under both names, though the most frequently used name is Victor. The designers Samuel Rubin (Si3.) and George Stangl who owned a jewellers laboratory in Paris (124 Faubourg St. Honoré), also worked for Silson. American designers such as Sue Harrison and Sally Stark also worked for the company. In 1940-41 Silson specialized in various types of patriotic jewelry production, though it also created other imaginative subjects and imitation jewelry. Designs by Victor Silson were also produced by the Mexican company Spratling Co., which specialized in Sterling Silver jewellery (Si2.).

There is no further information about Silson after the 1940s.

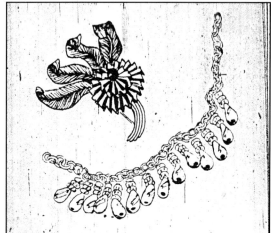

Inspired jewelry. The forthcoming Korda production. "Four Feathers", provided inspiration for this Silson jewelry. There's a feeling of fine primitive carving in the pendant necklace. About $3 with a matching bracelet. . . . Next to it, a four-feathered gold metal pin, centered with a bright enamel fluted pinwheel. Under $2. Best's, New York: Halle Bros., Cleveland

*Glamour*, November 1939: "Four Feathers" Jewelry by Silson, Inc.

Si1. "Running Unicorn," Silson 1938****
Manufacturer Silson Co.
Designer Vally Wieselthier.
Patent n° 108,902 Vally Wieselthier, New York, 22nd March 1938, filed on 1st February 1938, assignor to Victor Silberfeld and Jack Silberfeld, New York, doing business as Silson Co.

Gold-plated metal brooch, black and white enamel, of a running unicorn. 4.3x11cm.
Marked Silson Patented.

Si2. "Wise Owl," Silson 1940***
Manufacturer Silson, Inc.
Designer Victor Silson.
Patent n° 123,824 Victor Silson, New York, 3rd December 1940, filed on 30th October 1940.

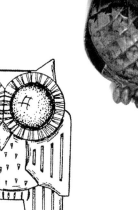

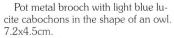

Pot metal brooch with light blue lucite cabochons in the shape of an owl. 7.2x4.5cm.
Unmarked.
This item was reproduced in *Glamour*, December 1940, where it stated that it was a Silson copy from an original Mexican piece. The item does in fact exist in silver marked with the name Spratling. The price was $1.95.

Gold-plated metal pin clip, with black enamel and rhinestones, of a tiger making a toast with a glass of champagne. 7.5x6.5cm.
Marked Silson Patented.
There are also other variants of this brooch, one with the tiger holding an umbrella and one with a glass that has no bubbles, but it was drilled, in order to double as a perfume holder.

Si3. "Drunk Tiger," Silson 1940***
Manufacturer Silson Inc., New York.
Designer Samuel Rubin.
Patent n° 123,216 Samuel Rubin, New York, 22nd October 1940, filed on 18th September 1940.

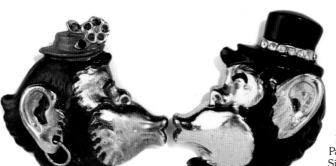

Gold-plated metal pin clips, brown, green black and red enamel, of two gorilla heads, male and female, kissing each other. 4x4.5cm.
Marked Silson Patented.

Si4. "Mrs. & Mr. Gorilla," Silson 1940***
Manufacturer Silson, Inc.
Designer Victor Silson
Patents n° 124,399 (male) 124,400 (female), Victor Silson, New York, 31st December 1940, filed on 6th December 1940.

Pair of gold-plated metal brooches, green, white, black, red and pink enamel, of Harlequin and Columbine who are holding hands and dancing. Harlequin 6x5cm, Columbine 6x4.5cm.
Marked Silson Patented.

Si5. "Harlequin and Columbine," Silson 1941****
Manufacturer Silson, Inc.
Designer Victor Silson.
Patent Harlequin n° 125,043, Columbine n° 125,042
Victor Silson, New York, 4th February 1941, filed on 28th December 194

Gold-plated metal pin clip with black, red, green, yellow and golden enamel, of a black woman's head with a scarf tied up in a large bowknot and with a gold-plated metal hoop earring. 7.5x4.5cm.
Marked Silson Patented.

Si6. "Black Woman," Silson 1941*****
Manufacturer Silson Inc. New York.
Designer Victor Silson.
Patent n° 125,041 Victor Silson, New York, 4th February 1941, filed on 28th December 1940.

Si7. "Key with figural charms," Silson 1939**
Manufacturer Silson Inc. New York.
Designer Victor Silson.
Not patented.
    Gold-plated metal brooch of a key with three humanoid figurines (idols or extraterrestrials?) hanging from it. 6.5x6.7cm.
    Marked Silson.

Si8. "Winged Foot," Silson 1940***
Manufacturer Silson, Inc.
Designer Victor Silson.
Not patented.
    Gold-plated metal brooch with rhinestones, of Mercury's winged foot. 4.5x8.5cm.
    Marked Silson.

# STARET

There is little information about Staret Jewellery Co, Inc., a company based in Chicago with a head office at 322 South Franklin Street. The name of the company was registered in the Jewellery Board of Trade Directory from 1941 to 1947.

From an article in *Women's Wear Daily,* 28th March 1941, information is given about the recent change in company name which had previously been known as the Star Novelty Jewelry Co., Inc. This company had been around at least from 1935 when the "Star Novelty" trademark seems to have been registered.

In 1940 and in 1941 there were two advertisements in *Vogue,* one on 1st September 1940 and the second on 1st December 1941. The first showed a set of rhodium-plated metal bracelet, brooch and earrings with white and coloured crystals with the caption "Jewel of the Month." The second was of another set of gold-plated or rhodium-plated metal bracelet, brooch, and earrings with white crystals, topaz, ruby, emerald, sapphire and amethyst with the caption "Costume Brilliants."

The brooch, on sale for $10, was of a bow which was similar to an Eisenberg creation. The article in *WWD* stated that Staret had presented a collection characterized by large brooches with floral designs. The pieces in general were very similar to Eisenberg designs: large, with mainly abstract or floral subjects and a use of high quality crystals. It is not clear whether Staret manufactured its own goods or had them made. However, the existence of identical items with and without a mark leads to the conclusion that the company used an external manufacturer. This could have been H.M. Schrager & Co., Inc., of 305 Fifth Avenue, N.Y., a manufacturing company that presented as its own, a large brooch in the shape of a butterfly in *Jewellers' Circular Keystone,* January 1942, with colored crystals on the wings, identical to one marked by Staret (U5.). Rice-Weiner & Co., could also have manufactured for Staret, as apparent in the identical design between an enamelled horse rider marked Staret (St10.) and a non-enamelled one marked "Thief of Baghdad Korda" ( RW3.)

Staret items had the mark Staret stamped on a rectangular disk applied or melted onto the base metal. The mark Staret was not registered.

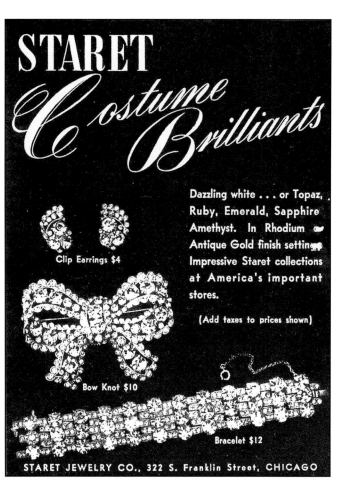

*Vogue,* December 1, 1941: "Costume Brilliants" by Staret.

St1. "Chrysanthemum," Staret 1941***
Manufacturer Staret Jewelry, Co., Inc.
   Gold-plated metal brooch, with green and blue enamel, square crystals, aquamarines and rhinestones, depicting a chrysanthemum. 11.5x11cm.
   Marked Staret.
   In 1944 Trifari manufactured a brooch with the same design. Trifari's brooch however was made of sterling, without enamel, and was more compact and three-dimensional (T188.).
Since Staret's brooch certainly dates from an earlier period, as shown by its workmanship and materials, Trifari's item, whose design was patented, should not be considered a copy, but as an item originating from a common source of inspiration.

St3. "Bellflowers," Staret 1940****
Manufacturer Staret Jewelry Co., Inc.
Pot metal brooch, pearls and rhinestones
pavé, of two bellflowers. 6.5x7cm.
Marked Staret.

St4. "Owl," Staret
1940****
Manufacturer Staret Jew-
elry, Co., Inc.
    Rhodium plated metal
brooch of an owl head with
rhinestone pavé and red
stones for its eyes. 5.7x6cm.
    Marked Staret.

St2. "Columbine," Staret 1940***
Manufacturer Staret Jewelry, Co., Inc.
    Rhodium plated metal brooch with rhinestone pave,
depicting a columbine. 13x6cm.
    Marked Staret.
    This item is identical to Boucher's "Columbine" (B5.),
except for its larger size and less accurate manufacturing. Assuming that this is not a copy, both items probably
originated from a common source of inspiration, possibly a
piece of precious jewelry.

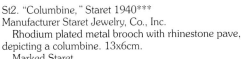

St5. "Trembling Parrots," Staret 1940****
Manufacturer Staret Jewelry Co., Inc.
    Pot metal brooch with brown, green, red,
orange and blue enamel and rhinestones, of three
parrots on a branch. The parrots were attached to
springs to produce a quivering effect. 7.5x5cm.
    Marked Staret.

St6. *"Lion Mask,"* Staret 1941*****
Manufacturer Staret Jewelry Co., Inc.
   Rhodium plated metal brooch, red, blue and green crystals, rhinestone pavé, of a lion-like mask. 10x8.5cm.
   Marked Staret.

St7. *"Parrot,"* Staret 1940*****
Manufacturer Staret Jewelry Co., Inc.
   Pot metal brooch, green and yellow enamel, red stones and rhinestones, of a parrot on a perch. 8x5cm.
   Marked Staret.

St8. *"Clown,"* Staret, 1942*****
Manufacturer Staret Jewelry Co., Inc.
   Gold-plated metal brooch, various colors enamel and rhinestones, of a clown. 7.2x4.5cm.
   Marked Staret.

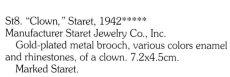

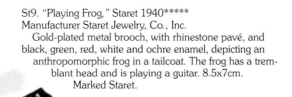

St9. "Playing Frog," Staret 1940*****
Manufacturer Staret Jewelry, Co., Inc.
  Gold-plated metal brooch, with rhinestone pavé, and black, green, red, white and ochre enamel, depicting an anthropomorphic frog in a tailcoat. The frog has a tremblant head and is playing a guitar. 8.5x7cm.
  Marked Staret.

St10. "Rider," Staret 1940****
Manufacturer Staret Jewelry Co., Inc.
  Gold-plated metal brooch, blue, and green, white, red and black enamel, of a galloping horseman with a whip. 6x6.5cm.
  Marked Staret.
  An identical but not enameled item produced by Rice-Weiner and marked "Thief of Bagdad Korda" (RW3.), confirms the supposition that Rice-Weiner also worked for Staret.

St11. "Fish," Staret 1941*****
Manufacturer Staret Jewelry Co., Inc.
  Pot metal brooch, large blue crystal in the center, green enamel and rhinestone pavé, in the shape of a fish. 5.5x7cm.
  Marked Staret.

# ERNEST STEINER & CO., INC.

ES1. "Blackamoor," Ernest Steiner. 1937-39***
Manufacturer Ernest Steiner & Co., Inc., New York.
Designer Ernest Steiner.
Not patented.
  Gold-plated metal brooch, with black, red and green enamel, a pearl and rhinestones, depicting the head and bust of a turbaned Moor. 3.5x2cm.
  Marked Ernest Steiner Original on a polylobate plaque.
  Unlike the others (U17.), this is a non-identical imitation of the famous Cartier brooch "Esclave Noir" (1936).
  Ernest Steiner was the owner of the firm Ernest Steiner & Co., Inc., which had headquarters and a showroom in New York at 339 Fifth Avenue, but he also worked as a designer for other companies, including Albert Manufacturing and Go-Gay Products Corp., 347 Fifth Avenue, New York, which, in 1941 (*WWD*, 25th April 1941) merged with Ernest Steiner. Ernest Steiner was the owner of some patents registered between the end of the 1930s and the first half of the 1940s.

# TRIFARI

Trifari was the second largest company after Coro, but, then as now, is considered to be one of the most important for collectors.

It was founded in 1925 by Gustavo Trifari, Leo F. Krussman, and Carl M. Fishel as Trifari, Krussman & Fishel, Inc., with offices in New York, at 377 Fifth Avenue. Gustavo Trifari was born in Naples on 27th September 1883 to Raimondo and Giuseppina Nascia. After working for four years, from 1900 to 1904, in his grandfather Luigi Trifari's goldsmith workshop, he emigrated to New York where he arrived on 26th February 1904. In New York he first

*WWD*, October 31, 1952: Gustavo Trifari.

worked for Weinberg & Sudzen, a jewelry manufacturer, and later on, in 1912, he started his own business. In 1918, with the arrival of Leo Krussman, a salesman at Rice & Hochster, the greatest manufacturer of hat ornaments of the time, the company name was changed to Trifari & Krussman.

Trifari & Krussman mainly produced hair ornaments, but also costume jewelry, as documented by the existence of a few remaining items of scarce esthetic or qualitative value, which are nevertheless significant items for the collectors' market. These items were marked with TK in block letters. When Carl Fishel joined the company in 1925, the managerial positions were taken up by Krussman as president, Trifari as vice-president responsible for production, and Fishel in charge of marketing and sales.

Gustavo Trifari's role is confirmed by the patent of a brooch clip that "offers a combination of brooch and clip in a new ornamental form. The brooch consists of two separate, detachable

*WWD*, May 19, 1939: Leo F. Krussman.

*WWD*, July 22, 1938, Carl M. Fishel.

components attached to a small bar. Each component can be assembled to a separate bar with a clip to be worn as a clip." Patent n° 1,878,028, 20th September 1932, for Trifari, Krussman & Fishel, Inc.

The hiring in 1930 of Alfred Philippe, first as a designer and later as head designer, was a decisive factor in the company's success. Alfred Philippe worked uninterruptedly for the company until his retirement in 1968. He was born in Paris on 24th February 1900 and studied at the Ecole Boulle in Paris. After emigrating to the United States, he worked for William Scheer Inc. of New York, one of the most important companies in the field of precious jewelry, which collaborated with Cartier and Van Cleef & Arpels. This experience strongly influenced Philippe's creations which were characterized by elaborate design and accurate manufacture. An echo of Cartier's style is perceivable in the "Fruit Salad" items, a jewelry line manufactured during the second half of 1930s, which featured small red, blue and green cut stones variously combined and set in rhodium-plated metal with rhinestone accents. The delicate deco style designs are inspired by Louis Cartier's "Indian Style" jewelry dating from the end of the 1920s, which were made of platinum and precious stones. Jewelry made in 1928 for the maharajah of Patiala were especially famous. The "costume" version of this jewelry became very fashionable in the mid-1930s, after apparently being brought in by Philippe, who produced the whole range of this jewelry using a manufacturing technique typically used for precious jewelry. This motif was taken up again and revisited in 1941 in an extraordinary line which included large tridimensional brooches, also available in a version with white and blue cut stones ("Chalcedony"). With the same "Indian Style" theme, Philippe ended his career in 1965 with a jewelry line called "Jewels of India," a modern revisitation of the former models, featuring large smooth multi-colored cabochons set in glazed gold-plated metal. In the course of his long career, in which he witnessed the coming and going of different tastes and requirements, Alfred Philippe always showed himself to be a great artist, endowed with talent, technique, and great sensibility for fashion and the market, with an ability to interpret all materials – including the most innovative – at the highest possible level. He designed nearly all the Trifari collections and many patents were registered in his name. His style was always extremely refined. Alfred Philippe died in December 1970.

Trifari became more and more successful and, in 1939, this success led to the need to expand its productive structure, so the company moved its plant to Providence, R.I., while its offices and design department remained in New York at the same address. By 1952 the company had four plants in Providence.

At the beginning of 1930s Trifari made some exclusive jewelry designs for some of the most famous Broadway musicals of the time, such as *Roberta* in 1933, *The Great Waltz* in 1934, and *Jubilee* by Cole Porter in 1935. Trifari carried on working for the theatre and cinema, albeit discontinuously, in the following years.

During the war, the rationing of metals and the partial conversion of plants for the production of precision components for the Navy, did not interrupt Trifari's costume jewelry production business, or impair the quality of production. On the contrary, it was precisely in this period, that Trifari made some of its most beautiful collector's items, such as the jelly bellies. The use of sterling which had begun in the second half of 1942, continued until 1947 when Gustavo Trifari invented and patented "Trifanium," a special metal alloy – the best made in that period – which allowed for a quality melting process and an excellent output in the gold- and rhodium-plating phases. Moreover, Trifanium was heavy and presented a compact appearance similar to sterling.

Towards the end of 1940s, the company began to follow the new fashion trends which favored simple lines and lightweight constructions. The last great Trifari collection of the period under review was presented in 1949: the series known as "Moghul," a complete line of golden Trifanium jewelry with multicolor "melon-" and "rose-" cut cabochons, made according to patented designs.

In 1950 Trifari celebrated its "Silver Anniversary" with much advertising fanfare and a special collection. In the 1950s the "real look" was all the rage, but Trifari's collections were still very popular, even in Europe. In Paris, they had been brought by the Countess of Polignac, madame Lanvin's daughter and director of Lanvin. In London, where they were exhibited in Norman Hartnell's salon. Hartnell designed the clothes for the coronation of Queen Elizabeth II in 1953. For the Queen's coronation, Trifari launched the "Coronation Gems" line, which was made up of three sets composed of brooch and earrings shaped like the crown, and the globe and scepter which are the symbols of the British monarchy (T225.).

Some popular events helped to strengthen the image and success of Trifari, such as the creation of two pearl sets designed by Alfred Philippe for the first lady Mamie Doud Eisenhower for the inauguration balls celebrating the Presidency of Dwight Eisenhower on 20th January 1953 and in 1957.

On 28th October 1952 at 69 years of age, Gustavo Trifari died, followed a month later by Leo F. Krussman, on 27th November, at the age of 64 (1888-1952). Carl M. Fishel continued to work until 1964 when he died, on 2nd February, at the age of 86, (1878-1964). He was the eldest of the three partners. The founders' children, Gustavo Trifari Jr. (1915-1982), Louis F. Krussman, and Carlton M. Fishel – the first two had already been working for the company from 1937 and the third from 1932 – became, respectively, president, vice-president, and general manager. In 1975, in the year of its "Golden Anniversary," the company became part of Hallmark Cards, Inc., which, in turn, was purchased in 1988 by Crystal Brands Jewelry, Inc., which had also taken over Marvella, Inc., a famous manufacturer of fake pearls in 1982. In 1989 Trifari and Marvella joined Monet, a subsidiary of Crystal Brands Jewelry Inc. and set up the Crystal Brands Jewelry Group or Monet Group, a subsidiary of Crystal Brands, Inc. The trademark was still used and the modern production was on sale at department stores all over the world. In 2000 the Monet Group, on the brink of bankruptcy, was purchased by the Liz Claiborne Group, which closed down all its plants and offices in the United States and moved the production of costume jewelry to Puerto Rico.

Two events in the history of Trifari are important for the collectors' market.

After winning a legal case for the protection of the copyright on the "Bolero" line against Charel in 1955, as minutely detailed in the section on patents and copyrights, Trifari practically did not patent any of its designs. As a consequence, today it is very difficult to track down the production of the post 1955 years due to lack of documentation. As a matter of fact, unlike patents, which can be consulted online, it is not possible to view copyrighted designs, unless one is ready to spend a lot of time and money. In fact, in order to obtain complete documentation, it is necessary to apply to the competent office and wait at least one week and pay about $80 for each dossier.

From 1955 onwards, Trifari, like most companies, added the copyright © symbol to its trademark. Nowadays this is a useful tool for collectors in dating Trifari jewelry made after 1955.

In the course of the years Trifari reproposed some of its designs from the 1940s. These items are similar, but not identical, to the originals, and could not deceive an expert or even an informed amateur at all. From a collector's point of view, these items have no value. A famous re-visitation of older items dates from 1965. The reproduced items include: the "Jelly Belly Small Sail Fish," "Jelly Belly Rooster," "Jelly Belly Hummingbird," "Ming Small Dragon," "Ming Fish," "Ming Turtle," "Ming Horse," and "Ming Lion" (regarding the originals, see their respective information cards). This jewelry was made of glazed gold-plated metal with a pale yellow hue, using lower quality stones, little glossy enamel, was lightweight and was marked © Trifari. Other models were reproduced in different periods, always using different materials from the originals. A "Retro Collection" was made between 1988 and 1992 in the wake of the success of antique items. These collections came complete with a "Retro Collection" authenticity certificate, detailing the history and data of the model and, to avoid confusion, the production year of these items was punched on the items themselves. Apparently this initiative did not last long, due to the high production costs involved.

From the very start Trifari made good quality, accurately manufactured jewelry aimed at a medium-high market segment. Its collections were always worthy of the attention *Women's Wear Daily* dedicated to them, starting as early as 1927, with the presentation of rhinestone jabot pins (3rd March) and two rhinestone and enamel brooches reproducing Lindbergh's plane, the "Spirit of St. Louis" (3rd June). In 1936 *Vogue* also mentioned Trifari jewelry in several articles, and its first *Vogue* advertisements date from March and May 1938 and were of brooches (flowers, fobs, a frog, and a leaf) of metal and rhinestones that sold for 3 dollars and, advertisements for the summer collection, of other floral brooches (anemone, gardenia, lilac and narcissus) and of a cane with a top hat and a bowtie with enamel and rhinestones.

*Vogue*, March 15, 1938: Jewels by Trifari.

*Vogue*, May 1, 1938: Jewels by Trifari.

Some of these designs were patented, and even then the company constantly emphasized the existing protection of its rights over its designs. Trifari's distinguishing feature was its style of imitating precious jewelry, with elaborate and sophisticated designs, accurate manufacturing technique and top quality materials. In particular the stones that were used, whether they were white or colored, were treated and set according to the strict rules of the goldsmith's craft – for example its rhinestone pavés which were mixed with glass paste stones or cut stones, or the first "invisible settings." Trifari earned the nickname "The Rhinestone Kings" due to its predilection for rhinestone packed jewelry. In 1937 Alfred Philippe created his first ever "tailored" line, i.e. elegant jewelry for daywear, with no stones.

The company always remained faithful to this style, though account was always taken of current fashion. Trifari never indulged in the use of prystal or other plastic materials, or in gadget-like items that had no stylistic value. The only exception was in the company's products dating from the end of 1920s and this was limited to their sports line. In the decade between 1925-35 Trifari created deco style jewelry only sporadically. An example of this occurred in 1928 when Trifari followed the fashion of the time by creating Chanel and Lelong imitation jewelry. The collections created during these years possessed personality and elegance. For example, in 1929 the company presented its first sterling silver line, called "Mayfair," which was made up of jewelry items with baguettes and pearls combined in intricate designs. In 1934 Trifari created the "Cleo Gems," a line of jewelry with fake rubies, emeralds, sapphires and diamonds, which were not made of glass, but, as reported in Women's Wear Daily, were obtained through changes in the structure of the corresponding precious stones, of which they retained certain characteristics, such as their hardness. This was Trifari's way of meeting the requirements of its top-notch clientele who requested very high quality. With this in mind, in January 1934, Trifari launched the "Scheherazade" line, a complete series of items characterized by the presence of a large, colored, central stone, surrounded by multicolored stones, baguettes and rhinestones. The name and concept of this line were reproposed in 1949, with the "Moghul" collection.

As reported in Women's Wear Daily, at the end of 1933, the company Trifari Krussman and Fishel was considered an important manufacturer of "fine jewelry," capable of fulfilling the high expectations of a clientele who were willing to pay higher prices in return for high quality.

Its managers were highly visible and active in the social and collective life of the sector, in which they held prestigious posts. In July 1938, Carl Fishel became president of the World Fair Committee for the Jewelry Industry, with the task of planning the costume jewelry industry's participation in the jewelry hall of the World Fair. Also in the following years Fishel and Krussman (though not Trifari, who apparently had no public role) remained highly visible.

There are no data on the company structure, but it is reasonable to surmise that it was a medium-sized company with a good, solid in-house organization which permitted strict quality policy and market selection. In 1945 the company turnover was about four million dollars.

Entry of New Trifari Showroom

WWD, June 3, 1949: the new Trifari showroom at 16 East 47th Street, New York.

Trifari relied on a number of in-house and freelance designers working under the supervision of Alfred Philippe. In addition to Philippe, who has been already extensively dealt with, here are the names of some of these important collaborators:

**Joseph Wuyts** was a freelancer who also worked for Mazer Bros for whom he patented some designs (see Mazer). In the spring of 1940 he designed a series of eighteen rhodium-plated brooches with enamel some of which had a special coating of mother-of-pearl-like material applied to the metal. The subjects of these brooches were small ethnic or fantasy figures, animals, flowers and bows. In the spring of 1941, Wuyts also designed a bracelet and a matching brooch. It is not known whether all these items had been designed for Trifari, since the patents made do not report the name of the customer. After this date there are no more patented designs in the name of Wuyts. In keeping with the fashion of the time, the items made after his designs were generally small, but extremely precise in details. This jewelry showed a skillful use of enamel, tiny colored stones and rhinestones, which were sparingly used.

**David Mir** was another freelancer who worked for Trifari at the end of 1941 and in January 1942 as well as for Leo Glass in 1941. He produced a total of nine designs of very beautiful brooches. In addition to those reproduced herein (T107., T112., T132., T154., and JB8.), Mir was the creator of: another brooch of a fantastic bird with Lucite wings on 21st October 1941, des. n° 130,082; an enamel elephant on 28th October 1941, des. n° 130,154 and a double flower on 17th February 1942, des. n° 131,425.

**Alfred Spaney** collaborated in the making of the fall 1941 and spring 1942 collections, creating several brooch designs mainly with floral subjects – i.e., large flowers studded with rhinestones, as well as convex, oblong colored stones which are one of his signature designs – and also figurative subjects. He was a good designer, a good interpreter of the "real look" style and had a somber, classic touch which was very much in tune with Trifari's parameters of excellence. His "novelties" were also remarkable.

**Norman Bel Geddes**. Norman Melancton Geddes was born in 1893 in Adrian, Michigan, and later went by the name of Bel Geddes. He studied at the Cleveland School of Arts and briefly attended the Art Institute in Chicago. His first work experience was at an advertising agency in Chicago designing billboards for General Motors and Packard.

Norman Bell Geddes
(1893-1958).

In 1918 he began a brilliant career as a set designer for the Metropolitan Opera in New York and in 1927 turned to industrial design, establishing his own company, without however abandoning his work as a costume and set designer.

His most famous creation was probably "Futurama the Metropolis of Tomorrow," for the Highways and Horizons hall of General Motors at the World Fair in New York in 1939. He died in 1958 leaving a daughter, the actress Barbara Bel Geddes (1922 - 2005).

In August 1941 he designed two Jelly Belly brooches for Trifari; the "Swan" (JB4.) and the "Sailfish" (JB1.). Later on and up to 1950 he apparently did not design any jewelry apart from some accessories for his theatre and movie costumes. In 1950 he began to collaborate with Rice-Weiner Co. for whom he designed a fall collection called "Flow Motion" (see Rice-Weiner).

After 1942 and throughout the period under review, only designs patented by Alfred Philippe are traceable,

with a single exception represented by a heart-shaped brooch patented on 5th June 1945 by George Bachner, n° 141,435.

The following designers collaborated with Trifari in chronological order:

**1958 to 1965**: Jean Paris who had also worked for Cartier and Van Cleef & Arpels and, when his seven-year contract with Trifari expired, he went back to Cartier.

**1967 to 1979**: André Boeuf, former designer for Cartier Paris, who replaced Philippe when he retired; Jacques Philippe, Alfred Philippe's son.

**1971 to 1974**: Diane Love, a young artist who had worked for Bergdorf Goodman and who designed collections with classic themes, which she reinterpreted according to modern tastes. Her aim was to renew the firm's style in order to overcome the costume jewelry crisis of the time.

Two marks were used for stamping Trifari's jewelry: "KTF." (for Trifari, Krussman & Fishel) and "TRIFARI" with a small crown surmounting the "T," a possible reference to the company nickname "The Rhinestone Kings" given to Trifari in the 1930s on account of its rhinestone-packed jewelry.

The mark KTF. was registered in 1935 as demonstrated by the items where it is accompanied by the words Reg. (for registered) 1935. This trademark had probably been in use since 1925 or soon after this date. It stopped being used in November/December 1937. Items dating from this period often exhibit both the KTF. and the TRIFARI trademark. The change in trademark is ascribed to Abbot Kimball, an advertiser with contacts in the world of fashion who suggested the change on the grounds that the general public was very allured by the charm of Italy and would therefore feel attracted to an Italian name.

Generally speaking all items marked KTF. are interesting because they are older and relatively rare, with a good, although sometimes not particularly creative, design. All items dating from this period are of excellent quality. Among the items marked KTF. are the first "Fruit Salad" pieces, which displayed a deco taste, and the first "Pastel Fruit Salad" items, also in deco style with fake pink coral and turquoise made of paste. These were often a second version of the "Fruit Salad" models; small enamel and rhinestone pavé brooches, and the first two designs of the "Invisible Setting" jewelry made with a special high-precision setting technique similar to the one used for precious jewelry. Only a few figurative items marked KTF. exist.

The trademark TRIFARI with the crown appeared on all Trifari items starting from December 1937.

In 1955 the © for copyright appeared next to the name TRIFARI, while the logo JEWELS BY TRIFARI served only an advertising purpose together with other trademarks of the single collections.

From March 1937 Trifari systematically patented its designs. The first three designs patented by Alfred

Philippe (except for two mechanisms patented in 1936) are an anemone, a gardenia, and a narcissus with enamel accents and rhinestone pavé of 16th March 1937, which were subsequently advertised in Vogue in May 1938. The number of patent registrations decreased in 1943 due to a drop in production caused by the war effort. It increased again in 1947 and 1948, but decreased again at the beginning of 1950s. From 1954-55 there were practically no new patent registrations. The name of the firm on behalf of which the patent was registered, was usually reported in the patents. The only exception to this was patents registered in the first half of 1940s, in which only the designer's name was mentioned.

The huge effort made by Trifari to protect its designs, which was evident also in its advertisements (especially during the second half of the 1940s), since mention was always made of the fact that the design was patented or that all original items were marked Trifari, accounts for the habit of stamping the jewelry (though not always) with the additional words, "Pat. Pend." (for Patent Pending) or "Des. Pat. No" (Design Patented No.) followed by the patent number. Sometimes a figure with one or two digits, or a letter were also stamped on the items: these were in-house reference numbers, used for control purposes, which identified the stone setter.

The items were characterized by perfect manufacture, the choice of top quality materials, refined details, creative spirit mitigated by good taste and imitations of precious jewels that were never banal. Each collection was composed of several different lines with varying inspirational themes and materials. Among the most successful lines – apart from the already mentioned "Fruit Salad," "Moghul," and the Jelly Bellies, (dealt with in a special section) – were small rhodium-plated and enamel brooches with figurative subjects manufactured between 1939 and 1942. In the fall of 1939, Trifari began to produce larger brooches made of metal, sometimes in two colors, with rhinestone accents. This trend was continued in the following seasons until the mid 1940s.

The "Ming" line is also worthy of mention. It was an oriental inspired series of gold-plated metal brooches studded with rhinestones, with red lacquer or black enamel, and a central fretwork jade-green, blue or pink stone, or a white pearl. The designs, most of which were of animal subjects, were made by Alfred Philippe and many of them were patented and made in two color versions of enamel and stone.

In 1943, at the same time as the peak in the war effort in the country, Trifari's production decreased and was practically limited to just the Jelly Bellies line. Production in 1944-45 was more plentiful, albeit somewhat monotonous with its large, massive designs, sterling and colored stone execution. The "Crown," launched in 1944, is the most famous Trifari product: It was manufactured in large quantities, featured in the collections of several seasons and was reproposed at different times and in different materials. The original items (see T182.) were made of sterling, whereas the later versions were first made of golden Trifanium and then of gold-plated metal.

The period herein under review ends with the "Silver Anniversary" jewelry, the most significant of which belongs to the "Clair de Lune" line (see T222.) which was characterized by delicate designs and was ornamented with moonstones.

T1. "Deco Necklace," KTF. 1930-35***** Manufacturer Trifari, Krussman & Fishel. Designer Alfred Philippe? Not patented. Rhodium-plated metal necklace with pavé rhinestone motif in the center, green and red stones in Deco style. Knit-chain and invisible clasp with green and red stones. 3x10cm motif in center. Marked KTF.

T2. "Deco Pin," KTF. 1935***
Manufacturer Trifari, Krussman & Fishel.
Designer Alfred Philippe?
Not patented.
    Rhodium-plated metal brooch, rhinestone pavé,
white baguettes and blue stones 2.8x5.3cm.
    Marked KTF. "45".
    The number marked on the piece refers to the
stone setter.

T3. "Deco Fan Clip," KTF. 1935***
    Manufacturer Trifari, Krussman & Fishel.
Designer Alfred Philippe?
Not patented.
    Rhodium-plated metal clip, rhinestone pavé and
baguettes. 3.5x4cm.
    Marked KTF. "34".

T4. "Deco Clip," KTF.
1930****
Manufacturer Trifari,
Krussman & Fishel.
Designer Alfred Philippe.
Not patented.

*WWD*, November 28, 1930: models from Trifari, Krussman
& Fishel, Inc.

    Rhodium-plated metal clip, rhinestone pavé and ba-
guettes. 6.2x4cm.
    Marked KTF. "42".
    *WWD*, 28th November 1930, printed the design of some
Trifari pieces of which two clips are identical to the one
catalogued.

T5. "Maggy Rouff Set," Trifari 1935*****
Manufacturer Trifari, Krussman & Fishel.
Designer Alfred Philippe.
Not patented.

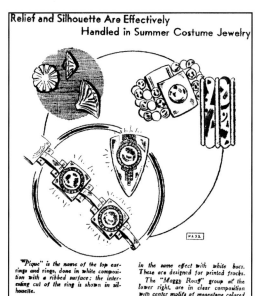

**Relief and Silhouette Are Effectively Handled in Summer Costume Jewelry**

*"Pique" is the name of the top earrings and rings, done in white composition with a ribbed surface; the interesting cut of the ring is shown in silhouette.*

*At the upper right, a bracelet of composition beads in a "printed" marbleised surface effect and a clip done*

*in the same effect with white bars. These are designed for printed frocks. The "Maggy Rouff" group at the lower right, are in clear composition with center motifs of moonstone colored cabochons outlined in rhinestone circles. Shown here are a clip and a bracelet. All from Trifari Krussmann & Fishel, Inc.*

*WWD*, May 24, 1935: "Maggy Rouff" bracelet and clip by Trifari.

Set made up of prystal-catalin clip and bracelet with conical blue cabochons and rhinestones. Clip 6x4cm. Bracelet 19cm length, 3.5cm width.

Clip marked KTF. Bracelet is unmarked.

*WWD*, 19th April 1935, reported that the: "American Catalin Corp., with headquarters in New York, 1 Park Avenue, purchased from the Societé Nobel Française of Paris, the trademarks and patent for 'Prystal' for the United States. This material is a virtually shatterproof imitation of crystal designed for use in costume jewelry and clothing accessory production.

On disclosing the purchase. E. J. Luster, president of the American company, stated that the material had already been in use for one year, however, due to technical problems concerning the registration of the trademark and patents, communication about the transfer had had to be delayed.

The registration numbers of the trademarks are 236,611 and 236,606 and the patent numbers are 1,645,848 and 1,691,427.

The material previously sold under the name of "Prystal" –Mr. Luster added – was an urea formaldehyde that was as transparent as water. However, it presented a number of limitations to its usability. Due to sensitivity to temperature and pressure changes, this kind of prystal broke easily, even without any apparent cause, whereas the Prystal manufactured by Catalin was a phenolic formaldehyde which was as transparent and beautiful as its predecessor and suitable for use in personal ornamental items. Moreover, it could be manufactured in a wider range of shapes, sizes and colors. One of the most recent types of this material was called "Star Dust" and consisted of a product containing minute suspended golden and silver particles."

The name "Maggy Rouff Jewelry" is original, and, *WWD*, 10th May 1935, in an article dedicated to Trifari's fall collection, reported that: "A series which the company has called "Maggy Rouff jewelry," is particularly showy, with its large transparent stones with the colors of real gems, cut in very thick cabochons, and set in massive prystal-catalin; among the most interesting items are the link bracelets which create an immediate impact, with matching earrings, clips and brooches. Another variant offers similar settings with slightly rounded cabochons the color of moonstones, that are proposed in two versions: a plain one for sports clothing, and one surrounded by a thin border of rhinestones for a more elegant effect". The clip and bracelet featured, together with other items from the same collection, in *WWD*, 24th May 1935.

Maggy Rouff was a French fashion designer who was very popular in the United States in those years.

She was born in Paris to British parents, who founded the maison Drecoll, where Maggy started her career as a fashion designer.

In 1928 she opened her own maison in the Champs Elysees and was immediately successful. She retired in 1948 and her daughter, the Countess of Dancourt, took over her role as company designer. Other famous designers such as Serge Matta, Michel Malard and Guy Douvier, worked for the maison Maggy Rouff, which remained in business until the end of the 1960s.

Maggy Rouff died in 1971 at the age of seventy-five.

T6. "Deco Bracelet," KTF. 1932-33*****
Manufacturer Trifari, Krussman & Fishel. Designer Alfred Philippe? Not patented.
Rhodium-plated metal bracelet, black enamel, rhinestone pavé and green baguettes. 2.7cm width. Marked KTF. "73".

T7. "Fruit Salad Set," KTF. 1936****
Manufacturer Trifari, Krussman & Fishel. Designer Alfred Philippe.
Patent clip-mates n° 2,050,804 Alfred Philippe, New York, 11th August 1936, filed on 23rd April 1936.

Set made up of rhodium-plated metal brooch, bracelet and earrings with multicolor engraved stones. The brooch is a Deco style, rhodium-plated double clip – clip-mates (i.e. twin clips) – in the shape of a triangle with a large blue engraved stone at the center, surrounded by small engraved red, blue and green stones. 3x7.5cm.
Small linked bracelet. Length: 18cm, width 1.5cm.
Round screwback earrings. 1.8cm.
Brooch mark: KTF. "74". Mechanism mark: CLIP-MATES Pat. No. 2050804.
Bracelet mark: KTF. "77".
Earring mark: "47".
Alfred Philippe patented the brooch joining mechanism which had a barrette on which the clips were inserted and slid into place. The clip mates were meant to be Trifari's answer to Coro's Duette. The clip design, however, is not patented.
On 17th November 1936 Alfred Philippe also patented the mechanism (n° 2,061,479) of a bangle with clip mates attached to its top part. Thus the bangle could be taken apart to become a brooch and two clips. The bangle was probably part of a set which included the brooch and was meant to be Trifari's version of Coro's Triquette. These are the only examples of mechanisms patented by Alfred Philippe.
"Fruit Salad" is a modern expression to indicate jewelry featuring variously combined small multicolor engraved stones. In the 1930s many manufacturers, some famous (such as Mazer) and some unknown, created "Fruit Salad" jewelry.

White metal clip with leaf shaped, carved glass paste stones, rhinestone pavé and baguettes, of a stylized bowknot with a baguette studded knot and concentric spiraling tassels with rhinestone pavé, with the outermost one made of blue, red and green glass paste stones. 5x4cm.
Marked Trifari Des. Pat. No. 105405 "76".
This item is part of a small series of patented "Fruit Salad" brooches made for the fall 1937 collection. Two versions were made of this and of most of the models belonging to this series: a "Fruit Salad" version and a "Pastel Fruit Salad" version, with pink and blue, i.e. coral and turquoise imitation glass paste engraved stones. This brooch also exists with the KTF mark. The fact that there are also items marked Trifari, indicates that the same model continued to be manufactured after the company trademark was changed (December 1937).

T8. "Fruit Salad Bow Clip," Trifari, 1937***
Manufacturer Trifari, Krussman & Fishel.
Designer Alfred Philippe.
Patent n° 105,405 Alfred Philippe, New York, 27th July 1937, filed on 13th February 1937, assignor to Trifari, Krussman & Fishel, New York.

T9. "Pastel Fruit Salad Set," KTF. 1937***
Manufacturer Trifari, Krussman & Fishel.
Designer Alfred Philippe.
Patent brooch n° 106,122 Alfred Philippe, New York, 21st September 1937, filed on 13th February 1937, assignor to Trifari, Krussman & Fishel, New York. The bracelet is not patented.

Set made up of rhodium-plated metal brooch and bracelet, pink and blue engraved leaf shaped coral and turquoise imitation stones, rhinestones and baguettes.
Round brooch with spiraling center and rhinestone pavé, white baguettes around the edge, and large half-circle made of pink and blue engraved stones. 5.5cm.
Link bracelet with alternated pink and blue stones, joined by square rhinestone studded plaques. Hidden clasp. Length: 18cm, width: 1.3cm.
Brooch marked Pat. Pend, "48". Bracelet marked KTF. "18".
This model also exists in a "Fruit Salad" version.

T10. "Apple with Butterfly," KTF. 1937*****
Manufacturer Trifari, Krussman & Fishel.
Designer Alfred Philippe.
Not patented.
Rhodium-plated metal pin clip, red and green stones, rhinestone pavé and white baguettes, of an apple with a butterfly on it. 4.7x6 cm.
Marked KTF. "28".
The brooch can be dated with accuracy to 1937 and attributed to Alfred Philippe because the green stones of the leaves and the 'invisible setting' technique used are the same as other designs patented in the same period (T11., T12. & T13.)

T11. "Invisible Setting Leaf," KTF. 1937****
Manufacturer Trifari, Krussman & Fishel.
Designer Alfred Philippe.
Patent n° 107,136 Alfred Philippe, New York, 23rd November 1937, filed 6th October 1937, assignor to Trifari, Krussman & Fishel, New York.
This model is a variant of the patented design with an added rhinestone pavé leaf as a base. The seeming superimposition of two layers – obtained by welding two separate elements together – was frequently used in Trifari jewelry dating from this period.

Rhodium-plated metal brooch shaped like two superimposed leaves. The lower leaf has a rhinestone pavé and baguette surface. The upper branch features five red leaves with red stones set using the "invisible setting" technique, and rhinestone veins. 8x5cm.
Marked KTF. "73".
The figure refers to the stone setter. The patented model was re-proposed in the 1960s.

T12. "Invisible Setting Leaf Bracelet," KTF. 1937****
Manufacturer Trifari, Krussman & Fishel.
Designer Alfred Philippe.
Not patented.
　Rhodium-plated metal bracelet, red stones and rhinestones with leaf motif. 1.5cm w.
　Marked KTF. "6".
　The bracelet matches the brooch T11.
　This is a copy of a gold bracelet with rubies by Van Cleef & Arpels set using the same technique.

T13. "Invisible Setting Duette," KTF. 1937****
　　　Manufacturer Trifari, Krussman & Fishel.
　　　Designer Alfred Philippe.
　　　Patent n° 107,135 Alfred Philippe, New York,
　　　23rd November 1937, filed on 6th October
　　　1937, assignor to Trifari, Krussman & Fishel,
　　　New York.

Double clip rhodium-plated metal brooch with small green glass stones and rhinestones. The brooch is of a leaf with rhinestone ornamented veins. The mechanism joining the two clips together; a thin, wide, contoured metal sheet, was apparently never patented, although it was definitely designed specifically for this model. 3.5x6.8cm.
　　Marked KTF. Pat. Pend.
　　The term "Invisible Setting" was coined by Van Cleef & Arpels in 1949 to indicate a highly accurate and expensive stone setting technique, which required good manual skills and extreme precision in the cutting and setting of stones.
　The result of using this technique is that the surface of the item of jewelry is completely covered with tiny, perfectly aligned stones, conveying the impression of being just one large stone, and the setting remains invisible.
　Trifari was a master in this technique, which the company started using in 1937. The fact that there are only two patented designs is evidence that this technique was probably used for just a few pieces. It began re-using it again, some time later, in the 1960s, for a series of gold-plated metal jewelry. The best known of these items from the 1960s were a brooch of a rose and a carnation-shaped brooch. In the same years Trifari reused some designs dating from 1937. These items were larger than the originals and were made of rhodium-plated metal and can be clearly distinguished from the older pieces, since they bear the Trifari © mark.
　The few 1937 items still circulating are of some significance, since they confirm the existence of older "Invisible Setting" items. The available variants feature green, red and blue stones.

T14. "Rhinestones Bracelet," KTF. 1935***
Manufacturer Trifari, Krussman & Fishel.
Designer Alfred Philippe?
Not patented.
　Rhodium-plated metal bracelet, rhinestones and baguettes. 2cm w.
　Marked KTF. "41".

T15. "Orchid," KTF 1936*****
Manufacturer Trifari, Krussman & Fishel.
Designer Alfred Philippe.
Not patented.

*Vogue* September 15, 1936: "Orchid" by Trifari.

Rhodium-plated metal brooch with rhinestones and small green baguettes, of an orchid, with rhinestone pavé and thin green veins. The central tremblant petal is set with a bright green crystal. 5.8x6.5cm.
Marked KTF.
A picture of this item appeared in a *Vogue* advertisement of costume jewelry, 15th September 1936, and was on sale at Bonwit Teller's. The brooch also featured in *Mademoiselle,* October 1936.
Production of this item continued in the following years, until at least 1938, as confirmed by pieces bearing the Trifari mark, in a larger size and without the tremblant petal. There are also matching earrings for this brooch. Color variants: blue and ruby red.
A remake of this brooch appeared in the mid-1950s (marked Trifari©) in a larger size and with tremblant petals. Likely contemporary copies of the brooch are still in circulation, but they are easily recognizable by their rather slapdash manufacture and by the lack of a trademark.

T16. "Swallow," KTF. 1937****
Manufacturer Trifari, Krussman & Fishel.
Designer Alfred Philippe.
Patent n° 106,120 Alfred Philippe, New York, 21st September 1937, filed on 2nd January 1937, assignor to Trifari, Krussman & Fishel, Inc., New York.

Metal base brooch, red, blue and black enamel, rhinestone pavé, depicting a swallow on a branch. 7.5x5cm.
Unmarked.

T17. "Flower Basket," Trifari 1937****
Manufacturer Trifari, Krussman & Fishel.
Designer Alfred Philippe.
Patent n° 107,133 Alfred Philippe, New York, 23rd November 1937, filed on 6th October 1937, assignor to Trifari, Krussman & Fishel, New York.

Rhodium-plated metal brooch with black enamel and rhinestones, of a flower basket. 5.5x5.8cm.
Marked KTF.

T18. "Flying Swallow," Trifari 1937*****
Manufacturer Trifari, Krussman & Fishel.
Designer Alfred Philippe.
Patent n° 106,145 Alfred Philippe, New York, 21st September 1937, filed on 2nd January 1937, assignor to Trifari, Krussman & Fishel, New York.

Rhodium and gold-plated metal brooch with black enamel and rhinestone pavé, of a swallow in flight, with a tremblant twig in its beak. 9.5x6.5cm.
Marked Pat. Pend.
This item appeared in an advertisement in Harper's Bazaar, March 1937.

T19. "Lovebirds," Trifari 1937****
Manufacturer Trifari, Krussman & Fishel.
Designer Alfred Philippe.
Patent n° 106,121 Alfred Philippe, New York, 21st September 1937, filed on 2nd January 1937, assignor to Trifari, Krussman & Fishel, New York.

Rhodium-plated metal brooch, with green, blue and black enamel and rhinestones, of two parakeets perched on a branch in bloom. 8x6.5cm
Marked Pat. Pend "77".

T20. "Riding Jockey," KTF. 1937****
Manufacturer Trifari, Krussman & Fishel.
Designer Alfred Philippe.
Not patented.
Rhodium-plated metal brooch, red, black, pink and brown enamel with rhinestone pavé, depicting a jockey on horseback. 2.5x5cm.
Marked KTF.

T21. "Pierrot," Trifari 1936****
Manufacturer Trifari, Krussman e Fishel.
Designer Alfred Philippe.
Not patented.
    Rhodium-plated metal clip with black
enamel, green marquise cut stones for its
eyes, a lozenge shaped red stone for its
mouth and rhinestones, depicting a Pierrot.
1.8x1.5cm.
    Marked KTF. L.M. E.L.M. (graffiti, probably
a dedication).

T22. "Masks," Trifari 1936****
Manufacturer Trifari, Krussman & Fishel.
Designer Alfred Philippe.
Not patented.
    Pair of rhodium-plated clips of two masks, with green triangular stones
for eyes, a red stone for the mouth, and rhinestones. 3.9x3cm.
    One brooch is marked KTF the other "22".

T23. "Poodle," KTF. 1936****
Manufacturer Trifari, Krussman & Fishel.
Designer Alfred Philippe.
Not patented.

*Mademoiselle*, December 1937: Trifari's pins at Hammacher
Schlemmer.

    Rhodium-plated metal brooch, black and red enamel with
rhinestones, of a French poodle. 3.5x3cm.
    Marked KTF. "16".
    This piece was photographed in *Mademoiselle*, October 1936,
was on sale at Saks for $5, and again, along with T24. T25. &
T26., in *Mademoiselle*, December 1937, on sale for $5 at Ham-
macher Schlemmer, New York.

T24. "Bulldog," KTF. 1937****
Manufacturer Trifari, Krussman & Fishel.
Designer Alfred Philippe.
Not patented.
    Rhodium-plated metal brooch, brown enamel and rhinestones, of a
bulldog. 3.5x3.5cm.
    Marked "14".
    This piece was photographed in '*Mademoiselle*," December 1937,
and was on sale for $5 at Hammacher Schlemmer, New York.

T25. "Penguin," KTF. 1937****
Manufacturer Trifari, Krussman & Fishel.
Designer Alfred Philippe.
Not patented.
   Rhodium-plated metal brooch, black, yellow and red enamel
with rhinestone pavé, of a penguin. 4x2.5cm.
   Marked KTF.
   This piece was photographed in *Mademoiselle*, December
1937, and was on sale for $5 at Hammacher Schlemmer, New
York.

T26. "Horse Head," Trifari 1937****
Manufacturer Trifari, Krussman & Fishel.
Designer Alfred Philippe.
Not patented.
   Rhodium-plated metal brooch, with black and red enamel,
a green cabochon, a red stone and rhinestones, of a horse's
head. 4x3.5cm.
   Marked Trifari H "5".
   The brooch was advertised in "*Mademoiselle*" Decem-
ber 1937, and was on sale for $5 at Hammacher Schlemmer,
New York, together with items T23., T24., and T25. There is
also a specimen of this brooch marked KTF. which means that
it was made towards the end of 1937 (December) when the
company trademark was changed from KTF. to Trifari.

T27. "Snow White Jewelry," Trifari 1938*****
Manufacturer Trifari, Krussman & Fishel.
Designer Alfred Philippe after Walt Disney.
Not patented.
   Rhodium-plated metal brooch, with white, brown, red, azure, blue and black enamel, of Snow
White (written on a metal scroll) and two of the seven dwarfs: Sleepy (written on a metal scroll
under the figure) and Sneezy (also written on a metal scroll under the figure). 3x3cm.
   Marked Trifari.
   On 21st January 1938 *WWD* reported: " Philadelphia – The Snow White bracelet with seven
dwarf charms proved one of the hits of a Wanamaker Fashion Show on Wednesday, with wom-
en stopping the mannequin on the run-way for a closer inspection of this accessory." And again
on 11th March: "Records were broken at Radio City Music Hall when "Snow White" played for four weeks, and
records are reported being broken at Trifari, Krussman & Fishel by reorders on the charm bracelet and pins in Snow
White likeness, and sketched earlier in Women's Wear Daily".
   Unlike with other manufacturers (Coro, Wertheimer & Sons), the "Snow White Jewelry" was apparently not
manufactured on a Walt Disney license, as confirmed by the lack of the usual WDP marking.
   Walt Disney's "Snow White," inspired by the tale of "Schneewittchen" by the Grimm brothers, was made in 1937
and distributed in time for Christmas that same year. It was the first ever color animation movie and one of the
greatest success stories in the history of cinema.

T28. "Mr. & Mrs. Monkey," Trifari 1939*****
Manufacturer Trifari, Krussman & Fishel.
Designer Alfred Philippe.
Patents n° 113,786 & n° 113,787 Alfred Philippe,
New York, 14th March 1939, filed on 17th Febru-
ary 1939, assignor to Trifari, Krussman & Fishel,
New York.

   Pair of rhodium-plated pin clips of two elegantly
dressed chimpanzees.
   Mr. Monkey is wearing a black enamel top hat and
jacket with red enamel lapels and rhinestone buttons,
red enamel trousers, black enamel bowtie and rhinestone vest. His hairy face has rhinestone accents. His
hands and feet are grey enameled. 5.2x2cm.
   Mrs. Monkey is wearing a light green enamel dress
with black enamel piping and flounces, a rhinestone petticoat and a large black enamel hat with a red enamel
feather. Her rhinestone bordered face, arms and feet are
grey enameled. 5.3x2cm.
   The male is marked Trifari Des. Pat. No. 113786. The
female is marked Trifari Pat. Pend.

Rhodium-plated metal pin clip, green, brown, blue, white and red enamel, rhinestones, of a monkey hanging from a branch. 5.8x5cm.
Marked Trifari Pat. Pend.

T29. "Dangling Monkey," Trifari 1939*****
Manufacturer Trifari, Krussman & Fishel.
Designer Alfred Philippe.
Patent n° 114,235 Alfred Philippe, New York, 11th April 1939, filed on 9th March 1939.

T30. "Peter and Helen," Trifari 1939****
Manufacturer Trifari, Krussman & Fishel.
Designer Alfred Philippe.
Patent Helen n° 113,523, Peter n° 113,524 Alfred Philippe, New York, 28th February 1939, filed on 23rd January 1939, assignor to Trifari, Krussman & Fishel, New York.

Rhodium-plated metal pin clips, red, black and pink enamel, rhinestones, baguettes and green stones, of a Swiss couple in traditional costume. Helen 6.7x3.8cm, Peter 6x3cm.
Marked Helen Trifari Des.Pat.No. 113523, Peter Trifari Pat.Pend.
The set of brooches was on sale at Saks Fifth Avenue for $7.50 and was advertised in *WWD*, 17th February 1939, under the name "Peter and Helen" with the indication that it was a Swiss couple in traditional costume, made with rhinestones and enameled, to be worn for carnival.

T31. "Gypsy," Trifari 1939***
Manufacturer Trifari, Krussman & Fishel.
Designer Alfred Philippe.
Patent n° 114,236 Alfred Philippe, New York, 11th April 1939, filed on 9th March 1939.

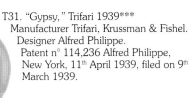

Rhodium-plated metal pin clip of a gypsy with a yellow enamel blouse, wide green enamel and rhinestone skirt and vest, a tied kerchief on her head, and red and yellow enamel shoes. Accurately designed enamel face and hair. 5.5x4cm.
Marked Trifari Pat. Pend.
The gypsy is one of a pair with a dancing male gypsy, with patent no. 114,237.

T32. "French Couple," Trifari 1939****
Manufacturer Trifari, Krussman & Fishel.
Designer Alfred Philippe.
Patent Woman n° 113,788, Man n° 113,789 Alfred Philippe,
New York, 14th March 1939, filed on 17th February 1939,
assignor to Trifari, Krussman & Fishel, New York.

Rhodium-plated metal pin clips, pink, black,
brown and red enamel, rhinestones, of the male
and female heads of a typically French "Belle
Époque" couple. Woman 3.8x2.5cm, Man
3.5x2.7cm.
Marked Woman Trifari Pat. Pend., Man Trifari
Des. Pat. No. 113789
In 1939 Alfred Philippe patented a series of
couple brooches: "Mr. & Mrs. Monkey" (T28.),
"Peter and Helen" (T30.), "Gypsies" (T31.), "Rodeo Couple" (T33.) "Odds of March" (T35.).

T33. "Rodeo Couple," Trifari 1939*****
Manufacturer Trifari, Krussman & Fishel.
Designer Alfred Philippe.
Patents n° 113,791 girl, 113,792 boy Alfred Philippe, New York,
14th March 1939, filed on 17th February 1939, assignor to Trifari,
Krussman & Fishel, New York.

Pair of rhodium-plated metal brooches with brown,
white, azure, blue, red, pink, yellow, and black
enamel and rhinestones, of a horse mounted cowgirl
and a horse mounted cowboy, showing off their skills
at a rodeo. Girl 4.7x4cm; boy 5.3x5cm.
The girl is marked Des. Pat. 113791; the boy is
marked Des. Pat. No 113792.

T34. "Laughing Horse," Trifari 1939*****
Manufacturer Trifari Krussman & Fishel.
Designer Alfred Philippe.
Patent n° 114,297 Alfred Philippe, New
York, 11th April 1939, filed on 9th March
1939.

Rhodium-plated metal pin clip with light green,
white, red, black, and pink enamel and rhinestones, of a laughing horse's head. 5.5x4.7cm.
Marked Trifari Pat. Pend.
Available in several color variants (red, white,
blue).

T35. "Odds of March," Trifari 1939****
Manufacturer Trifari, Krussman & Fishel.
Designer Alfred Philippe.
Patents Lion n° 113,793 14th March 1939, filed on 17th February 1939; Lamb n° 114,135 4th April 1939, filed on 4th March 1939
Alfred Philippe, New York, assignor to Trifari, Krussman & Fishel, New York.

Rhodium-plated metal brooch (lion) and pin clip (lamb) conceived of as a pair.

The lion has a blue enamel body with black enamel claws and rhinestone pavé mane. 4x5.3cm.

The lamb's body is rhinestone studded with small blue enamel spots, and its mouth, ears, eye and hooves have black enamel accents, and it has a black enamel nose. 4.5x2.5cm.

Lion marked Des. Pat. No. 113793. Lamb marked Trifari Des. Pat. No. 114135 "41".

The lion and lamb were presented with the name "Odds of March" in *WWD*, 17th March 1939, as a representation of the saying "March comes in like a lion and goes out like a lamb". The pair was on sale at Saks Fifth Avenue.

T36. "Pink Elephant," Trifari 1939****
Manufacturer Trifari, Krussman & Fishel.
Designer Alfred Philippe.
Not patented.

*WWD*, February 17, 1939: "Lapel loot" at Saks and Lord & Taylor. "Pink Elephant" and "Peter and Helen" by Trifari.

Rhodium-plated metal pin clip, pink and white enamel, rhinestones, of an elephant. 5x5.5cm.

Marked Trifari.

The brooch was published in 'WWD', 17th February 1939. It was on sale at Lord & Taylor, New York, for $4.95 and was described as being an "elephant clip pin in shocking pink".

T37. "Shoe-Button Grapes," Trifari 1938***
Manufacturer Trifari, Krussman & Fishel.
Designer Alfred Philippe.
Patent n° 110,292 Alfred Philippe, New York,
28th June 1938, filed 2nd May 1938, assignor to
Trifari, Krussman & Fishel, New York.

Gold-plated metal pin clip with black enamel,
pearls with a rhinestone set in the middle (shoe
button), and grape shaped rhinestones. 5.4x4cm.
Marked Trifari Des. Pat. No. 110292.
The name "shoe button" was used by Trifari
to indicate pearls and cabochons set with
a rhinestone in the center, like a shoe button
(WWD, 29th April 1938).

T38. "Calla-lilies," Trifari 1939**
Manufacturer Trifari, Krussman &
Fishel.
Designer Alfred Philippe.
Patent n° 114,138 Alfred Philippe
New York, 4th April 1939, filed
on 4th March 1939.

Gold-plated metal brooch, azure,
green and pink enamel, rhinestones, of two calla-lilies. 6.5x3cm.
Marked Trifari.

Rhodium-plated metal and
enamel pin clip of a flower with
yellow enamel petals, rhinestone
pistils and green enamel and
rhinestone pavé leaves. 7x5.5cm.
Marked Trifari Des. Pat. No.
118757.

T39. "Enameled Flower," Trifari 1940**
Manufacturer Trifari Krussman & Fishel.
Designer Alfred Philippe.
Patent n° 118,757 Alfred Philippe, New York,
30th January 1940, filed on 29th December 1939.

T40. "Tiger Lily," Trifari 1940****
Manufacturer Trifari, Krussman &
  Fishel.
  Designer Alfred Philippe.
  Patent n° 119,094 Alfred Philippe,
  New York, 20th February 1940, filed
  on 17th January 1940.

Rhodium-plated metal pin clip,
brown, green and pink enamel-
ing, rhinestones pavé, of a tiger lily.
7.5x4.8cm.
  Marked Trifari Des. Pat. No. 119094.

T41. "Leaves and Flowers," Trifari 1939****
Manufacturer Trifari, Krussman & Fishel.
Designer Alfred Philippe.
Patent n° 115,294 Alfred Philippe, New York, 20th June
1939, filed on 18th February 1939.

Gold-plated metal pin clip, pink
enamel, white and sky-blue rhinestones, of a branch with leaves and
flowers. 8x5.5cm.
  Marked Trifari Pat.Pend.

T42. *"Bunch of Flowers,"* Trifari 1940****
Manufacturer Trifari, Krussman & Fishel.
Designer Joseph Wuyts.
Patent n° 119,837 Joseph Wuyts, New York, 2nd
April 1940, filed on 21st February 1940.

Rhodium-plated metal pin clip,
with blue, yellow, red and brown
enamel and rhinestones, of a bunch
of flowers. 7.5x6.2cm
   Marked Trifari Des. Pat. No.
119837.

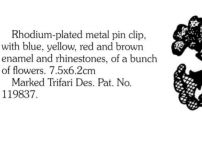

T43 *"Flower Basket,"* Trifari 1940***
Manufacturer Trifari, Krussman & Fishel.
Designer Alfred Philippe.
Patent n° 119,434 Alfred Philippe, New York,
12th March 1940, filed on 30th January 1940.

Rhodium-plated metal pin clip, red, yellow, green and blue enamel, rhinestones,
depicting a basket of flowers. 4x6cm.
Marked Trifari.

T44. *"Flower Pot,"* Trifari 1939****
Manufacturer Trifari, Krussman & Fishel.
Designer Alfred Philippe.
Patent n° 114,296 Alfred Philippe,
New York, 11th April 1939, filed on 9th
March 1939.

Rhodium-plated metal pin clip, red,
blue, green, pink, sky-blue and yellow
enamel, rhinestones, depicting a vase of
flowers. 4.5x3cm.
Marked Trifari.

T45. "Posy," Trifari 1940****
Manufacturer Trifari, Krussman &
Fishel.
Designer Joseph Wuyts.
Patent n° 119,836 Joseph
Wuyts, New York, 2nd April
1940, filed on 21st February 1940.

Rhodium-plated metal pin clip, sky-blue,
green and pink enamel, rhinestones, depicting a posy of flowers. 5x3.5cm.
Marked Trifari Pat. Pend.
From 1939-41 freelance designer Joseph Wuyts worked for Trifari and Mazer
Bros. His designs for both companies
were few and are rare items.

T46. "Carnation," Trifari 1940***
Manufacturer Trifari, Krussman & Fishel.
Designer Alfred Philippe.
Patent n° 118,759 Alfred Philippe, New York,
30th January 1940, filed on 29th December
1939.

Rhodium-plated metal pin clip, with green, brown and
red enamel and rhinestones, of a carnation. 7x4.5cm.
Marked Trifari Des. Pat. No. 118759.
There are also matching earrings and a bracelet to go
with this pin clip, with patent no. 120,590.

T47. "Flowers," Trifari 1940**
Manufacturer Trifari, Krussman & Fishel.
Designer Alfred Philippe.
Not patented but see patent n° 118,758 Alfred Philippe, New York, 30th January 1940,
filed on 29th December 1939.

Rhodium-plated metal pin clip, red and green enamel,
rhinestones, of two flowers with leaves. 7.5x6.5cm.
Marked Trifari Pat. Pend.
As the mark 'Patent Pending' indicates, this design was created from other designs, patented in the same period.

T48. "Reindeer", Trifari 1939*****
Manufacturer Trifari, Krussman & Fishel.
Designer Alfred Philippe.
Patent n° 114,238 Alfred Philippe, New York,
11th April 1939, filed on 8th March 1939.

Rhodium-plated metal brooch,
with lilac, white and black enamel,
and rhinestones. The brooch is of a
reindeer. 6x5cm.
Marked Trifari.

Rhodium-plated metal and enamel pin
clip, of a hummingbird among flowers,
with yellow enamel beak, blue and red
enamel body with rhinestones, twig in
bloom with green-brown enamel and
rhinestone flowers with tiny central blue
cabochons. 4.5x7cm.
Marked Trifari Pat. Pend.

T49. "Hummingbird," Trifari 1940***
Manufacturer Trifari, Krussman & Fishel.
Designer Alfred Philippe.
Patent n° 119,096 Alfred Philippe, New York,
20th February 1940, filed on 17th January
1940.

Rhodium-plated metal brooch, rhinestone pavé, red blue and green stones, brown, green and yellow enamel, of a bird perched on a branch. 5x6cm.
Marked Trifari "85".

T50. "Bird on a Branch," Trifari 1940****
Manufacturer Trifari, Krussman & Fishel.
Designer Alfred Philippe.
Patent n° 119,456 Alfred Philippe, New York, 12th March 1940, filed on 1st February 1940.

T51. "Fly," Trifari 1940****
Manufacturer Trifari, Krussman & Fishel.
Designer Alfred Philippe.
Patent n° 119,098 Alfred Philippe, New York, 22nd February 1940, filed on 17th January 1940.

Rhodium-plated metal brooch, transparent pale blue moonstones, green, blue and red rhinestones, of a fly with outspread wings. 4x6.8cm.
Marked Trifari Pat. Pend.
The cabochons with a rhinestone in the center are called "shoe-button" because they look like shoe buttons and were used by Trifari as early as 1938 for necklaces, bracelets and brooches (WWD, 29th April 1938). Some of these designs are patented (T37.). There is also a pawn shop number engraved on the brooch.

T52. "Pearl Belly Fly," Trifari 1940****
Manufacturer Trifari, Krussman & Fishel.
Designer Alfred Philippe.
Patent n° 120,303 Alfred Philippe, New York, 30th April 1940, filed on 18th January 1940.

Rhodium-plated metal pin clip of a resting fly with a baroque pearl for its body, a red and blue enamel head and wings with rhinestones, yellow enamel eyes and black enamel legs. 5x5.3cm.
Marked Trifari Pat. Pend.
In 1940 Alfred Philippe patented a series of brooches with various subjects (T52. T55. T56. T57. T58.) which all had in common the use of a mother-of-pearl material applied to a metal plaque, simulating a baroque pearl placed at the center of the subject. Similar items were made according to designs patented by Joseph Wuyts (T63. T64.).

T53. "Robins," Trifari 1940****
Manufacturer Trifari, Krussman & Fishel.
Designer Alfred Philippe.
Patent n° 119,102 Alfred Philippe, New York, 20th
February 1940, filed on 18th January 1940.

Rhodium-plated metal pin clip, with red,
black, white, yellow, brown, and green enamel
and rhinestones, of two robins on a branch.
5.5x4.5cm.
   Marked Trifari Des. Pat. No. 119102.

Brooch gold-plated with red gold,
white baroque pearl rhinestones
pavé, of a mallard in mid-flight.
5x6cm.
   Marked Trifari.

T54. "Pearl Belly Mallard," Trifari 1940****
Manufacturer Trifari, Krussman & Fishel.
Designer Alfred Philippe.
Patent n° 119,457 Alfred Philippe, New York,
12th March 1940, filed on 1st February 1940.

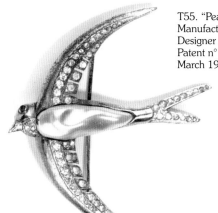

T55. "Pearl Belly Swallow," Trifari 1940\*\*\*\*
Manufacturer Trifari, Krussman & Fishel,
Designer Alfred Philippe.
Patent n° 119,435 Alfred Philippe, New York, 12th
March 1940, filed on 30th January 1940.

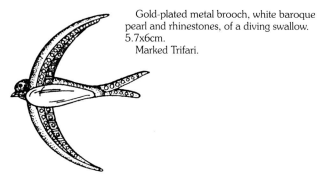

Gold-plated metal brooch, white baroque
pearl and rhinestones, of a diving swallow.
5.7x6cm.
Marked Trifari.

Rhodium-plated metal brooch of a flying bird
with outspread wings. Its body is made of a large
baroque pearl, its head is a large red cabochon,
while its wings and tail are studded with rhinestones
and blue baguettes. 7.3x6cm.
Marked Trifari Pat. Pend. "73".

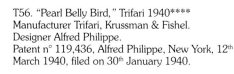

T56. "Pearl Belly Bird," Trifari 1940\*\*\*\*
Manufacturer Trifari, Krussman & Fishel.
Designer Alfred Philippe.
Patent n° 119,436, Alfred Philippe, New York, 12th
March 1940, filed on 30th January 1940.

Rhodium-plated metal pin clip, blue
and red enamel, white baroque pearl,
rhinestone pavé and green stones, of a
fish with small air bubbles coming out of its
mouth. 5x4cm.
Marked Trifari Pat. Pend.

T57. "Pearl Belly Fish," Trifari
1940****
Manufacturer Trifari, Krussman &
Fishel.
Designer Alfred Philippe.
Patent n° 119,093 Alfred Philippe, New
York, 20th February 1940, filed on 17th
January 1940.

T58. "Pearl Belly Elephant," Trifari
1940****
Manufacturer Trifari, Krussman & Fishel.
Designer Alfred Philippe.
Not patented.
Rhodium-plated metal brooch, red and
blue enamel, rhinestone pavé and white
baroque pearl, of an elephant. 3.8x5cm.
Marked Trifari.

Rhodium-plated metal pin clip, blue, pink, white,
mustard and yellow enamel, rhinestones, of a
Dutch woman holding a basket under her arm
with a goose in it. 5x3.8cm.
Marked Trifari Pat.Pend.

T59. "Dutch Woman," Trifari
1940*****
Manufacturer Trifari, Krussman
& Fishel.
Designer Joseph Wuyts.
Patent n° 119,529 Joseph Wuyts,
New York, 19th March 1940, filed
on 7th February 1940.

T60. "Dutch Girl Herding a Goose," Trifari
1940*****
Manufacturer Trifari, Krussman & Fishel.
Designer Joseph Wuyts.
Patent n° 119,445 Joseph Wuyts, New York,
12th March 1940, filed on 3rd February 1940.

Rhodium-plated metal brooch, with
blue, pink, yellow and brown enamel,
red baguettes and rhinestone pavé, of
a girl in traditional Dutch folk costume,
herding a goose with a forked stick.
5.7x4.7cm.
Marked Trifari.

T61. "Tenor Fish," Trifari 1940*****
Manufacturer Trifari, Krussman &
Fishel.
Designer Joseph Wuyts.
Patent n° 119,107 Joseph Wuyts,
New York, 20th February 1940, filed
on 18th January 1940.

Rhodium-plated metal pin clip, with
blue, green, white and black enamel,
a red cabochon and rhinestones, of a
fish wearing a tailcoat and singing while
holding a music score in its right fin.
4.6x2.5cm.
Marked Trifari Pat. Pend.

T62. "Soldier's Fiancée," Trifari 1940****
Manufacturer Trifari, Krussman & Fishel.
Designer Joseph Wuyts.
Patent n° 119,531 Joseph Wuyts, New York,
19th March 1940, filed on 7th February 1940.

Rhodium-plated metal and enamel pin clip of a young woman
wearing an elegant turn of the century dress. The yellow enamel
dress features rhinestone ornaments and a rhinestone pavé
petticoat. The woman has a black enamel bag and shoes,
white enamel stockings and long gloves, and a rhinestone hat
with a yellow pompom. The girl has a pink enamel face and
black enamel hair. 5.2x2.5cm.
Marked Trifari Pat. Pend.
The pin clip is one of a pair, the other being a pin clip of
a soldier in ceremonial uniform, also made according to a
design by Joseph Wuyts and patented with n° 119,530.

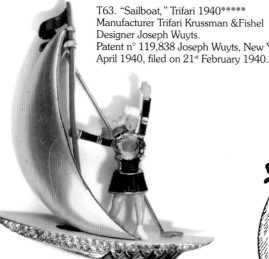

T63. "Sailboat," Trifari 1940*****
Manufacturer Trifari Krussman &Fishel
Designer Joseph Wuyts.
Patent n° 119,838 Joseph Wuyts, New York, 2nd
April 1940, filed on 21st February 1940.

Rhodium-plated metal brooch of a sailboat with metal
full sail coated with faux mother-of-pearl. The boat hull is
enameled and ornamented with rhinestone pavé and green
baguettes, the mast is coated with light brown enamel and the
flag is red and blue enameled. A female sailor is standing on
deck, holding on to the mast with one hand and waving
with the other. The figure is enameled and features an aqua
green stone for her chest, a rectangular red stone for her
waist, four rectangular azure stones for her skirt and green
baguette arms. She is wearing a white enamel hat and stockings, has yellow enamel hair, a pink enamel neckerchief and a
pink enamel body. 7.5x6.2cm.
Marked Trifari Des. Pat. No. 119838 "34".

T64. "Mexican," Trifari 1940*****
Manufacturer Trifari, Krussman & Fishel.
Designer Joseph Wuyts.
Patent n° 119,467 Joseph Wuyts, New
York, 12th March 1940, filed on 3rd
February 1940.

Rhodium-plated metal pin clip, black,
pink, yellow, red, blue, green and azure
enamel, rhinestone pavé, baroque pearl,
of a standing Mexican. 5.5x3cm.
Marked Trifari Pat. Pend.

T65. "Red Indian Chief Head," Trifari 1939****
Manufacturer Trifari, Krussman & Fishel.
Designer Alfred Philippe (?)
Not patented.
Gold-plated metal pin clip, dark brown, white,
blue and black enamel, depicting the head of a Red
Indian chief. 3x3cm.
Marked Trifari.

This brooch was probably inspired by
a Cartier piece, manufactured by Cartier,
New York, designed by George A.J.
Bezault, Juvisy-sur-Orge, France, des.
n° 110,635, 26th July 1938 (see also by
Bezault des. n° 114,055, 4th April 1939).

T66. "Ice Cream Barrow, Trifari 1939***
Manufacturer Trifari, Krussman & Fishel.
Designer Alfred Philippe?
Not patented.
Rhodium-plated metal pin clip of an ice cream cart with rhinestone pavé, black, green, yellow and red enamel, a black enamel
moving wheel and a small red stone for the wheel hub. The
cart is fitted with a red and white enamel and rhinestone sun
umbrella and with a red cabochon lantern. 5x4cm.
Marked Trifari.
This was a typical summer novelty brooch, which, based on
other designs and product characteristics of this period, can be
dated to the spring of 1939 or, at the latest (though less likely), to
the spring of 1940.

T67. "Bowknot," Trifari 1940****
Manufacturer Trifari, Krussman & Fishel.
Designer Joseph Wuyts.
Patent n° 120,560 Joseph Wuyts, New York,
14th May 1940, filed on 8th March 1940.

Rhodium-plated metal brooch, with red
enamel and rhinestones, of a bowknot.
5.7x6cm.
Marked Trifari.
Another version of the brooch was made in
patriotic red and blue colors. On the same dates
Joseph Wuyts patented four other enamel and
rhinestone bowknot shaped brooches very similar to this one, the difference being in a more or
less elaborate decoration.

T68. "Watering Can," Trifari 1940\*\*\*\*
Manufacturer Trifari, Krussman & Fishel.
Designer Joseph Wuyts.
Patent n° 120,052 Joseph Wuyts, New York, 16th
April 1940, filed on 8th March 1940.

Rhodium-plated metal pin clip, red, blue, green
and yellow enamel, rhinestones, of a watering can
used as a vase for flowers. 3.5x4.5cm.
Marked Trifari Des. Pat. No. 120052.

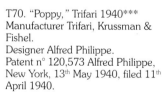

T69. "Daffodil," Trifari 1940\*\*\*
Manufacturer Trifari, Krussman & Fishel.
Designer Alfred Philippe.
Patent n° 121,254 Alfred Philippe, New York, 25th June 1940,
filed on 22nd May 1940.

Rhodium-plated metal pin clip, blue, green,
brown and yellow enamel, rhinestones in the
shape of a daffodil. 7x4.5cm
Marked Trifari Pat. Pend.

T70. "Poppy," Trifari 1940\*\*\*
Manufacturer Trifari, Krussman &
Fishel.
Designer Alfred Philippe.
Patent n° 120,573 Alfred Philippe,
New York, 13th May 1940, filed 11th
April 1940.

Rhodium-plated metal pin clip, with red,
brown, green and blue enamel and rhinestones,
of a poppy. 7.2x4.2cm.
Marked Trifari.
A matching necklace (patent n° 120,591) and
bracelet (patent n° 120,896) complete the set.

T71. *"Carnation Necklace,"* Trifari 1940***
Manufacturer Trifari, Krussman & Fishel.
Designer Alfred Philippe.
Patent n° 120,589 Alfred Philippe, New
York, 14th May 1940, filed on 13th April
1940.

Rhodium-plated metal necklace with red and
green enamel, and rhinestones with a red flower
at the center. Central motif: 10.5cm; width: 4cm.
Marked Trifari Pat. Pend.
The set is completed by a matching brooch
with patent n° 120,572.

T72. "Flowers," Trifari 1940***
Manufacturer Trifari, Krussman & Fishel.
Designer Alfred Philippe.
Patent n° 121,253 Alfred Philippe, New York,
June 25th 1940, filed May 22nd 1940.

Rhodium-plated metal pin clip,
green, pink, red and white enamel,
rhinestones, of a bunch of flowers.
7.5x5cm.
   Marked Trifari Des. Pat. No.
121253.

T73. "Glass Flower," Trifari 1940***
Manufacturer Trifari, Krussman & Fishel.
Designer Alfred Philippe.
Patent n° 121,255 Alfred Philippe, New York,
25th June 1940, filed on 25th May 1940.

Gold-plated metal pin clip, red and green enamel,
white pearls, of three flowers with white glass petals.
9x6cm.
   Marked Trifari.
   An identical brooch was patented with the number
121,350 with six flowers, and other brooches and
two necklaces were patented using the same type of
flower.

T74. "Lily of the Valley," Trifari 1940***
Manufacturer Trifari, Krussman & Fishel.
Designer Alfred Philippe.
Patent n° 121,252 Alfred Philippe, New York, 23rd
June 1940, filed on 22nd May 1940.

Rhodium-plated metal pin clip shaped like a lily of the
valley with red enamel flowers and green enamel leaves
ornamented with rhinestones. 8x4.5cm.
Marked Trifari Des. Pat. No. 121252.
As usual, this model was also made in other color variants, for example with white and blue enamel flowers.
It belongs to a series of floral brooches designed by
Philippe for the fall 1940 collection. The brooches had a
simple line and design, but were interesting for the skilful
use of enamel, typical of this period.

Rhodium-plated metal brooch, rhinestone pavé, white pearls, orange and
blue carved glass stones, of a flower
basket. 5.3x6cm.
Marked Trifari.

T75. "Basket," Trifari 1940***
Manufacturer Trifari, Krussman & Fishel.
Designer Alfred Philippe.
Patent n° 123,301 Alfred Philippe, New
York, 29th October 1940, filed on 26th
September 1940.

T76. "Enameled Orchid," Trifari 1940***
Manufacturer Trifari, Krussman & Fishel.
Designer Alfred Philippe (?)
        Not patented.
        Rhodium-plated metal pin clip of a pink enamel and rhine-
stone orchid. 8x7.7cm.
        Marked Trifari Pat. Pend.
        In spite of the Pat. Pend. mark, the patent was actually
never issued. However, the item can be accurately dated to the
spring of 1940, since, during this time, Philippe patented a series of
very similar floral designs.

T77. "Cornucopia," Trifari 1940***
Manufacturer Trifari, Krussman & Fishel.
Designer Alfred Philippe.
Not patented.
  Rhodium-plated metal pin clip, rhinestone pavé,
green, blue and red stones, green, pink, yellow and
white enamel, of a cornucopia with leaves and flowers
in it. 9x6.5cm.
  Marked Trifari.

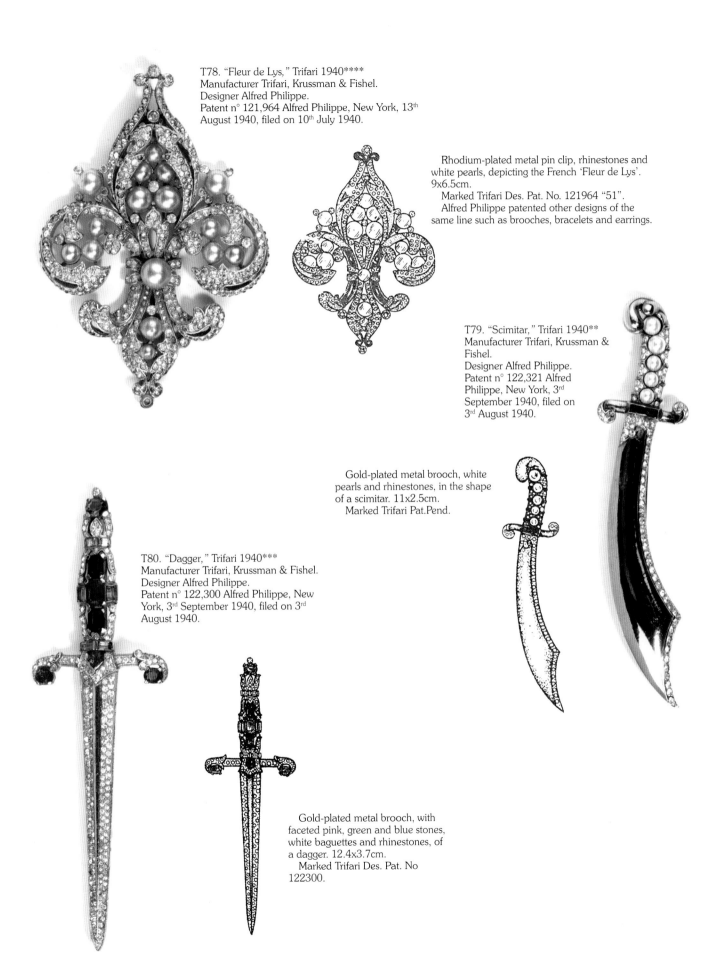

T78. "Fleur de Lys," Trifari 1940****
Manufacturer Trifari, Krussman & Fishel.
Designer Alfred Philippe.
Patent n° 121,964 Alfred Philippe, New York, 13th
August 1940, filed on 10th July 1940.

Rhodium-plated metal pin clip, rhinestones and
white pearls, depicting the French 'Fleur de Lys'.
9x6.5cm.
Marked Trifari Des. Pat. No. 121964 "51".
Alfred Philippe patented other designs of the
same line such as brooches, bracelets and earrings.

T79. "Scimitar," Trifari 1940**
Manufacturer Trifari, Krussman &
Fishel.
Designer Alfred Philippe.
Patent n° 122,321 Alfred
Philippe, New York, 3rd
September 1940, filed on
3rd August 1940.

Gold-plated metal brooch, white
pearls and rhinestones, in the shape
of a scimitar. 11x2.5cm.
Marked Trifari Pat.Pend.

T80. "Dagger," Trifari 1940***
Manufacturer Trifari, Krussman & Fishel.
Designer Alfred Philippe.
Patent n° 122,300 Alfred Philippe, New
York, 3rd September 1940, filed on 3rd
August 1940.

Gold-plated metal brooch, with
faceted pink, green and blue stones,
white baguettes and rhinestones, of
a dagger. 12.4x3.7cm.
Marked Trifari Des. Pat. No
122300.

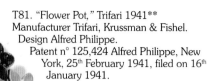

T81. *"Flower Pot,"* Trifari 1941**
Manufacturer Trifari, Krussman & Fishel.
Design Alfred Philippe.
Patent n° 125,424 Alfred Philippe, New
York, 25th February 1941, filed on 16th
January 1941.

Rhodium-plated metal pin clip,
yellow, red, green and blue enamel,
rhinestones, of a bunch of flowers in a
vase. 5.5x3cm.
Marked Trifari Des. Pat. No.
125424.

T82. *"Arum Lilies,"* Trifari 1940****
Manufacturer Trifari, Krussman & Fishel.
Designer Alfred Philippe.
Patent n° 122,340 Alfred Philippe, New York, 3rd
September 1940, filed on 3rd August 1940.

Rhodium-plated metal pin clip,
rhinestone pavé, red and blue stones,
black enamel, of a bunch of arum lilies.
12x6.5cm.
Marked Trifari.

T83. *"Pastel Fruit Salad Flower Pot,"*
Trifari 1941**
Manufacturer Trifari, Krussman & Fishel.
Designer Alfred Philippe.
Patent n° 125,162 Alfred Philippe, New York, 11th February 1941, filed on 9th January 1941.

Gold-plated metal pin clip, red and blue carved stones, rhinestones, of a bunch of flowers in a vase. 5.5x3cm.
Marked Trifari "15".
There is also a "fruit salad" version, "chalcedony" and white transparent stones.

Rhodium-plated metal pin clip, green, red and blue carved stones, rhinestones and baguettes, of a flower. 11x5cm.
Marked Trifari "5".

T84. *"Fruit Salad Flower,"* Trifari 1941*****
Manufacturer Trifari, Krussman & Fishel.
Designer Alfred Philippe.
Patent n° 125,157 Alfred Philippe, New York, 11th February 1941, filed on 8th January 1941.

T85. "Fruit Salad Butterfly," Trifari
1941*****
Manufacturer Trifari, Krussman & Fishel.
Designer Alfred Philippe.
Patent n° 125,166 Alfred Philippe, New
York, 11th February 1941, filed on 9th January
1941.

Rhodium-plated metal brooch, rhinestones and
green, red and blue carved stones, of a butterfly.
4.5x7cm.
Marked Trifari Pat.Pend. "41".
This item forms part of a series of extraordinarily
beautiful brooches both in design and elaboration,
produced in the 'fruit salad' version and 'chalcedony' version. The term "fruit salad" is modern
and indicates jewelry characterized by small multi-
colored carved stones first launched by Cartier in
1929 as "style indien" o "Hindou".

T86. "Fruit Salad Basket," Trifari 1941***
Manufacturer Trifari, Krussman & Fishel.
  Designer Alfred Philippe.
    Patent n° 125,156 Alfred Philippe, New York, 11th
    February 1941, filed on 8th January 1941.

Rhodium-plated metal pin clip with rhinestones, baguettes and
red, blue and green engraved stones, of a flower basket. 5x3.2cm.
Marked Trifari Des. Pat. No. 125156.
In 1941 Alfred Philippe, patented two designs, one smaller, the
other bigger, which were very similar to "Basket". The cataloged
item is the bigger version. The basket was made of rhodium-plated
metal and multicolor "Fruit Salad" engraved stones, and of gold-
plated metal and engraved white (crystal), azure (chalcedony) or
pink stones, used alone and together.

Rhodium-plated metal brooch of a peacock in flight, with rhinestone pavé body
with blue cabochon accents, red enamel
beak and legs, small red cabochon for
its eye, baguettes for its tail and
wings with engraved red, green
and blue stones. 5x8cm.
Marked Trifari "92".

T87. "Fruit Salad Peacock," Trifari 1941*****
Manufacturer Trifari, Krussman & Fishel.
Designer Alfred Philippe.
Patent n° 125,165 Alfred Philippe, New York,
11th March 1941, filed on 6th February 1941.

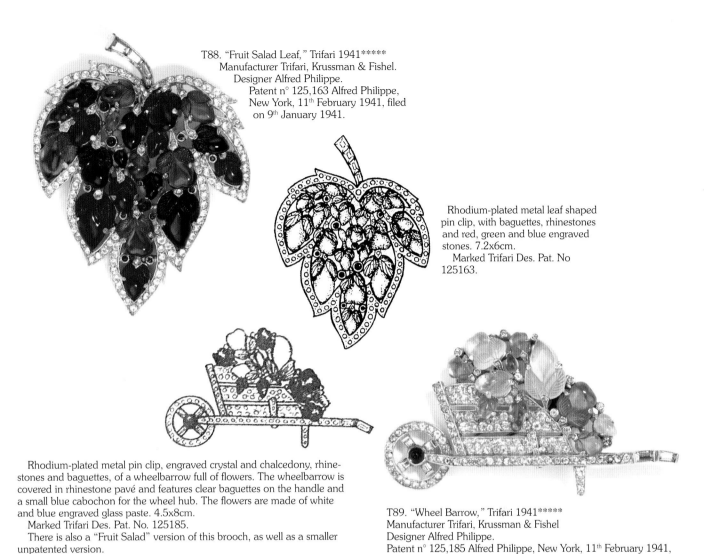

T88. "Fruit Salad Leaf," Trifari 1941*****
Manufacturer Trifari, Krussman & Fishel.
Designer Alfred Philippe.
Patent n° 125,163 Alfred Philippe,
New York, 11th February 1941, filed
on 9th January 1941.

Rhodium-plated metal leaf shaped
pin clip, with baguettes, rhinestones
and red, green and blue engraved
stones. 7.2x6cm.
Marked Trifari Des. Pat. No
125163.

Rhodium-plated metal pin clip, engraved crystal and chalcedony, rhinestones and baguettes, of a wheelbarrow full of flowers. The wheelbarrow is
covered in rhinestone pavé and features clear baguettes on the handle and
a small blue cabochon for the wheel hub. The flowers are made of white
and blue engraved glass paste. 4.5x8cm.
Marked Trifari Des. Pat. No. 125185.
There is also a "Fruit Salad" version of this brooch, as well as a smaller
unpatented version.

T89. "Wheel Barrow," Trifari 1941*****
Manufacturer Trifari, Krussman & Fishel
Designer Alfred Philippe.
Patent n° 125,185 Alfred Philippe, New York, 11th February 1941,
filed on 8th January 1941.

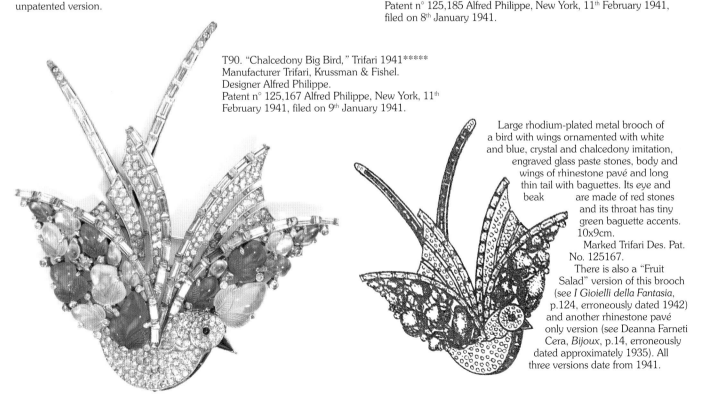

T90. "Chalcedony Big Bird," Trifari 1941*****
Manufacturer Trifari, Krussman & Fishel.
Designer Alfred Philippe.
Patent n° 125,167 Alfred Philippe, New York, 11th
February 1941, filed on 9th January 1941.

Large rhodium-plated metal brooch of
a bird with wings ornamented with white
and blue, crystal and chalcedony imitation,
engraved glass paste stones, body and
wings of rhinestone pavé and long
thin tail with baguettes. Its eye and
beak      are made of red stones
and its throat has tiny
green baguette accents.
10x9cm.
Marked Trifari Des. Pat.
No. 125167.
There is also a "Fruit
Salad" version of this brooch
(see I Gioielli della Fantasia,
p.124, erroneously dated 1942)
and another rhinestone pavé
only version (see Deanna Farneti
Cera, Bijoux, p.14, erroneously
dated approximately 1935). All
three versions date from 1941.

T91. "*Chalcedony Turtle,*" Trifari 1941\*\*\*\*\*
Manufacturer Trifari, Krussman & Fishel.
Designer Alfred Philippe.
Not patented.
    Rhodium-plated metal pin clip, baguettes, rhinestones, clear and blue, crystal and chalcedony, engraved stones, of a turtle. 8.4x6cm.
    Marked Trifari.
    There was also an engraved red stone version of this brooch.

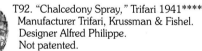

T92. "*Chalcedony Spray,*" Trifari 1941\*\*\*\*
Manufacturer Trifari, Krussman & Fishel.
Designer Alfred Philippe.
Not patented.
    Gold-plated metal pin clip shaped like a spray of flowers made of blue engraved and contoured glass paste stones. The pin clip features a safety lock. 9.5x5cm.
Marked Trifari "31".
    There is also a "Fruit Salad" version of this pin clip, manufactured in the same period, made of rhodium-plated metal with tree spirals.

T93. "*Posy,*" Trifari 1941\*\*\*
Manufacturer Trifari, Krussman & Fishel.
Designer Alfred Philippe.
Patent n° 125,348 Alfred Philippe, New York, 18th February 1941, filed on 16th January 1941.

    Rhodium-plated metal pin clip, red, blue, white, green and brown enamel, rhinestones, in the shape of a bunch of flowers. 9x5cm.
    Marked Trifari Des. Pat. No. 125348.
    There is also a smaller version.

T94. "Flower," Trifari 1941***
Manufacturer Trifari, Krussman & Fishel.
Designer Alfred Philippe.
Patent n° 126,246 Alfred Philippe, New
York, 1st April 1941, filed on 18th February
1941.

Rhodium-plated metal pin
clip, with green, red and yellow
enamel and rhinestones, of a flower.
8.1x4.2cm.
Marked Trifari.

T95. "Flower Vase," Trifari 1941***
Manufacturer Trifari, Krussman & Fishel.
Designer Alfred Philippe.
Patent n° 125,846 Alfred Philippe, New York,
11th March 1941, filed on 6th February 1941.

Rhodium-plated metal pin clip, with blue,
green, red and yellow enamel and rhinestones, of a flower vase. 5.5x4.2cm.
Marked Trifari.

T96. "Hyacinths," Trifari 1941*****
Manufacturer Trifari, Krussman & Fishel.
Designer Alfred Philippe.
Patent n° 125,820 Alfred Philippe, New York,
11th March 1941, filed on 6th February 1941.

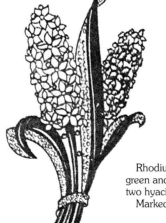

Rhodium-plated metal pin clip, pink, blue,
green and brown enamel, rhinestones, of
two hyacinths. 11x6cm.
Marked Trifari Des. Pat. No. 125820.

T97. "Clematis," Trifari 1941****
Manufacturer Trifari, Krussman & Fishel.
Designer Alfred Philippe.
Patent n° 125,421 Alfred Philippe, New
York, 25th February 1941, filed on 16th
January 1941.

Rhodium-plated metal pin clip, with red
and green enamel and rhinestones, of a
clematis. 9.8x6.8cm
    Marked Trifari Sterling Pat. Pend.
    The original Sterling hallmark is a
peculiarity, since the metal used for
this pin clip was not silver. A possible
explanation for this is that a marking
mistake may have occurred.

Rhodium-plated metal pin clip, red and
green enamel, rhinestones, in the shape of a
flower. 8x4.5cm.
    Marked Trifari Des. Pat. No. 125422.

T98. "Red Flower," Trifari 1941***
Manufacturer Trifari, Krussman & Fishel.
Designer Alfred Philippe.
Patent n° 125,422 Alfred Philippe, New York,
25th February 1941, filed on 16th January 1941.

T99. "Stork," Trifari 1941*****
Manufacturer Trifari, Krussman & Fishel.
Designer Alfred Philippe.
Patent n° 125,847 Alfred Philippe,
New York, 11th March 1941, filed on
6th February 1941.

Rhodium-plated metal brooch of a stork with a rhinestone studded body, yellow enamel bill and legs, a red stone for its eye, and blue enamel crest, wing and tail tips. The stork is portrayed drinking from a pond which is a large, rectangular, narrow pink crystal, with bright shaded pink enamel borders and ornamented with four green enamel and rhinestone water lilies. 7x7.3cm.
Marked Trifari.
The reproduced brooch does not fit exactly the design patented, which is for a pin clip and has a different, not framed stone. Even more the mark should have been on the clip and not on the piece. However it does not look like a modern fake but or Trifari made at the same time another, cheaper version of the patented model, or the brooch was repaired as good as possible.

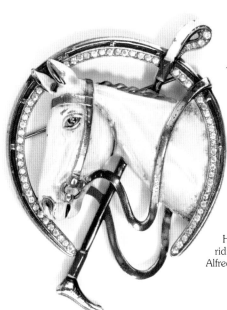

T100. "Horse Head," Trifari 1942*****
Manufacturer Trifari, Krussman & Fishel.
Designer Alfred Spaney (?)
Not patented.
Brooch plated with red gold, white and red enamel, rhinestones, of a horse's head and whip within a horseshoe. 6x8cm.
Marked Trifari Pat. Pend.
The mark "Patent Pending" is applied to the whip, which is almost identical to a design by Alfred Spaney (Des. No. 131,247, 27th January 1942, filed on 23rd December 1941). Another whip, with a riding cap was also patented by Alfred Spaney, 3rd March 1942 (Des. No. 131,458, filed on 3rd January 1942). The catalogued Horse Head goes well with these items inspired by horse riding and it is highly probable that it too was designed by Alfred Spaney.

T101. "Flying Heron," Trifari 1941*****
Manufacturer Trifari, Krussman & Fishel.
Designer Alfred Philippe.
Patent n° 126,247 Alfred Philippe, New York,
1st April 1941, filed on 18th February 1941.

Rhodium-plated metal pin clip, blue,
red and yellow enamel, large green
center stone, rhinestones, of a flying
heron. 9x7.5cm.
Marked Trifari Pat. Pend.

T102. "Frog," Trifari 1941*****
Manufacturer Trifari, Krussman & Fishel.
Designer Alfred Philippe.
Patent n° 125,848 Alfred Philippe, New York,
11th March 1941, filed on 6th February 1941.

Rhodium-plated metal pin clip, green enamel, large green
center stone, red and blue rhinestones, in the shape of a frog.
7x7cm.
Marked Trifari Des. Pat. No. 125848.
This piece was produced with the central stone in various
colors and without enamel, which was replaced by rhinestones.

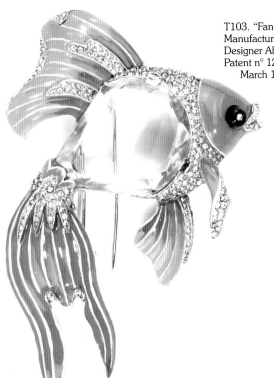

T103. "Fan Tail Fish," Trifari 1941*****
Manufacturer Trifari, Krussman & Fishel.
Designer Alfred Philippe.
Patent n° 125,817 Alfred Philippe, New York, 11th
  March 1941, filed 6th February 1941.

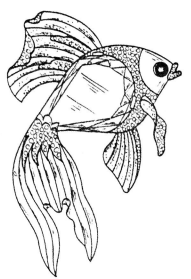

Rhodium-plated metal pin
clip of a fish, with blue, white
and pink enamel, rhinestones,
a red shoe-button cabochon
for its eye, and large, oval,
faceted, aqua blue central
stone. 10x7.5cm.
  Marked Trifari Pat. Pend.
  This item is exceptional for
its design, size, and colors.

T104. "Rooster," Trifari 1941****
Manufacturer Trifari, Krussman &
Fishel.
Designer Alfred Philippe.
Patent n° 125,350 Alfred Philippe,
New York, 18th February 1941, filed on
16th January 1941.

Rhodium-plated metal brooch,
blue, red and pink cut stones,
rhinestones and blue cabochon,
of a rooster. 4.4x6cm.
  Marked Trifari.

T105. *"Déco Swallow,"* Trifari 1941\*\*\*
Manufacturer Trifari, Krussman & Fishel.
Designer Alfred Philippe.
Patent n° 125,818 Alfred Philippe, New
York, 11th March 1941, filed on 6th February
1941.

Rhodium-plated metal pin clip,
with red and blue enamel, central
green stone, red cabochon and
rhinestones, of a stylized swallow in
flight. 5x3.5cm.
Marked Trifari Pat. Pend.

T106. *"Owl,"* Trifari 1941\*\*\*\*
Manufacturer Trifari, Kruss-
man & Fishel.
Designer Alfred Philippe.
Patent n° 125,184 Alfred
Philippe, New York, 11th
February 1941, filed on 8th
January 1941.

Rhodium-plated metal pin
clip, large blue cut-stone, red
cabochons and green stones,
yellow enamel, rhinestone pavé,
of an owl perched on a branch.
4.3x2.8cm.
Marked Trifari Des. Pat. No.
125184.

T107. *"Sinbad Head,"* Trifari 1941\*\*\*\*\*
Manufacturer Trifari, Krussman & Fishel.
Designer David Mir.
Patent n° 129,439 David Mir, New
York, 9th September 1941, filed on
2nd August 1941.

Two-color gold-plated metal brooch, red, blue
and green cut stones, white pearls, rhinestones,
of an oriental head with turban and jewelry.
8x5.5cm.
Marked Trifari Des. Pat. No. 129439.
Similarly to other Oriental heads of the same
period and by different producers, this item is
called 'Sinbad' however there is no reference
to the same period. 'Sinbad the Sailor' was the
adventurous character in 'A Thousand and One
Nights' who traveled the World.

T108. "Pierrot," Trifari 1942*****
Manufacturer Trifari, Krussman & Fishel.
Designer David Mir (?)
Not patented.
   Rhodium-plated metal pin clip, with
black, red and white enamel and rhine-
stones, of the head of a Pierrot with a
wide, rhinestone studded collar, and black
enamel mask and skull cap. 5.2x5.5cm.
   Marked Trifari.

T109. "Bar Tender," Trifari 1941*****
Manufacturer Trifari, Krussman & Fishel.
Designer Alfred Philippe.
Patent n° 125,845 Alfred Philippe, New York,
11th March 1941, filed on 6th February 1941.

   Rhodium-plated metal pin clip, black
and white enamel, large green and red
cut stones, rhinestones, of a bar tender
holding a shaker. 6x3.5cm.
   Marked Trifari Des. Pat. No. 125845.
   "6th CG to EG," is inscribed on the
brooch which was probably a wedding
anniversary present.

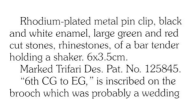

T110. "Jack in the Box," Trifari 1941*****
Manufacturer Trifari, Krussman & Fishel.
Designer Alfred Philippe.
Patent n° 125,821 Alfred Philippe, New
York, 11th March 1941, filed on 6th February
1941.

   Rhodium-plated metal pin clip,
red and blue enamel, large violet,
green, blue and pink cut stones,
rhinestones, of a jack-in-the-box.
7x4cm.
   Marked Trifari Des. Pat. No.
125821.

T111. "Toasting Drinker," Trifari 1941*****
Manufacturer Trifari, Krussman & Fishel.
Designer Alfred Philippe.
Patent n° 125,826 Alfred Philippe, New York,
11th March 1941, filed on 8th February 1941.

Gold-plated metal brooch,
large hexagonal violet cut stone,
red stone and rhinestones,
of a drinker making a toast.
7x3.5cm.
Marked Trifari Pat.Pend.

T112. "Ivan and Tania," Trifari
1942*****
Manufacturer Trifari, Krussman
& Fishel.
Designer David Mir.
Patent Tania n° 131,233, Ivan n°
131,234 David Mir, New York, 27th
January 1942, filed on 17th December 1941.

Rhodium-plated metal pin clips of a couple of dancing Russian peas-
ants. Tania is wearing a blue, white and red enamel dress, a green beret and
rhinestone vest. Ivan is wearing red enamel trousers, white enamel boots, a
rhinestone and green enamel tunic, and black, red and yellow tricorn hat.
Tania: 6.5x3.5cm, Ivan: 5.5x6cm.
    Marked Trifari Pat. Pend. (both)
    WWD, 8th February 1942, reported that "Ivan and Tania are two enameled
peasant figures said to be favored in reorders". The names and clothing suggest that the figures were inspired by Russian folklore, as in 1947 "Tasha and
Sasha" (T176.).
    David Mir, about whom no further information is available, is the creator of
the designs of some of Trifari's most beautiful items.

T113. *"Treble Clef,"* Trifari 1941***
Manufacturer Trifari, Krussman &
Fishel.
Designer Alfred Philippe.
Patent n° 125,824 Alfred Philippe,
New York, 11th March 1941, filed on
6th February 1941.

Rhodium-plated metal brooch,
pink and blue enamel, red and
blue cabochons, rhinestones, in the
shape of a violin stick. 8x3.2cm.
Marked Trifari Pat. Pend.

T114. *"Axe,"* Trifari 1941***
Manufacturer Trifari, Krussman & Fishel.
Designer Alfred Philippe.
Patent n° 125,825 Alfred Philippe, New
York, 11th March 1941, filed on 6th Febru-
ary 1941.

Gold-plated metal and rhinestone brooch
of an axe with a large faceted blue stone at
the top and pink and blue stones at the base
of the handle. 8.5x3.9cm
Marked Trifari "15".

T115. *"Lyre,"* Trifari 1941***
Manufacturer Trifari, Krussman & Fishel.
Designer Alfred Philippe.
Patent n° 125,353 Alfred Philippe, New York, 19th
February 1941, filed on 16th January 1941.

Rhodium-plated metal brooch, with pink and
blue enamel and rhinestones, of a lyre with pink
shaded enamel strings and base, and a blue
enamel structure ornamented with pink and blue
crystals and rhinestone pavé. 5.2x4.8cm.
Marked Trifari Pat. Pend.

T116. "Triple Flower," Trifari 1941****
Manufacturer Trifari, Krussman & Fishel.
Designer Alfred Philippe.
Patent n° 126,633 Alfred Philippe, New
York, 15th April 1941, filed on 10th March
1941.

Two-color gold-plated metal
brooch with rhinestones, of
three flowers. 12x7.5cm.
Marked Trifari Des.Pat.No.
126633.
As with many other pieces made
at this time, this item was also
made in an enameled version.

T117. "Flower Spray," Trifari 1941***
Manufacturer Trifari, Krussman & Fishel.
Designer Alfred Spaney.
Patent n° 130,087 Alfred Spaney, New
York, 21st October 1941, filed on 19th
September 1941.

Rhodium-plated metal brooch
shaped like a flower spray, with green
enamel, blue marquise cut stones and
rhinestones. 10.2x3.4cm.
Marked Trifari Pat. Pend.

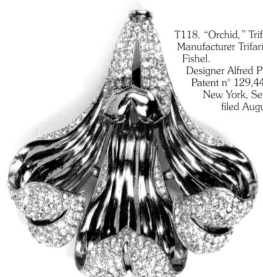

T118. "Orchid," Trifari 1941*****
Manufacturer Trifari Krussman &
Fishel.
Designer Alfred Philippe.
Patent n° 129,441 Alfred Philippe,
New York, September 9th 1941,
filed August 2nd 1941.

Gold-plated metal and rhinestone pin clip
shaped like an orchid. 7.7x7cm.
Marked Trifari Pat. Pend.
This is a copy of an identical
design created for a precious item
of jewelry by Fulco della Cerda,
Duke of Verdura, in 1940 and
manufactured by Jewels Verdura
Inc., 712 Fifth Avenue. The
fine jewel was made of gold and
diamonds and appeared in a Vogue
advertisement in 1940.

T119. "Double Flower," Trifari 1941***
Manufacturer Trifari, Krussman & Fishel.
Designer Alfred Spaney.
Patent n° 129,553 Alfred Spaney, New York,
16th September 1941, filed on 16th August
1941.

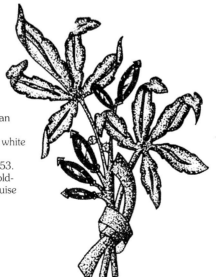

Rhodium-plated metal brooch of an
elaborate double flower joined by a
rhinestone pavé bowknot with large white
marquise cut stones. 11.3x7.5cm.
Marked Trifari Des. Pat. No. 129553.
This design was used also for a gold-
plated metal brooch with blue marquise
cut stones.

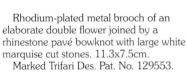

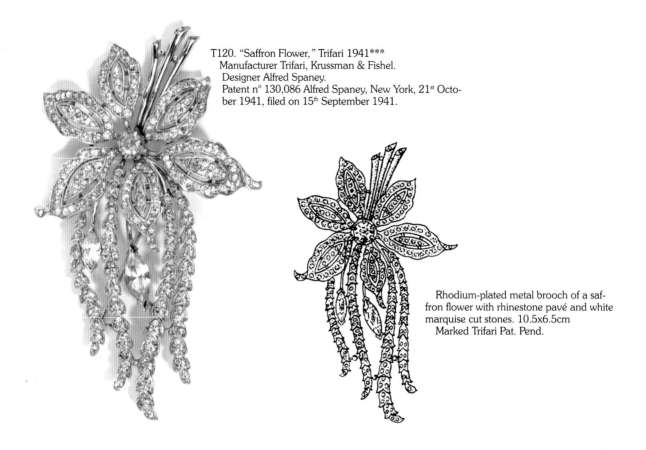

T120. "Saffron Flower," Trifari 1941***
Manufacturer Trifari, Krussman & Fishel.
Designer Alfred Spaney.
Patent n° 130,086 Alfred Spaney, New York, 21st October 1941, filed on 15th September 1941.

Rhodium-plated metal brooch of a saffron flower with rhinestone pavé and white marquise cut stones. 10.5x6.5cm
Marked Trifari Pat. Pend.

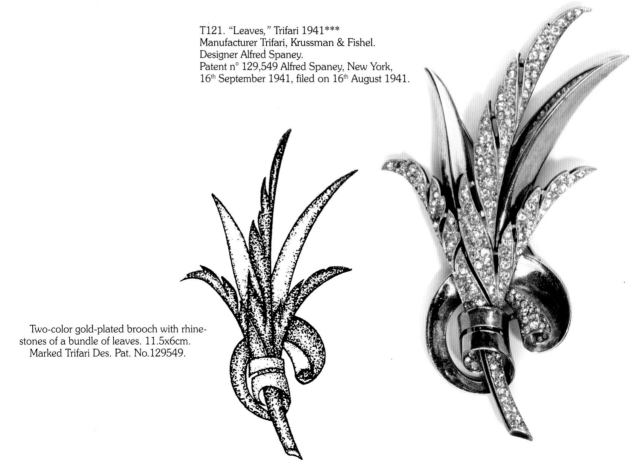

T121. "Leaves," Trifari 1941***
Manufacturer Trifari, Krussman & Fishel.
Designer Alfred Spaney.
Patent n° 129,549 Alfred Spaney, New York,
16th September 1941, filed on 16th August 1941.

Two-color gold-plated brooch with rhinestones of a bundle of leaves. 11.5x6cm.
Marked Trifari Des. Pat. No.129549.

T122. "Palm," Trifari 1942**
Manufacturer Trifari, Krussman & Fishel.
Designer Alfred Philippe.
Patent n° 131,367 Alfred Philippe, New
York, 10th February 1942, filed on 30th
December 1941.

Gold-plated metal brooch, with rhinestones and
blue stones, of a palm tree with two coconuts and a
rhinestone pavé crescent moon in the background.
6x4.5cm.
    Marked Trifari Des. Pat. No. 131367.
    Similarly to many other items made in this period,
this brooch was made in two versions: enameled and
gold-plated.

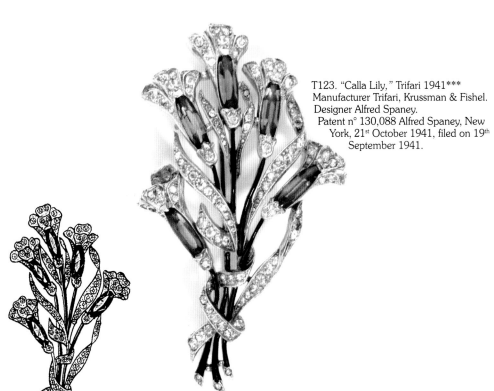

T123. "Calla Lily," Trifari 1941***
Manufacturer Trifari, Krussman & Fishel.
Designer Alfred Spaney.
Patent n° 130,088 Alfred Spaney, New
York, 21st October 1941, filed on 19th
September 1941.

Rhodium-plated metal brooch,
with oval citrine stones, black
enamel and rhinestones, of a
bunch of lilies. 10x6cm.
    Marked Trifari Des. Pat. No.
130088.

T124. *"Cherries,"* Trifari 1941****
Manufacturer Trifari, Krussman & Fishel.
Designer Alfred Philippe.
Patent n° 127,327 Alfred Philippe, New
York, 20th May 1941, filed on 9th April 1941.

Rhodium-plated metal pin clip, red,
green and brown enamel, of a cherry-
blossom branch. 7.3x4.5cm.
Marked Trifari Pat.Pend.

T125. *"Moon and Star,"* Trifari 1941****
Manufacturer Trifari, Krussman & Fishel.
Designer Alfred Philippe.
Not patented.
　　Gold and rhodium-plated metal pin clip, with black
and red enamel, pearls, small red cabochons and
rhinestones, of a crescent moon outlined with pearls
and with a star in the middle. 5x5cm.
　　　　Marked Trifari.

Rhodium-plated metal pin clip
shaped like a pineapple with rhinestone
and reddish-brown enamel fruit,
and green enamel and rhinestone
leaves. 6x5.2cm.
　　Marked Trifari Pat. Pend.

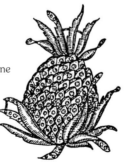

T126. *"Pineapple,"* Trifari 1941***
Manufacturer Trifari, Krussman & Fishel.
Designer Alfred Philippe.
Patent n° 129,516 Alfred Philippe, New
York, 16th September 1941, filed on 19th
March 1941.

Rhodium-plated metal pin clip, with black and red enamel, small green and red cabochons and rhinestones, of a seated greyhound wearing a coat and collar. 9x5.2cm.
Marked Trifari.

T127. "Greyhound," Trifari 1942*****
Manufacturer Trifari, Krussman & Fishel.
Designer Alfred Philippe.
Patent n° 131,240 Alfred Philippe, New York, 27th January 1942, filed on 20th December 1941.

Rhodium-plated metal pin clip, red and blue enamel, rhinestone pavé, of a bird perched on a branch with outspread wings. 10.5x6cm.
Marked Trifari Des. Pat. No. 127329.

T128. "Bird," Trifari 1941****
Manufacturer Trifari, Krussman & Fishel.
Designer Alfred Philippe.
Patent n° 127,329 Alfred Philippe, New York, 20th May 1941, filed on 9th April 1941.

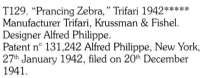

Rhodium-plated metal pin clip, with red and black enamel, green cabochons and rhinestones, of a prancing zebra. 7.3x5cm.
Marked Trifari Pat. Pend.

T129. "Prancing Zebra," Trifari 1942*****
Manufacturer Trifari, Krussman & Fishel.
Designer Alfred Philippe.
Patent n° 131,242 Alfred Philippe, New York, 27th January 1942, filed on 20th December 1941.

T130. "Elephant," Trifari 1942*****
Manufacturer Trifari, Krussman & Fishel.
Designer Alfred Philippe.
Patent n° 131,236 Alfred Philippe, New York, 27th January 1942, filed on 17th December 1941.

Gold-plated metal brooch, with white, red, black, turquoise enamel and rhinestones, of an elephant with parade saddle cloth and earring. 7.2x5cm.
Marked Trifari Pat. Pend.

T131. "Perching Bird," Trifari 1941***
Manufacturer Trifari, Krussman & Fishel.
Designer Alfred Philippe.
Patent n° 126,634 Alfred Philippe, New
    York, 15ᵗʰ April 1941, filed on 10ᵗʰ
    March 1941.

Gold-plated metal pin clip with
green, blue, yellow and ochre
enamel and rhinestones, of a bird
perching on a branch. 5.5x3.5cm.
Marked Trifari Des. Pat. No.
126634.

Gold-plated metal brooch, white,
blue and red enamel, blue, green
and red cabochons, rhinestones, of
a horse with elaborate decorative
trimmings. 6.5x7cm.
Marked Trifari Pat. Pend.

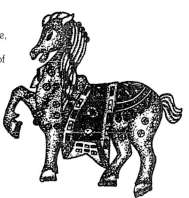

T132. "Carousel Horse," Trifari
1941*****
Manufacturer Trifari, Krussman & Fishel.
Designer David Mir.
Patent n° 130,338 David Mir, New York, 11ᵗʰ
November 1941, filed on 18ᵗʰ October 1941.

T133. "Tree," Trifari 1941*****
Manufacturer Trifari, Krussman & Fishel.
Designer Alfred Philippe.
Patent n° 131,369 Alfred Philippe, New York,
    10ᵗʰ February 1942, filed on 30ᵗʰ December
    1941.

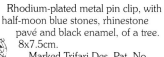

Rhodium-plated metal pin clip, with
half-moon blue stones, rhinestone
    pavé and black enamel, of a tree.
    8x7.5cm.
    Marked Trifari Des. Pat. No.
131369.
    The pin clip was made in several
color variants.

T134. "Small Tree," Trifari 1942**
Manufacturer Trifari, Krussman & Fishel.
Designer Alfred Philippe.
Patent n° 131,539 Alfred Philippe, New York,
10th March 1942, filed on 12th January 1942.

Rhodium-plated metal pin clip,
yellow, red and green enamel, of a
small tree. 5x4cm.
Marked Trifari Pat. Pend.

Gold-plated metal brooch, red enamel,
rhinestones, green cabochons, of a willow tree in
bloom. 8x6cm.
Marked Trifari Pat. Pend.
The willow featured in *WWD*, 20th February
1942. There are also versions enameled in red,
green, white and blue.

T135. "Willow Tree," Trifari 1942*****
Manufacturer Trifari, Krussman & Fishel.
Designer Alfred Philippe.
Patent n° 131,366 Alfred Philippe, New York,
10th February 1942, filed on 30th December
1941.

Gold-plated metal brooch, with green and pink crystals and rhinestones, of two birds on a branch. One of the birds has an aqua
green crystal for its body, whilst the other has a pale pink one.
6.3x6.5cm.
Marked Trifari Pat. Pend. "56".
Like many other pieces from the year 1942, several color
variants were made of this brooch with different enamel
colors and stones. Trifari also made matching earrings with the
same design, only smaller. The earrings had patent n° 131,974, 7th
April 1942.
The brooch appeared in the "Ladies' Home Journal," April 1942.

T136. "Two Birds on a Branch," Trifari 1942****
Manufacturer Trifari, Krussman & Fishel.
Designer Alfred Philippe.
Patent n° 131,365 Alfred Philippe, New York, 10th
February 1942, filed on 30th December 1941.

T137. "Windmill," Trifari 1942*****
Manufacturer Trifari, Krussman & Fishel.
Designer Alfred Spaney.
Patent n° 131,245 Alfred Spaney, New York, 27th
January 1942, filed on 17th December 1941.

Rhodium-plated metal brooch,
green and red enamel, yellow, pink,
blue and red stones, rhinestones, in
the shape of a windmill. 6x4cm.
Marked Trifari Pat. Pend.

Rhodium-plated metal pin clip, with yellow,
red and blue enamel, red and blue rhinestone
set cabochons and rhinestones, of a tree trunk
with two birds, one perched on a branch, the
other one inside a birdhouse. 6x2.8cm.
Marked Trifari Pat. Pend.

T138. "Birds and Birdhouse", Trifari 1942*****
Manufacturer Trifari, Krussman & Fishel.
Designer Alfred Philippe.
Patent n° 131,243 Alfred Philippe, New York, 27th
January 1942, filed on 23rd December 1941.

Gold-plated metal brooch of a bumblebee
with white, black and burgundy enamel and two
small cabochons for its eyes, and rhinestones.
5x4cm.
Marked Trifari.

T139. "Bumblebee," Trifari 1942****
Manufacturer Trifari, Krussman & Fishel.
Designer Alfred Philippe.
Patent n° 131,267 Alfred Philippe, New York, 27th January
1942, filed on 20th December 1941.

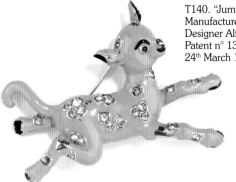

T140. "Jumping Lamb," Trifari 1942***
Manufacturer Trifari, Krussman & Fishel.
Designer Alfred Philippe.
Patent n° 131,746 Alfred Philippe, New York,
24th March 1942, filed on 20th January 1942.

Rhodium-plated metal and pink
enamel brooch of a jumping lamb, with
pink enamel coat and rhinestone pavé
spots, red stones for its eye and mouth,
and black enamel for its hooves, lashes
and ears. 4.5x6.2cm.
Marked Trifari.

T141. "Snail," Trifari 1942*****
Manufacturer Trifari, Krussman & Fishel.
Designer Alfred Philippe.
Patent n° 131,265 Alfred Philippe, New York, 27th
January 1942, filed on 17th December 1941.

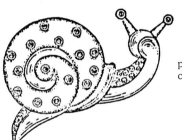

Gold-plated metal pin clip, black and
pink enamel, rhinestones and green cabochons, of a snail. 5x8.8cm.
Marked Trifari "51".

T142 "Bear," Trifari 1942***
Manufacturer Trifari, Krussman & Fishel.
Designer Alfred Philippe.
Patent n° 131,783 Alfred Philippe, New York,
24th March 1942, filed on 20th January 1942.

Rhodium-plated metal pin clip, black
and blue enamel and rhinestones, of an
upright bear with a black enamel coat,
outlined in blue enamel and ornamented
with rhinestones. Its mouth has red
enamel accents and its eye is a red stone.
5x2.9cm.
Marked Trifari Pat. Pend.

T143. "Prancing Horse," Trifari 1942****
Manufacturer Trifari, Krussman & Fishel.
Designer Alfred
Philippe.
Patent n°
131,368 Alfred
Philippe, New
York, 10th Feb-
ruary 1942,
filed on 30th
December 1941.

Rhodium-plated metal brooch, with blue and red enamel,
baguettes and rhinestones, of a prancing horse with blue
enamel body outlined with red enamel, red enamel eyes,
mouth and hooves, white baguettes for its mane, a rhinestone studded tail and rhinestones set in its
neck and legs. 4.5x5.5cm.
Marked Trifari "56".
In 1942 Alfred Philippe designed and patented a remarkable series of rhodium-plated,
colored enamel brooches with
animal, figurative and floral
subjects.

## "MING COLLECTION" 1942

T144. "Ming Dragon Bracelet," Trifari 1942*****
Manufacturer Trifari, Krussman & Fishel.
Designer Alfred Philippe.
Patent n° 131,439 Alfred Philippe, New York, 17th February 1942, filed on 7th January 1942.

Gold-plated metal link bracelet with red enamel, faux green jade, small cabochons and rhinestones, of two dragons and three jade squares. 17.6x2cm.
Marked Trifari Des. Pat. No. 131439.
The patented design refers to the larger version with four dragons and four jade squares. Other items in this series were also made in two versions; a larger one and a smaller one, such as the "Ming Bat" (T158.).

# Chinese Goes Modern in Luxury Pieces Worked in Stone, Enamel

Tribute to elegant Chinese inspiration registers in the new collection of Trifari, Krussman & Fishel, Inc., as reported earlier in "Women's Wear Daily."
The graceful tree is done in red enamel, with green and white stones as flowers; the fire-eating dragon is particularly ferocious in simulated jade, rhinestones and gold, while the earring, sketched at the upper right, is in light amethyst with green enamel; it suggests a warrior figurine.

*WWD*, February 20, 1942: "Ming Collection" by Trifari.

The "Ming" collection by Trifari is described by *WWD*, 8th February 1942, as "A Chinese series, "Ming" leads off the spring jewelry collection at Trifari, Krussman & Fishel, Inc. What effective use can be made of jewelry materials which are not 'substitutes' in the sense that wood is, perhaps, but whose use is inspired by consciousness of shortages is seen in these designs. Large, flat pieces of simulated jade are set in black and red enamel, set off with rhinestone paving, to make such Oriental figures as mandolins, bats, daggers and pagodas. Very grandiose is the fire eating dragon. "Ming" group is also featured in baroque pearls studded with small colored faceted stones, instead of the jade. Earrings and bracelets complete the pin group."

Apart from the information given in this article, these pieces were also made with blue enamel and the 'jade' came in blue and pink.

All pieces were patented except for the "Fire Eating Dragon" and the "Ming Axe" (T159.)

Some models, "Dragon" (T146.), "Fish" (T153.), Horse (T145.) and "Lyon" (T161.), were remade by Trifari in 1965, in gold-plated, glazed metal with central pearl, and are recognizable both for their workmanship and the symbol ©.

T145. "Ming Horse," Trifari 1942*****
Manufacturer Trifari, Krussman & Fishel.
Designer Alfred Philippe.
Patent n° 131,428 Alfred Philippe, New York, 17th
February 1942, filed on 7th January 1942.

Gold-plated metal brooch, green carved
jade, red enamel, rhinestones, of a horse
looking back. 5.5x6.5cm.
Marked Trifari Pat.Pend.

Gold-plated metal brooch, with red enamel,
green, engraved, fretwork stone and rhinestones, of a dragon. 3x7.5cm.
Marked Trifari Des. Pat. No. 131426.
This is the first patented item of this series.

T146. "Ming Dragon," Trifari 1942****
Manufacturer Trifari, Krussman & Fishel.
Designer Alfred Philippe.
Patent n° 131,426 Alfred Philippe, New York,
17th February 1942, filed on 7th January 1942.

T147. "Ming Duck," Trifari 1942\*\*\*\*
Manufacturer Trifari, Krussman & Fishel.
Designer Alfred Philippe.
Patent n° 131,533 Alfred Philippe, New York, 10th
March 1942, filed on 12th January 1942.

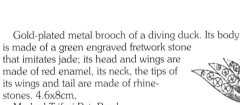

Gold-plated metal brooch of a diving duck. Its body
is made of a green engraved fretwork stone
that imitates jade; its head and wings are
made of red enamel, its neck, the tips of
its wings and tail are made of rhinestones. 4.6x8cm,
Marked Trifari Pat. Pend.
There are also matching earrings with the same
design.
This item appeared in the "Ladies' Home Journal,"
April 1942.

Gold-plated metal brooch, green carved
jade, red enamel, rhinestones, of a tiger.
6x9cm.
Marked Trifari Pat. Pend.

T148. "Ming Tiger," Trifari 1942\*\*\*\*\*
Manufacturer Trifari, Krussman & Fishel.
Designer Alfred Philippe.
Patent n° 131,535 Alfred Philippe, New York, 10th
March 1942, filed on 12th January 1942.

T149. "Ming Camel," Trifari 1942*****
Manufacturer Trifari, Krussman & Fishel.
Designer Alfred Philippe.
Patent n° 131,429 Alfred Philippe, New
York, 17th February 1942, filed on 7th January 1942.

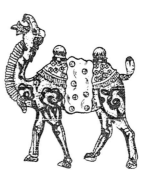

Gold-plated metal brooch, with red
enamel, central green faux jade, and
rhinestones, of a camel. 6x6.8cm.
Marked Trifari Pat. Pend.

T150. "Ming Cow," Trifari 1942*****
Manufacturer Trifari, Krussman & Fishel.
Designer Alfred Philippe.
Patent n° 131,563 Alfred Philippe, New York,
10th March 1942, filed on 12th January 1942.

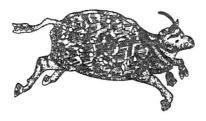

Gold-plated metal brooch, with red enamel,
green faux jade and rhinestones, of a running
cow. 7.5x5cm.
Marked Trifari Pat. Pend.

Gold-plated metal pin clip, with red enamel, green faux jade, pearl and rhinestones, of an acrobat-monkey, carrying an elastic trampoline for somersaulting under one arm and holding a ball, made of a pearl, in its hand. 7x4.2cm.
Marked Trifari Pat. Pend.

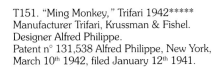

T151. "Ming Monkey," Trifari 1942*****
Manufacturer Trifari, Krussman & Fishel.
Designer Alfred Philippe.
Patent n° 131,538 Alfred Philippe, New York,
March 10th 1942, filed January 12th 1941.

T152. "Ming Turtle," Trifari 1942*****
Manufacturer Trifari, Krussman & Fishel.
Designer Alfred Philippe.
Patent n° 131,536 Alfred Philippe, New York,
10th March 1942, filed on 12th January 1942.

Gold-plated metal pin clip, white baroque pearl, black enamel, green rhinestones, of a turtle. 5x3.5cm.
There are also matching earrings.
Marked Trifari Pat.Pend.

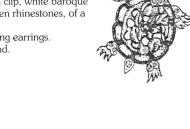

T153. "Ming Fish," Trifari 1942****
Manufacturer Trifari, Krussman & Fishel.
Designer Alfred Philippe.
Patent n° 131,565 Alfred Philippe, New York,
10th March 1942, filed on 12th January 1942.

Gold-plated metal and black enamel pin clip of a fighting fish. The fish's body is made of a baroque pearl encrusted with small faceted green stones, its head, fins and tail are black enameled with gold-plated metal and rhinestone borders. 6x4.5cm.
Marked Trifari Pat. Pend.

T154. "Royal Swan," Trifari 1941*****
Manufacturer Trifari, Krussman & Fishel.
Designer David Mir.
Patent n° 129,535 David Mir, New York, 16th September
1941, filed on 16th August 1941.

Gold-plated metal brooch, baroque white pearls,
black enamel, rhinestones, red and white baguettes,
green and red cabochons, of a swan wearing a
crown. 12.3x8cm.
    Marked Trifari Des. Pat. No. 129535.
    For baroque pearls see T52.
    References to Tchaikovsky's "Swan Lake" ballet
or the "The Ugly Duckling" fairy tale by Andersen
are enticing but there is no documented evidence to
support such sources of inspiration.

T155. "Ming Swan," Trifari 1942*****
Manufacturer Trifari, Krussman & Fishel.
Designer Alfred Philippe.
Patent n° 131,564 Alfred Philippe, New York, 10th March
1942, filed on 12th January 1942.

Gold-plated metal brooch, white baroque
pearl, black and yellow enamel, rhinestones, in
the shape of a swan. 6x10.5cm.
    Marked Trifari Pat. Pend.

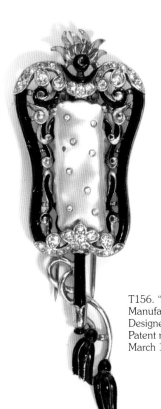

Gold-plated metal pin clip, white baroque pearl, black enamel, rhinestones, of a Chinese processional flag. 10.3x3.8cm.
Marked Trifari.

T156. "Ming Processional Flag," Trifari 1942*****
Manufacturer Trifari, Krussman & Fishel.
Designer Alfred Philippe.
Patent n° 131,566 Alfred Philippe, New York, 10th
March 1942, filed on 12th January 1942.

T157. "Ming Elephant," Trifari 1942*****
Manufacturer Trifari, Krussman & Fishel.
Designer Alfred Philippe.
Patent n° 131,534 Alfred Philippe,
New York, 10th March 1942, filed
on 12th January 1942.

Gold-plated metal brooch, white
baroque pearl, black enamel, white
and green rhinestones, of a running
elephant. 5x8cm.
Marked Trifari Pat. Pend.

Large gold-plated metal brooch, with black enamel and rhinestones, of a bat, with metal and rhinestone antennae, body made of a white baroque pearl encrusted with small faceted green stones and black enamel and rhinestone wings. 8x7cm.
Marked Trifari Pat. Pend.
There is also a smaller version of this brooch.

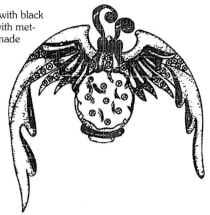

T158. "Big Ming Bat," Trifari 1942*****
Manufacturer Trifari, Krussman & Fishel.
Designer Alfred Philippe.
Patent n° 131,430 Alfred Philippe, New York,
17th February 1942, filed on 7th January 1942.

T159. "Ming Axe," Trifari 1942****
Manufacturer Trifari, Krussman & Fishel.
Designer Alfred Philippe.
Not patented.
Gold-plated metal and red enamel brooch of a ceremonial axe with two engraved, fretwork faux jade stones set at the base of the handle and in the middle of the blade. The handle and blade are red enameled with golden borders and there are rhinestones both on the handle and the blade. 9.5x4cm.
Marked Trifari.

Gold-plated metal pin clip, blue carved jade, red enamel, rhinestones, of a frog. 8x6.8cm.
Marked Trifari Pat. Pend.

T160. "Ming Frog," Trifari 1942*****
Manufacturer Trifari, Krussman & Fishel.
Designer Alfred Philippe.
Patent n° 131,537 Alfred Philippe, New York, 10th March 1942, filed on 12th January 1942.

T161. "Ming Lyon," Trifari 1942*****
Manufacturer Trifari, Krussman &
Fishel.
Designer Alfred Philippe.
Patent n° 131,782 Alfred
Philippe, New York, 24th March
1942, filed on 20th January 1942.

Gold-plated metal brooch, white
baroque pearl (probable substitu-
tion), red enamel and rhinestones,
of a winged lion. 4.5x4.5cm.
Marked Trifari Pat. Pend.

T162. "Ming Pagoda," Trifari 1942*****
Manufacturer Trifari, Krussman & Fishel.
Designer Alfred Philippe.
Patent n° 131,567 Alfred Philippe, New
York, 10th March 1942, filed on
12th January 1942.

Gold-plated metal pin clip, with a baroque
pearl, encrusted with multicolor rhinestones,
red and black enamel and rhinestones, of a
pagoda. 7.6x5.5cm.
Marked Trifari Pat. Pend.

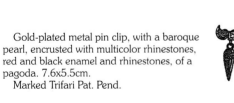

T163. "White Blossom," Trifari 1942****
Manufacturer Trifari, Krussman & Fishel.
Designer Alfred Philippe.
Patent n° 131,268 Alfred Philippe, New
York, 27th January 1942, filed on 20th
December 1941.

Gold-plated metal pin clip, white
enamel, red stones and rhinestones,
in the shape of a flower. 8x8cm.
Marked Trifari Pat. Pend.

T164. "Bow," Trifari 1942**
Manufacturer Trifari, Krussman & Fishel.
Designer Alfred Philippe.
Patent n° 131,868 Alfred Philippe, New York, 31st
March 1942, filed on 29th January 1942.

Rhodium-plated metal and blue enamel
brooch, of a bowknot. 5x10.5cm.
Marked Trifari Pat. Pend.

Rhodium-plated metal brooch, with
enamel and rhinestones, of an angry duck.
Red enamel body, rhinestone pavé and
green enamel wing, rhinestone bordered
breast and tail, green enamel head with
a small red cabochon for its eye, yellow
enamel beak, red enameled inside, red and
black enamel webbed feet. 3x4.8cm.
   Marked Trifari.

T165. "Angry Duck," Trifari 1942***
Manufacturer Trifari, Krussman & Fishel.
Designer Alfred Philippe.
Patent n° 131,865 Alfred Philippe, New York,
31st March 1942, filed on 29th January 1942.

T166. "Lovebirds," Trifari 1942***
Manufacturer Trifari, Krussman & Fishel.
Designer Alfred Philippe.
Patent n° 131,883 Alfred Philippe, New York, 31st
March 1942, filed on 7th February 1942.

Rhodium-plated metal pin clip of two birds on
a branch with flowers, with green, red and black
enamel, small cabochons for the eyes and rhinestones. 4.7x4.2cm.
   Marked Trifari Pat. Pend.

T167. "Perching Swallow," Trifari 1942***
Manufacturer Trifari, Krussman & Fishel.
Designer Alfred Philippe.
Patent n° 131,884 Alfred Philippe, New York,
31st March 1942, filed on 7th February 1942.

Rhodium-plated metal pin clip of
a swallow perched on a branch, with
green, blue, ochre, red, yellow and
black enamel. Small green cabochon
for its eye and rhinestones. 6.5x5.7cm.
Marked Trifari "5".

Rhodium-plated metal pin clip, green, yellow
and blue enamel, rhinestones, of a bird perched
on a leafy branch. 5.5x7.7cm.
Marked Trifari Pat. Pend.

T168. "Bird on a Leaf," Trifari 1942***
Manufacturer Trifari, Krussman & Fishel.
Designer Alfred Philippe.
Patent n° 131,886 Alfred Philippe, New York, 31st March
1942, filed on 7th February 1942.

T169. "Fuchsia," Trifari 1942***
Manufacturer Trifari, Krussman & Fishel.
Designer Alfred Philippe.
Patent n° 131,889 Alfred Philippe, New York, 31st March
1942, filed on 7th February 1942.

Two-toned gold-plated metal pin clip (with
yellow and red gold-plating), of a fuchsia
branch, with half-moon and oval blue crystals,
pink crystals and rhinestones. 7.7x5.5cm.
Marked Trifari Pat. Pend.
There are several variants of this piece in different enamel colors.

Gold-plated sterling pin clip of a peacock in flight, with green, red and blue stones, small green cabochons and rhinestones. 5.2x5cm.
Marked Trifari Sterling.

T170. *"Flying Peacock,"* Trifari 1942****
Manufacturer Trifari, Krussman & Fishel.
Designer Alfred Philippe.
Patent n° 134,031 Alfred Philippe, New York, 6th October 1942, filed on 12th September 1942.

T171. *"Heraldic Bird,"* Trifari 1942****
Manufacturer Trifari, Krussman & Fishel.
Designer Alfred Philippe.
Patent n° 134,028 Alfred Philippe, New York, 6th October 1942, filed on 12th September 1942.

Gold-plated sterling brooch, green, red and blue drop stones, rhinestones, of a heraldic bird. 6.2x6cm.
Marked Trifari Sterling.

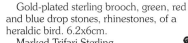

T172. *"Firebird,"* Trifari 1942****
Manufacturer Trifari, Krussman & Fishel.
Designer Alfred Philippe.
Patent n° 134,027 Alfred Philippe, Providence, R.I., 6th October 1942, filed on 12th September 1942.

Gold-plated sterling brooch, large blue center stone, red and green stones, rhinestones, depicting an imaginary bird. 8.5x8cm.
Marked Trifari Sterling.
There is also a version without the long tail.

T173. "Peacock," Trifari 1942\*\*\*
Manufacturer Trifari, Krussman & Fishel.
Designer Alfred Philippe.
Patent n° 134,026 Alfred Philippe, Providence, R.I., 6th
October 1942, filed on 12th September 1942.

Gold-plated sterling brooch, green stones
and rhinestones, of a peacock. 4.3x4cm.
Marked Trifari Sterling.
Trifari started manufacturing in sterling
from the middle of 1942 due to the rationing of other metals.

T174. "Nenette & Rintintin," Trifari 1943\*\*
Manufacturer Trifari, Krussman & Fishel.
Designer Alfred Philippe.
Patents Nenette n°136,079, Rintintin n° 136,080
Alfred Philippe, Cranston, R.I., 3rd August 1943, filed
on 17th June 1943.

Pair of sterling brooches with green cabochons and rhinestones, of two dolls of the kind made in 1918 with
wool or silk yarn for the "poilus," as French infantry soldiers were called. The yarn effect was achieved by
means of engravings in the metal. Nenette 4.3x3cm; Rintintin 4x3.5cm.
Nenette is marked Trifari Sterling Patent No. 136079. Rintintin is marked Trifari Sterling Patent No. 136080.
These are the original names taken from a Gerlou Fifth Avenue advertisement published in *Vogue* on 1st Oc-
tober 1944. The advertisement also gave information about the original source of inspiration for the dolls. The
brooches were on sale at $10 each. The advertisement also specified that the brooches were made of sterling.
Gerlou was a regular Trifari distributor at the time. The same brooches also appeared in a *Harper's Bazaar*
Christmas advertisement, December 1943, for I. Magnin & Co. California, a famous department store, and in
*Town & Country*, again in December 1943.
The "poilus" dolls also appealed to Philippe, who, in 1949, portrayed them in two patented designs, which
were used for a pair of colored glass brooches, called "Pom-Pom & Tom-Tom".
The same subject also cropped up in two designs by Adolph Katz, which were patented in 1945.
The brooches were blatantly copied by Alpha-Craft, Inc., a New York company with headquarters in 303
Fifth Avenue, which advertised them under the name of "Punch 'n' Judy" and sold them for $1.95 a pair and
$13.50 a dozen pairs. The items were available both in sterling and in pink or yellow gold-plated metal (*WWD*,
5th April 1946).

T175. "Pom-Pom and Tom-Tom," Trifari 1949***
Manufacturer Trifari, Krussman & Fishel.
Designer Alfred Philippe.
Patents Pom-Pom n° 153,551; Tom-Tom 153,552 Alfred
Philippe, Scarsdale, NY., 26th April 1949, filed on 18th
February 1949.

A pair of rhodium-plated metal brooches with blue contoured glass paste stones, of two yarn dolls. 4.5x2.5cm.

Pom-Pom is marked Trifari Pat. Pend. Tom-Tom is marked Trifari Des. Pat. No. 153552.

The model resembled "Nenette & Rintintin" and was produced in blue, red and green variants. This pair of brooches appeared in *Harper's Bazaar*, June 1949, and in the *Jewelers' Circular Keystone*, June 1949, with the name of "Pom-Pom and Tom-Tom". The pair of brooches were on sale for $15 plus taxes.

T176. "Tasha and Sasha," Trifari 1947***
Manufacturer Trifari, Krussman & Fishel.
Designer Alfred Philippe.
Patents n° 147,865, "Tasha," n° 147,866, "Sasha"
Alfred Philippe, Scarsdale, NY., 11th November,
1947, filed on 28th March 1947.

A pair of gold-plated sterling brooches, each with a white pearl, red baguette and rhinestones, of two Russian dancers.

"Tasha" is wearing a wide skirt with fretwork lozenges, a rhinestone pavé vest, and rhinestone-studded shoes. Her face is a white pearl and her headdress is a red baguette. 4.5x3.2cm

"Sasha" is wearing rhinestone pavé vest and boots, his face is a white pearl, and he has a red baguette for a hat. 4.5x3.5cm.

Marked Trifari © Sterling.

The two brooches "Tasha and Sasha" were mentioned with these names by *Women's Wear Daily*, 18th July 1947, as the only sterling items of the fall collection, thus indirectly confirming that the new alloy Trifanium had replaced the more expensive sterling as a material. The name of the item is the original one, which was mentioned in two other advertisements in *Vogue*, on 15th May 1947: one by Browning, an East Greenwich, Rhode Island store, where the brooches were on offer for $30 the pair, or $15 each, the other advertisement was by Trifari itself, which offered the brooches at $12.50 each plus taxes. The same advertisement was published in *Town & Country*, April 1947. Similarly to the case of the "Talisman" (T183.), and for the same reasons, Trifari applied for copyright rights, hence the copyright symbol stamped on the item.

T177. "Jon & Metje," Trifari 1945**
Manufacturer Trifari, Krussman & Fishel.
Designer Alfred Philippe.
Patents Metje 142,664; Jon 142,665 Alfred Philippe,
Scarsdale, NY., 23rd October 1945, filed on 10th July
1945.

A pair of gold-plated sterling brooches, each with a white pearl, small
red stones and rhinestones, of a girl and a boy with stylized clothing,
each face was made of a white pearl, the spiky hair of red stones, and
they had rhinestone studded hands and feet. 3.5x2cm.
    Metje is marked Trifari Sterling Des. Pat. No. 142664. Jon is marked
Trifari Sterling Des. Pat. No. 142665.
    The patent design is much larger than the actual brooches.
    The names "Jon" and "Metje" appear on the original gouache by
Philippe, kept in the Trifari archives, dated 6th February 1945 and published by Price "Trifari l'eleganza di uno stile," p. 187.

T178. "Chess Men," Trifari 1945***
Manufacturer Trifari, Krussman & Fishel.
Designer Alfred Philippe.
Patents n° 140,843, "Queen," n° 140,844,
"King," n° 140,855, "Knight," n° 140,800, (filed
on 25th January 1945) earrings, Alfred Philippe,
Scarsdale, NY., 10th April 1945, filed on 20th Janu-
ary 1945.

Set made up of gold-plated pin clips and earrings, with black enamel, little faux
turquoises and rhinestones. These items are shaped like chess pieces: king,
queen, knight and pawn. 4x2cm. Clip earrings: 2.8cm.
    The Queen is marked Trifari Sterling Des. Pat. No. 140843. The King is
marked Trifari Sterling Des. Pat. No. 140844. The knight is marked Trifari Sterling Des. Pat. No. 144855. The earrings are marked Trifari Sterling Pat. Pend.
    The series was also made in a white enamel version. The set appeared in
Vogue, 1st September 1945, in Harper's Bazaar, September 1945, under the
name "Chess Men," and in Town & Country, September 1945. The original gouache by Philippe, dated 22nd November 1944 which depicted "The
Queen," was published by Price "Trifari l'eleganza di uno stile," p.183.

T179. "Flower Girl,"
Trifari 1947****
Manufacturer Trifari,
Krussman & Fishel.
Designer Alfred
Philippe.
Patent n° 148,087 Alfred
Philippe, Scarsdale, N.Y., 9th December
1947, filed on 11th January 1947
assignor to Trifari, Krussman &
Fishel, New York.

Gold-plated sterling brooch of a flower vendor with
a basket of flowers on her arm, in the act of offering
a bunch of flowers. The flower girl is wearing a
fretwork dress with a rhinestone studded skirt and hat
and a necklace with a green pendant. Her mouth is a
red cabochon. The basket has a fretwork motif and the flower
petals are made of red, green, blue and white stones. 8x5.8cm.
Marked Trifari Pat. Pend. Sterling.

This item was made in the period of transition from
sterling to Trifanium, which began to be used in June 1947.
For this reason the collections feature items alternately made
of one or the other metal, with a progressive dwindling in the
use of sterling. This state of affairs is confirmed by the design
patents deposited in January 1947: sterling for "Flower Girl,"
"Spider" and "Fan," and Trifanium for the "Ballerina". See also
"Romantique Necklace" (T200.).

T180. "Hand Pin," Trifari 1944**
Manufacturer Trifari, Krussman &
Fishel.
Designer Alfred Philippe.
Patent n° 138,203 Alfred Philippe,
Providence, R.I., 4th July 1944, filed on
12th February 1944.

Gold-plated metal pin clip, with rhinestones and white crystals, in the shape of a hand wearing a ring with a red stone and a puffed cuff richly ornamented with white stones. 5.7x3.5cm.
Marked Trifari Pat. Pend.

An advertisement by Gerlou Fifth Avenue with the picture and description of this brooch, on
sale for $20, was published in *Vogue*, 1st December 1945.

The Pat. Pend. mark shows that this item was manufactured between 12th February and 4th
July 1944, in the time between the patent application and its granting. However the brooch
was not made of sterling, like the one on sale at Gerlou's and advertised in *Vogue*. This piece
was actually an exception, together with a few other cases, to the extensive use made of sterling
during the war period, due to the temporary unavailability of metal. The pin clip was also
manufactured in sterling.

A similar brooch – of a gloved hand – by an unknown manufacturer and which appeared
in an advertisement in *Vogue* in December 1947 under the name of "Romantique Hand Pin,"
was on sale at Gerlou's for $12.50, i.e. at a much cheaper price than the original.

T181. "Ballerina," Trifari 1947***
Manufacturer Trifari, Krussman & Fishel.
Designer Alfred Philippe.
Patent n° 148,088 Alfred Philippe, Scarsdale,
N.Y., 9th December 1947, filed on 29th Janu-
ary 1947.

Two-color, golden and white Trifanium brooch with lu-
cite and rhinestones, of a ballet dancer wearing a fretwork
tutu ornamented with rhinestones, and white metal bodice.
Her face is a lucite cabochon. 7x3.5cm.
Marked Trifari Pat. Pend.
A sterling version of this brooch was also made.

T182. "Crown Set," Trifari 1944***
Manufacturer Trifari, Krussman & Fishel.
Designer Alfred Philippe.
Patent crowns n° 137,542 Alfred Philippe, Providence, R.I.,
28th March 1944, filed on 12th February 1944. Patent earrings n° 143,989 Alfred Philippe, Scarsdale, NY. 26th February 1946, filed on 25th July 1945.

Set made up of:
Two gold-plated sterling "King Crown" brooches. One features two emerald green cabochons, a smaller red cabochon, blue baguettes, red, green and blue stones and rhinestones; the other features two white moonstone cabochons and a smaller red one, blue baguettes, red and blue stones and rhinestones;
a "Queen Crown" brooch with two white moonstone cabochons and a smaller red one, red and blue stones and rhinestones;
two pairs of clip earrings, one with emerald green cabochons, a red stone and rhinestones, the other with white moonstone cabochons, a red stone and rhinestones. King Crowns: 4.8x4.5cm; Queen Crown 3.4x3.4cm. Earrings: 2.5x1.4cm.
The King Crowns are marked Trifari Sterling Des. Pat. No. 137542. The Queen Crown is marked Trifari Sterling Des. Pat. No. 137542 "5". The white earrings are marked Trifari Sterling, the green ones Trifari Sterling Des. Pat. No. 141907 (the number refers to another design by Philippe for a leaf-shaped brooch patented on 31st July 1945. The earring patent was issued as late as 1946, although its application had been submitted in July 1945. Hence the earrings were manufactured on this date and punched with a patent number which was already available although it referred to another design).
These are Trifari's most famous items, and they were an immediate success, as reported Elsie McCormick's article entitled *Merchants of Glitter* published in the Saturday Evening Post of 31st May 1947 with a picture of the King Crown with white moonstone cabochons and matching earrings. McCormick quoted a statement made by one of Trifari's agents: "If we had manufactured nothing else but these crowns in the last three years, we would be still clearing the orders".
*WWD*, 21st December 1945, stated that: "The crowns are popular in this week's advertising (Christmas week). Saks 34th presented two Trifari crowns, a large and a small one, with matching earrings: large crown $19.75, small crown $15, earrings $12.50."
The crowns remained in production for more than three years, as confirmed by the existence of both sterling and golden Trifanium examples, and were featured again in 1988, in the "retro collection".
In the following years Philippe designed other crowns, but none were as successful as these.
This model was also made with ruby red and sapphire blue cabochons and in clear, rock crystal imitation lucite.
The King and Queen Crowns with white moonstone cabochons and matching earrings were reproduced together with other items in a color advertisement, which appeared in *Town & Country,* December 1945.

T183. "Talisman Set," Trifari 1948***
Manufacturer Trifari, Krussman & Fishel.
Designer Alfred Philippe.
Patent n° 149,015, pin clip, n° 149,019,
earrings, Alfred Philippe, Scarsdale, NY.,
16th March 1948, filed on 21st February
1947 and 28th February 1947, respectively.

Oriental style gold-plated sterling pin clip and earrings, with imitation
moonstones, red and green stones and rhinestones. The pin clip has a
safety clasp. Pin clip: 8.5x3.5cm; earrings: 2.8 cm.
    The pin clip is marked Trifari © Sterling Pat. Pend. The earrings are
marked Trifari Sterling Pat. Pend. "L" and Pat. Pend. "8".
    In this period, due to the long waiting times for the issuing of patents,
probably caused by the reorganization of the patent office, Trifari copyrighted some of its designs (see "Tasha and Sasha," T176, also from this
period) and this is the reason why some items dating from these years bear
the copyright symbol. Copyright applications were filed only in the years
1947, 1948 and 1949.
    Several color variants were made of this set.
    The set appeared in a Trifari advertisement published in *Harper's Ba-
zaar,* May 1947, under the name of "Talisman".

T184. "Jewels of Tanjore," Trifari 1945***
Manufacturer Trifari, Krussman & Fishel.
Designer Alfred Philippe.
Patent Earrings n° 142,657, Brooch n° 142,658 Alfred
Philippe, Scarsdale, NY., 23rd October 1945, filed on
22nd June 1945.

Gold-plated sterling brooch and earrings, white lucite cabochons, red and blue stones, rhinestones, with an Indian-inspired design. Brooch 7.3x4cm, earrings 2.5x2cm.
    Marked Brooch Trifari Sterling Pat.Pend. "18," Earrings Trifari Sterling Pat. Pend.
    These items where advertised in *Vogue,* 1st October 1945, and in *Town & Country,* October
1945, under the name of "Jewels of Tanjore".
    Tanjore or Tanjavur is a sacred city in India, which has many splendid Dravidian temples. It was
one of the main cultural, political and religious centers in Southern India. Once again Philippe, following the creations of Cartier, was inspired by Indian art.
    For the fall-winter 1945 collection Trifari created a series of items featuring lucite cabochons in
various colors and sizes. The catalogued earrings match various different pieces.

T185. "Tank Bracelet," Trifari 1943****
Manufacturer Trifari, Krussman & Fishel.
Designer Alfred Philippe.
Not patented.

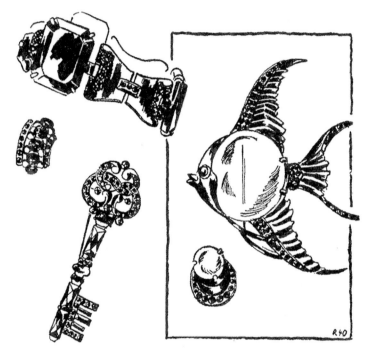

*WWD*, September 3, 1943: "Tank Bracelet," jelly belly "Angelfish" (JB19) and "Horse Shoe" earrings (JB28) by Trifari.

Sterling bracelet with large square red stones and rhinestones. 2.5cm w.
Marked Trifari Sterling.
The design of this item was published in *WWD*, 3rd September 1943, and the bracelet was advertised in *Vogue*, 15th December 1944, and *Harper's Bazaar*, January 1945.
There is also a gold-plated sterling version with green stones.

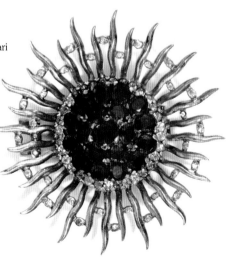

Gold-plated sterling pin clip, red crystals and rhinestones, of a beaming sun. 6.5cm diameter.
Marked Trifari Sterling Des. Pat. No. 142666.
The same brooch was manufactured in a smaller size and in several color variants. There were also matching earrings.
The design was inspired by jewelry by Fulco di Verdura (*Fortune*, December 1946, *Costume Jewelry*). This item, together with its matching earrings, appeared in a Trifari advertisement in *Vogue*, 1st June 1946, under the name of "Sunburst," and in *Fortune*, December 1946, together with many other brooches arranged round the jewel by the Duke of Verdura, which was their common source of inspiration. In addition, it appeared in *Mademoiselle*, August 1946, and in *Town & Country*, December 1945 and June 1946.
In the original gouache by Philippe, of 21st October 1944, published by Price *"Trifari l'eleganza di uno stile,"* p. 180, the brooch was called "Sea Flower": evidently Trifari later changed its mind and decided to launch the item under the name of "Sunburst" with an evident reference to the precious piece of jewelry by Fulco di Verdura.

T186. "Sunburst," Trifari 1945**
Manufacturer Trifari, Krussman & Fishel.
Designer Alfred Philippe.
Patent n° 142,666 Alfred Philippe, Scarsdale, NY., 23rd October 1945, filed on 27th June 1945.

Gold-plated sterling pin clip, ruby red stones and rhinestones, in the shape of a scroll. 6x3cm.
Marked Trifari Sterling Des. Pat. No. 137546.
This brooch is part of a set including earrings with the same shape. A picture of the brooch appeared in a color advertisement in *Vogue*, June 1944.

T187. "Scroll Pin," Trifari 1944**
Manufacturer Trifari, Krussman & Fishel.
Designer Alfred Philippe.
Patent n° 137,546 Alfred Philippe, Providence, R.I., 20th March 1944, filed on 12th February 1944.

T188. "Chrysanthemum," Trifari 1944***
Manufacturer Trifari, Krussman & Fishel.
Designer Alfred Philippe.
Patent n° 137,543 Alfred Philippe, Providence, R.I., 28th March 1944, filed on 12th February 1944.

Gold-plated sterling brooch, faux aquamarine crystals with carré cut and rhinestones. The brooch is of a chrysanthemum. 7.5x7.3cm.
Marked Trifari Sterling Des. Pat. No. 137543 "43".
The red-stoned version appeared with other items from the set, (i.e. the "Tank Bracelet" (T185.) and the earrings) in a Trifari advertisement in *Vogue* 14th December 1944 and in *Harper's Bazaar*, January 1945.
The subject is identical to an earlier Staret design, made of gold-plated metal, blue enamel and blue stones, with a larger, flatter line, and less accurate workmanship (St1.). It is likely that both items had a common source of inspiration, possibly an item of precious jewelry.

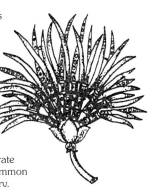

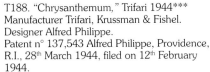

Gold-plated sterling brooch and earrings, small red and blue cabochons and rhinestones, of a butterfly.
Brooch 5.7x4.5cm; clip earrings: 3x2.5cm.
Marked Trifari Sterling Pat. Pend.
The brooch was made in two different sizes and was again remade for the "Retro Collection" of 1988. The set appeared in a Trifari advertisement published in *Vogue*, 15th September 1944, and in *Mademoiselle*, September 1944.

T189. "Butterfly Set," Trifari 1944**
Manufacturer Trifari, Krussman & Fishel.
Designer Alfred Philippe.
Patent n° 138,520 Alfred Philippe, Providence, R.I., 15th August 1944, filed on 28th June 1944.

T190. "Ruby Set," Trifari 1945****
Manufacturer Trifari, Krussman & Fishel.
Designer Alfred Philippe.
Not patented.

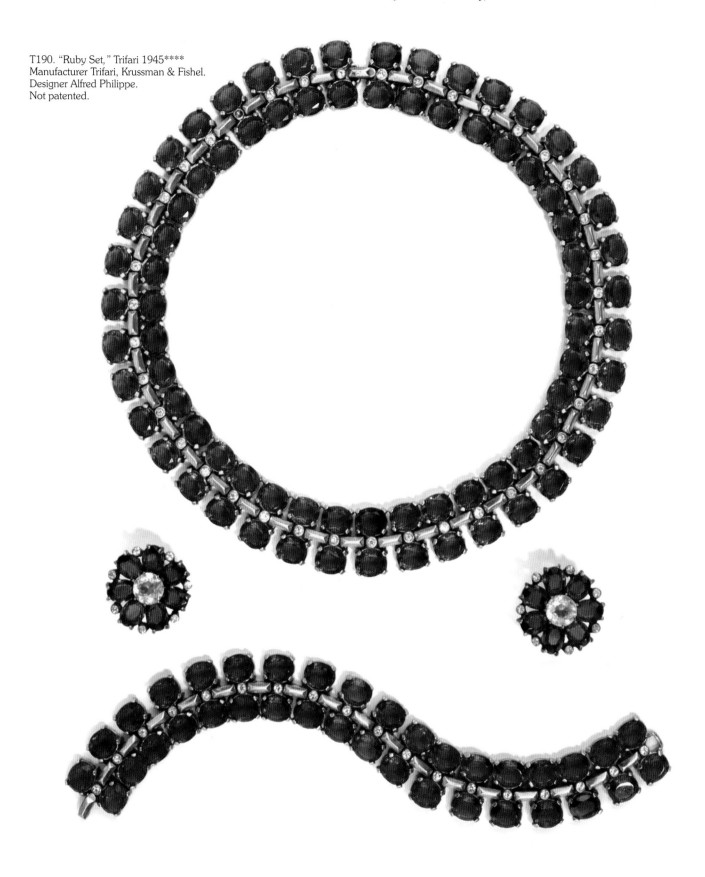

*Harper's Bazaar*, February 1946: "Ruby Set" by Trifari.

Gold-plated sterling choker, bracelet and earrings, red stones and rhinestones. Choker and bracelet 1.5cm w, earrings 2cm.
Marked Choker and bracelet Trifari Sterling, earrings Sterling.
Choker and bracelet can be clipped together transforming the choker into a necklace.
The set was advertised in *Harper's Bazaar*, February 1946.

Gold-plated sterling brooch, small red, green and blue stones and rhinestones, of fan. The manufacturing technique and the stones used are identical to those of the "Flower Girl". 4.5x7.2cm.

Marked Trifari Pat. Pend. Sterling "5".

Sixteen months elapsed between the patent application date and its issue. The mark Pat. Pend. indicates that the item was manufactured in 1947.

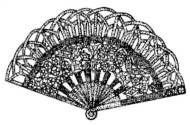

T191. "Fan," Trifari 1948***
Manufacturer Trifari, Krussman & Fishel.
Designer Alfred Philippe.
Patent n° 149,582 Alfred Philippe, Scarsdale, NY., 11th May 1948, filed on 31st January 1947.

T192. "Surrey," Trifari 1944***
Manufacturer Trifari, Krussman & Fishel.
Designer Alfred Philippe.
Patent n° 139,695 Alfred Philippe, New York, 12th December 1944, filed on 29th September 1944.

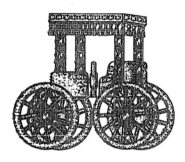

Gold-plated sterling brooch, rhinestones, baguettes and red cabochons, of a "Surrey," the American definition of a light four-wheel, two-seater. The two front wheels are mobile. 3x3.5cm.

Marked Trifari Sterling Des. Pat. No. 139695.

The brooch appeared in a B. Altman & Co advertisement in *WWD*, 1st December 1944, and was on sale for $30.

Gold-plated sterling pin clip, in the shape of a turtle, with central red cabochon, pink, azure and blue stones, tiny green cabochons for its eyes and rhinestones. 7x5cm.
Marked Trifari Sterling Pat. Pend.

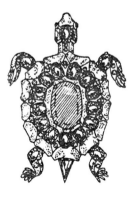

T193. "Turtle," Trifari 1945****
Manufacturer Trifari, Krussman & Fishel.
Designer Alfred Philippe.
Patent n° 142,587 Alfred Philippe, Scarsdale, NY., 16th October 1945, filed on 20th June 1945.

T194. "Frog," Trifari 1945****
Manufacturer Trifari, Krussman & Fishel.
Designer Alfred Philippe.
Patent n° 142,585 Alfred Philippe, Scarsdale,
NY., 16th October 1945, filed on 20th June 1945.

Gold-plated sterling brooch, green lucite cabochons, green stones, white and red rhinestones, of a frog. 6x5.5cm.
Marked Trifari Sterling "53".

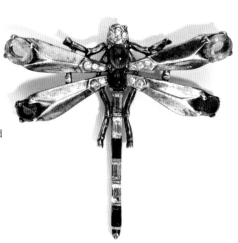

T195. "Dragonfly," Trifari 1945**
Manufacturer Trifari, Krussman & Fishel.
Designer Alfred Philippe.
Patent n° 142,584 Alfred Philippe, Scarsdale, NY., 16th October 1945, filed on 20th June 1945.

Gold-plated sterling brooch of a dragonfly, with pink and red stones on the tips of its wings, red cabochons on its body, pink, blue and white baguettes on its tail and rhinestones on its head. 5.8x6.3cm.
Marked Trifari Sterling Des. Pat. No. 142584.
There is also a gold-plated sterling version of this brooch, from the same period, with the tail curving slightly sideways.

T196. "Fish," Trifari 1945****
Manufacturer Trifari, Krussman & Fishel.
Designer Alfred Philippe.
Patent n° 142,661 Alfred Philippe, Scarsdale, NY., October 23rd 1945, filed June 27th 1945.

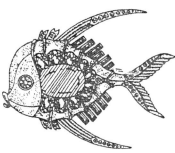

Gold-plated sterling brooch, red lucite cabochons, pink stones, blue baguettes and rhinestones, of a fish. cm 5x6.5.
Marked Trifari Sterling "15".

T197. "Lyre Bird," Trifari 1945***
Manufacturer Trifari, Krussman & Fishel.
Designer Alfred Philippe.
Patent n° 142,659 Alfred Philippe, Scarsdale,
NY., October 23rd 1945, filed June 27th 1945.

Gold-plated sterling brooch, citrine lucite, green baguettes,
red and yellow stones and rhinestones, depicting a lyre bird.
8x5.3cm.
Marked Trifari Pat. Pend. "53".
This item was made with different lucite versions for
the body: white, citrine, green and blue.
The brooch appeared in an advertisement in *Town
& Country*, December 1945.

T198. "Monkey," Trifari 1948*****
Manufacturer Trifari, Krussman & Fishel.
Designer Alfred Philippe.
Patent n° 148,563, Alfred Philippe, Scarsdale, NY.,
February 3rd 1948, filed January 29th 1947 assignor to
Trifari, Krussman & Fishel.

Gold-plated sterling brooch, big square cut
pale blue stone, red stones and rhinestones,
depicting a monkey dangling by its tail from
a branch and holding a large stone in its
hand. 7x3cm.
Marked Trifari Sterling Pat. Pend.

T199. "Spider," Trifari 1948**
Manufacturer Trifari, Krussman & Fishel.
Designer Alfred Philippe.
Patent n° 148,568 Alfred Philippe, Scarsdale, NY.,
February 3rd 1948, filed January 31st 1947, assignor
to Trifari, Krussman & Fishel.

Pink gold-plated sterling pin clip of a
spider, with red crystals, small green cabochons and rhinestones. 5x4.5cm.
Marked Trifari Sterling Pat. Pend.

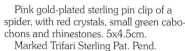

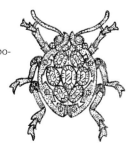

T200. *"Romantique Necklace,"* Trifari 1947***
Manufacturer Trifari, Krussman & Fishel.
Designer Alfred Philippe.
Patent n° 149,215 Alfred Philippe, Scars-
dale, NY., April 6th 1948, filed August 6th
1947, assignor to Trifari, Krussman &
Fishel.

White pearl necklace with golden Trifanium motif in the center, black
enamel, rhinestones, white pearls and pendant with drop-shaped white pearl.
5.5x5cm the center motif.

Marked Trifari Pat. Pend.

The necklace, which matches the bracelet and earrings (respectively des. n° 149,298
and n° 149,211) was advertised in *Town & Country,* October 1947, as a piece from the
"Romantique" series.

Note that a longer than usual period of time passed between the patent application date and
its issue. In July 1947 (*WWD,* July 18th 1947) Trifari started to manufacture items using a metal
alloy invented by Gustavo Trifari himself and called "golden Trifanium". As *WWD,* December
30th 1949, stated; "Trifanium is a compound word in which "Tri" indicates the customary three
(but elsewhere "Tri" is said to stand for Trifari), "fa" denotes famous, to which is added "-nium"
- the usual suffix for a metal.

T201. "Dewdrops Set," Trifari 1949***
Manufacturer Trifari, Krussman & Fishel.
Designer Alfred Philippe.
Patent necklace n° 152,735, February 15th 1949, filed December 14th 1949, earrings n° 153,628, May 3rd 1949, filed January 8th 1949 Alfred Philippe, Scarsdale, NY., assignor to Trifari, Krussman & Fishel.

Golden Trifanium necklace and earrings with white Lucite, carved with a flower and leaf motif in center, and rhinestones. 2x11cm the center motif, earrings 2x2cm.
Marked Necklace Trifari Pat.Pend., earrings one Trifari Pat.Pend., the other Trifari Des. Pat. 153026.
The marked patent number on one of the earrings refers to a similar but slightly different design. The exact number is 153,628. Errors in marking were rare and probably were due to problems in production.
The set was advertised under the name "Dewdrops" in Vogue, May 1st 1949, and "The Jewelers' Circular-Keystone," May 1949. The necklace was sold for $17.50, the earrings for $10 plus taxes.

## "Moghul Jewels," Trifari 1949

For the 1949 spring-summer collection, Alfred Philippe designed a complete jewelry line - necklaces, bracelets, brooches and earrings – made of golden Trifanium, with melon and rosette cut, engraved glass paste stones, combined with rhinestones and drop-shaped cabochons. The stone colors were red, green and blue, and the combinations were: red/blue, green/red, blue/green. The stone cuts and color combinations were inspired by Indian jewelry and the name "Scheherazade" was given by Trifari to some of these items in the advertisements. The name "Moghul" prevailed later and referred to jewelry made under the Mongolian dynasty that reigned over India from 1526 to 1858, which was famous for the splendor of its court and for having supported the creation of an original Muslim art. In English the name Moghul is commonly used as a synonym for pomp and oriental exoticism and it is no wonder that it was chosen for this extraordinary series of jewelry. The items belonging to this line are among the most beautiful ever designed by Philippe. For this reason and for their high level of workmanship, they are considered to be very important collector items. Apart from a few exceptions, all the designs were patented, or were a development of existing design patents. It is likely that the series was produced in a relatively limited number. At any rate, this kind of jewelry was not really in line with prevailing fashion trends of the time, which privileged more simple, unobtrusive designs, as exemplified by other Trifari items dating from the same period.

The "Moghul" items are difficult to find, and the most important pieces are extremely rare.

T202. "Moghul Pendant Necklace"*****
Patent n° 154,636 Alfred Philippe, Scarsdale, NY., July 26th 1949, filed April 23rd 1949, assignor to Trifari, Krussman & Fishel.

Golden Trifanium necklace with round link chain. The links are joined by rhinestone barrettes. The necklace features an elaborate central scroll motif with red melon cut cabochons, blue drop shaped cabochons and rhinestones. The central scroll is hung with a triangular pendant with red melon cut cabochons, blue drop shaped cabochons and a small azure cabochon on the tip.
Central motif: 13cm; pendant: 6x4cm.
Marked Trifari Pat. Pend. "19".
This is the most extraordinary item in the series.

T203. "Moghul Drop Earrings"\*\*\*\*
Patent n° 155,184 Alfred Philippe, Scarsdale,
NY., 13th September 1949, filed on 15th April
1949, assignor to Trifari, Krussman & Fishel.

Golden Trifanium dangle clip earrings with red "rosette" cabochon, blue
round and drop shaped cabochons
and rhinestones. 5x2cm.
Marked Trifari Pat. Pend.

T204. "Moghul Wasp Nest"\*\*\*\*\*
Patent n° 155,202 Alfred Philippe,
Scarsdale, NY., 13th September 1949,
filed on 14th May 1949, assignor to
Trifari, Krussman & Fishel.

Golden Trifanium brooch with
red melon cut cabochons, blue drop
shaped cabochons and rhinestones.
The design is of a metal branch with
a hanging wasp nest encrusted with
cabochons and rhinestones. 8x5cm.
Marked Trifari Pat. Pend. "23".

T205. "Moghul Staff Pin"\*\*\*\*\*
Patent n° 155,201 Alfred Philippe,
Scarsdale, NY., 13th September
1949, filed on 14th May 1949,
assignor to Trifari, Krussman
& Fishel.

Golden Trifanium brooch with rhinestones, red "rosette" cabochons and blue
cabochons, of a twisted staff with what
appear to be two bags attached to a metal
ring hanging from it. 9.5x4cm.
Marked Trifari Pat. Pend.

**T206. "Moghul Link Bracelet"*****
Not patented.

Golden Trifanium bracelet with hinged scroll shaped metal links with small blue cabochons and rhinestones joining together three star-shaped links with red central "rosette" cabochon, surrounded by round and drop shaped blue cabochons.

Length: 19cm, width: 3cm.

Marked Trifari Pat. Pend.

The bracelet design patent does not refer to the bracelet as a whole, but is the result of a combination of other patented designs, in particular a link bracelet with "rosette" cabochons at the center of each link (des. n° 155,203 of 13th September 1949) and another one with metal scroll shaped links (des. n° 155,224 of 13th September 1949).

**T207. "Scheherazade Earrings"***
Patent n° 156,655 Alfred Philippe, Scarsdale, NY., 27th December 1949, filed on 15th July 1949 assignor to Trifari, Krussman & Fishel.

Golden Trifanium clip earrings with green central "rosette" cabochon, three hanging drop shaped red cabochons and rhinestones, 3cm.

Marked Trifari Pat. Pend.

**T208. "Scheherazade Necklace"****
Patent n° 156,162 Alfred Philippe, Scarsdale, NY., 22nd November 1949, filed on 12th July 1949, assignor to Trifari Krussman & Fishel.

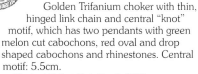

Golden Trifanium choker with thin, hinged link chain and central "knot" motif, which has two pendants with green melon cut cabochons, red oval and drop shaped cabochons and rhinestones. Central motif: 5.5cm.

Marked Trifari Pat. Pend. "18".

There are matching clip earrings with pendants for this choker. The choker, together with the "Leaf" (T211.) and the "Scheherazade" earrings (T 207.) appeared in a nationwide advertisement.

**T209. "Moghul Flower"\*\*\*\***
Not patented.
    Golden Trifanium pin clip in the shape of a flower, with a center consisting of melon and rosette cut green cabochons, red drop shaped cabochons and rhinestones. The metal petals are covered by a rhinestone pavé. Diameter: 6cm.
    Marked Trifari Pat. Pend.
    As in the case of other items of this series, the Patent Pending mark does not refer to the design as a whole, but to individual components.

**T210. "Moghul Choker"\*\*\*\***
Patent n° 155,194 Alfred Philippe, Scarsdale, N.Y., 13th September 1949, filed on 6th May 1949, assignor to Trifari Krussman & Fishel.

Golden Trifanium choker with thin hinged link chain and central festoon shaped motif with a green "rosette" cabochon in the middle, surrounded by red drop shaped cabochons, and with a small green melon cut cabochon and rhinestones at the top. Central motif: 5x3.5cm.
    Marked Trifari Pat. Pend. "19".
    The patent refers to a brooch and was also used for the manufacture of the choker.

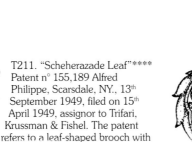

**T211. "Scheherazade Leaf"\*\*\*\***
Patent n° 155,189 Alfred Philippe, Scarsdale, NY., 13th September 1949, filed on 15th April 1949, assignor to Trifari, Krussman & Fishel. The patent refers to a leaf-shaped brooch with the same line, albeit simpler. This design therefore represents a further development of the brooch design.

Golden Trifanium leaf-shaped pin clip with green melon cut cabochons, red drop shaped cabochons and rhinestones. The pin clip has a safety clasp. 6.8x5cm.
    Marked Trifari Pat. Pend. "18".
    A picture of this item, together with the "Scheherazade" necklace and earrings appeared in a Trifari advertisement with information about the item names and sale prices in a page in *Life,* 5th December 1949, and in the "Jewelers Circular-Keystone," December 1949. The necklace was on sale for $20, the pin clip for $25, the earrings for $15.

Golden Trifanium brooch, with red melon cut, blue drop-shaped cabochons and rhinestones, of a peacock with a red round cabochon for its head. 5.5x4.8cm.
 Marked Trifari Pat. Pend.
 The design was revised by Trifari in 1965 resulting in a glazed gold-plated version.
 This item appeared in an advertisement published in *Town & Country,* September 1949.

T212. "Moghul Peacock"****
Patent n° 155,196 Alfred Philippe, Scarsdale, NY., 13th September 1949, filed on 6th May 1949, assignor to Trifari, Krussman & Fishel.

Golden Trifanium brooch, with red melon cut cabochon, blue drop shaped cabochons and rhinestones, of an elephant. 3x4cm.
 Marked Trifari Pat. Pend. "15".

T213. "Moghul Elephant"****
Patent n° 155,195 Alfred Philippe, Scarsdale, NY., 13th September 1949, filed on 6th May 1949, assignor to Trifari, Krussman & Fishel.

Golden Trifanium brooch of a parade horse with central red melon cut cabochon, rhinestone studded ears, mane, tail, hooves and saddle strap. Green and blue drop shaped cabochons hanging from round red cabochons. Small green cabochon for its eye. 5x6cm.
 Marked Trifari Pat. Pend. "15".

T214. "Moghul Horse"*****
Patent n° 155,219 Alfred Philippe, Scarsdale, NY., 13th September 1949, filed on 23rd June 1949, assignor to Trifari, Krussman & Fishel.

T215. "Moghul Fruit Holder," Trifari 1949***
Patent n° 155,209 Alfred Philippe, Scarsdale, NY., 13th September 1949, filed on 9th June 1949, assignor to Trifari, Krussman & Fishel, New York.

Golden Trifanium pin clip with three rosette cut stones, blue drop shaped and round cabochons, and rhinestones, depicting a fruit holder. 5.2x3cm.
 Marked Trifari Pat. Pend.

T216. "Moghul Poodle," Trifari 1950***
Patent n° 158,124 Alfred Philippe, Scarsdale,
NY., 11th April 1950, filed on 16th January
1950, assignor to Trifari, Krussman & Fishel.

Golden Trifanium brooch with central
green melon cut cabochon, green stones
and rhinestones, of a poodle. 4.3x2.7cm.
Marked Trifari Pat. Pend.

T217. "Moghul Cornucopia"***
Patent n° 155,210 Alfred Philippe,
Scarsdale, NY., 13th September 1949,
filed on 9th June 1949, assignor to
Trifari, Krussman & Fishel.

Golden Trifanium brooch with red
rosette cabochon, blue drop shaped
cabochons and rhinestones, of a cornucopia. 4.5x3.6cm.
Marked Trifari Pat. Pend.

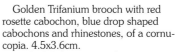

T218. "Moghul Butterfly"****
Patent n° 155,213 Alfred Philippe, Scars-
dale, NY. 13th September 1949, filed on 9th
June 1949, assignor to Trifari, Krussman &
Fishel.

Golden Trifanium brooch of a butterfly with green melon cut cabochons,
red drop shaped and round cabochons
and rhinestone pavé. 2.8x6.7cm.
Marked Trifari Pat. Pend. "18".

T219. "Moghul Tree"****
Patent n° 155,198 Alfred Philippe, Scarsdale,
NY., 13th September 1949, filed on 13th May
1949, assignor to Trifari, Krussman & Fishel.

Golden Trifanium pin clip with green
rosette cabochons, red drop shaped
cabochons and rhinestones, of a tree.
The pin clip has a safety clasp. 5x4cm.
Marked Trifari Pat. Pend.

T220. "Moghul Turtle"***
Patent n° 155,190 Alfred Philippe, Scarsdale, NY, 13th September 1949, filed on
15th April 1949, assignor to Trifari, Krussman & Fishel.

Golden Trifanium brooch with
green melon cut cabochon, small red
cabochons and rhinestones, of a turtle.
4x3cm.
    Marked Trifari Pat. Pend. "18".
    Another version of this item features a
central lucite cabochon (JB39.).

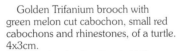

T221. "Moghul Bangle Bracelet and Ear-
rings"*****
Patent n° 156,165 Alfred Philippe, Scarsdale,
NY., 22nd November 1949, filed on 20th July
1949, assignor to Trifari, Krussman & Fishel.
The patent is for the bracelet.

Golden Trifanium bangle and clip earrings
with blue rosette cabochon, green drop shaped
cabochons and rhinestones. Bangle motif: 3cm,
earrings 2.5cm.
    Marked Trifari Pat. Pend. All items are
marked.

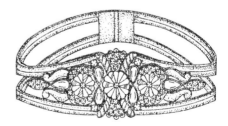

T222. *"Claire de Lune,"* Trifari 1950***
Manufacturer Trifari, Krussman & Fishel.
Designer Alfred Philippe.
Patents necklace n° 157,516, bracelet 157,518 Alfred
Philippe, Scarsdale, NY., 28th February 1950, filed
on 23rd November 1949, assignor to Trifari, Kruss-
man & Fishel.

Golden Trifanium choker with flexible link chain, double knot clasp, and central motif with half-moon shaped moonstones, small blue stones and rhinestones with three drop shaped moonstone pendants. Central motif: 7cm.

Golden Trifanium cuff bracelet with applied ornamental motif of half-moon shaped moonstones, blue and green stones and rhinestones. Spring lock with safety clasp. Motif: 10x2.5.

The choker is marked Trifari Pat. Pend. The bracelet is marked Trifari Pat. Pend. "18".

The "Claire de Lune" set is part of the "Silver Anniversary Collection". The complete set – choker, cuff bracelet and earrings – appeared in *Harper's Bazaar*, February 1950, and in the *"Jewelers Circular-Keystone,"* February 1950, under the name "Claire de Lune". The bracelet was on sale for $17.50, the choker for $13 and the earrings for $7. Two color variants of the set were made: moonstones and blue stones; moonstones and red stones. Other, less significant, lines designed for the "Silver Anniversary collection" were: "Golden Laurel," a modest, golden Trifanium set without any stones, with a laurel leaf motif, which sold for a low price ($ 7.50 for the necklace, $5 for the bracelet and $3 for the earrings); and "Bridal Bells," a set with delicate leaf-shaped stones. The necklace featured a pendant that doubled as a brooch.

T223. *"Tree of Life,"* Trifari 1950**
Manufacturer Trifari, Krussman & Fishel.
Designer Alfred Philippe.
Patent n° 157,200 Alfred Philippe, Scarsdale, NY.,
7th February 1950, filed on 15th October 1949,
assignor to Trifari, Krussman & Fishel.

Golden Trifanium brooch with half-moon
shaped moonstones, small red stones and
rhinestones, of a tree. 4.3x3.2cm.
Marked Trifari Pat. Pend. 28.
According to *Women's Wear Daily,* 20th
January 1950, the "Tree of Life" – the original name quoted by the paper – "is one of
the prettiest items of the 'Silver Anniversary'
collection," celebrating the 25th anniversary
of the setting up of Trifari, Krussman & Fishel, in
1925 with its third partner, Carl M. Fishel joining
the company. This item is a smaller version of the
patented design. The "Claire de Lune" set also belongs to
this collection.

T224. *"Scroll Bracelet & Earrings,"* Trifari
1950***
Manufacturer Trifari, Krussman & Fishel.
Designer Alfred Philippe.
Patent bracelet n° 161,049 Alfred
Philippe, Scarsdale, NY., 28th November
1950, filed on 22nd July 1950, assignor to
Trifari, Krussman & Fishel. Earrings not
patented.

Set made up of golden Trifanium bracelet and clip
earrings, with variously cut green and blue stones and
rhinestones. Bracelet: 6cm diameter. Earrings: 3cm.
Bracelet and earrings are marked Trifari.
The matching necklace bears patent n° 161,204.

T225. "Coronation Gems," Trifari 1953****
Manufacturer Trifari, Krussman & Fishel.
Designer Alfred Philippe.
     The crown and its matching earrings were patented
with No. 153,020 (the earrings), 8th March 1949, filed
on 16th December 1948 and 153,078 (the crown), 15th
March 1949, filed on 10th December 1948, Alfred Philippe,
Scarsdale, NY. In the original version the items were made
using lucite for the "Fairyland" (JB52.) series. The other
items are unpatented.

Trifari's original advertisement for the "Coronation Gems"
series (1953).

     Set made up of three pairs of brooches and clip earrings,
depicting the British crown jewels. The crown and earrings are
made of golden Trifanium, with red enamel, variously cut green
and blue stones, and rhinestones. According to tradition, the British crown may be lined with purple or red velvet, symbolizing the
Church color of penitence or the color of the blood of Christian
martyrs, respectively. The latter was used by Mary Stuart and
Elizabeth I, but purple was again reintroduced by James I. For the
coronation of Elizabeth II, as in the case of her predecessor with
the same name, the red of martyrdom was chosen.
     The scepter and matching earrings are made of golden
Trifanium, with a large central pear-shaped crystal, green and
red cabochons, red and white baguettes, a faceted amethyst
(scepter) and rhinestones. The crystal represents the "Great Star
of Africa," diamond, cut out of the Cullinan diamond, the largest diamond ever found (Transvaal 1905), which was donated
to Edward VII. The gem in the real scepter can be taken out and
worn as a pendant.
     The globe and globe earrings are made of golden Trifanium,
with red, blue and green stones, small pearls and rhinestones.
The items have a fretwork back.
     Crown: 4x4.3cm; earrings: 2.5x2cm.
     Scepter 10.4x2.3cm; earrings 2.6x1.8cm.
     Globe 5.6x3.7cm; earrings 2.1x1.7cm.
     All items are marked Trifari.
     The series appeared in color advertisements in major magazines.

# UNCAS MANUFACTURING COMPANY

*The Jewelers' Circular Keystone*, September 1948: advertisement by Uncas Manufacturing Co.

Brown plastic brooch of a gig being pulled by a horse. 8.4x4.2cm. Marked Pat. No. 133919.

This is the first of a series of brooches made of plastic, which was a popular alternative material during the war. The brooch was made by Uncas following a design by Barbieri. Most designs date from 1945.

Unc1. "Cabriolet," Uncas 1942*
Manufacturer Uncas Manufacturing Company.
Designer Nicholas Barbieri.
Patent n° 133,919 Nicholas Barbieri, Providence, R.I., 29th September 1942, filed on 25th February 1942, assignor to Uncas Manufacturing Company.

Unc2. "Hound," Uncas 1945*
Manufacturer Uncas Manufacturing Company.
Designer Nicholas Barbieri.
Patent n° 140,890 Nicholas Barbieri,
Providence, R.I., 17th April 1945, filed on
29th January 1945, assignor to Uncas
Manufacturing Company.

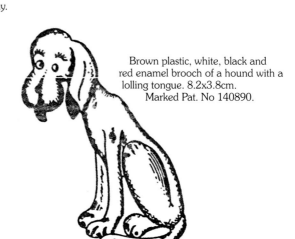

Brown plastic, white, black and
red enamel brooch of a hound with a
lolling tongue. 8.2x3.8cm.
Marked Pat. No 140890.

Unc3. 'Palm and Birds', Uncas 1938****
Manufacturer Uncas Manufacturing Company.
Designer Nicholas Barbieri.
Pat. n° 108,229 Nicholas Barbieri, Providence, R.I., 1st Feb. 1938, filed on 13th December 1937, assignor to Uncas Manufacturing Company.

Sterling brooch, green yellow and brown enamel, rhinestones, depicting two birds at the foot of two palm trees.
4.5cm.
Marked Sterling →U←
    The Uncas manufacturing Co. was founded in
1913 by Vincent Sorrentino (1892-1976) in Providence, R.I. and is still in business today. According to
advertising by the company itself ('Jewelers' Circular
Keystone', Sept. 1948) it produced rings, for which it
said it was 'America's Largest Ring House', costume
jewelry, novelties and plastics. The trademark was
'U-arrow' with the logo made up of a U with an arrow
going through it. Nicholas Barbieri was a designer of
novelties for Uncas from 1937 to 1948. Only one design
for a ring is patented (Des. n° 128,949, 19th August 1941)
for Uncas by George P. Wagner from Edgewood, Rhode
Island.

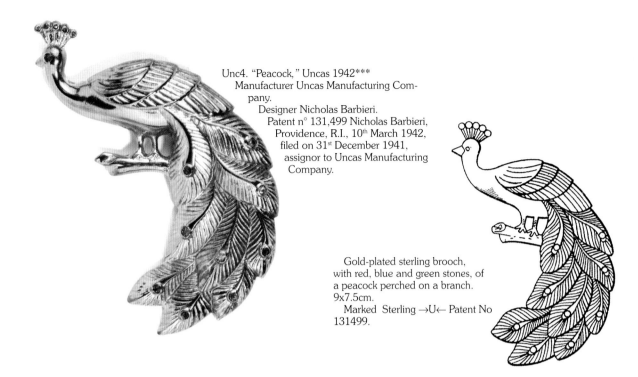

Unc4. "Peacock," Uncas 1942***
Manufacturer Uncas Manufacturing Company.
Designer Nicholas Barbieri.
Patent n° 131,499 Nicholas Barbieri, Providence, R.I., 10th March 1942, filed on 31st December 1941, assignor to Uncas Manufacturing Company.

Gold-plated sterling brooch, with red, blue and green stones, of a peacock perched on a branch. 9x7.5cm.
Marked  Sterling →U← Patent No 131499.

# E.K. WERTHEIMER & SON

U7. "Indian Chief," Cecil B. Demille 1940***
Manufacturer E.K.Wertheimer & Son, Inc.
   Gold-plated metal brooch of the head of an Indian Chief. 9x5.5cm.
   Marked North West Mounted Police Cecil B. Demille©.
   In the 1940s, especially in the first half of this decade, costume jewelry companies often bought the rights to produce jewelry inspired by films from the production companies. In this case, the movie in question was the 1940 film "North West Mounted Police" directed by Cecil B. Demille and starring Gary Cooper, Madeleine Carrol and Paulette Goddard.
   The manufacturer could be E.K. Wertheimer & Son, a New York based company, 27 West 33rd Street, which also produced jewelry inspired by the movies "Bambi" (1942) and "Saludos Amigos" (1943) under exclusive license from Walt Disney Novelty Jewelry. The company defined itself as "Creators of Tween Age Jewelry".
   The copyright refers to the rights of the film.

# UNSIGNED

**U8.** *"Woman with Dogs,"* Unsigned 1940\*\*\*
Manufacturer and designer unknown.
  Base metal brooch, with black and red enamel, crystals and rhinestones, of a woman with a pair of terriers on a leash. The woman's face and muff are made of white crystals. The woman is wearing a rhinestone pavé jacket bordered with red enamel, a black enamel skirt with rhinestone border, a black and red enamel hat, shoes and gloves. The rhinestone pavé dogs are mounted on a spring in order to achieve a tremblant effect. 7.5x4.8cm.
  This item is unmarked, but perfectly identical items marked Staret exist

**U9.** *"Cocktail Face,"* P.ʃ. © 1940\*\*\*\*\*
  Manufacturer unknown.
Designer Stanley MacNeil.
Patent n° 120,170 Stanley MacNeil, New York, 23th April 1940, filed on 12th March 1940.

  Base metal and rhodium plated metal pin clip, with green, red, yellow, brown and orange enamel, red cabochons, green, red and blue rhinestones, depicting a face whose features are formed by cocktail materials: a stem glass for its mouth and chin, two stirring sticks for the hollows of its cheeks, two cherries for a nose, two lemon slices for eyes and two orange slices for ears. A garland of vine leaves and grapes, topped by a crescent moon, adorns the head. A curved metal strip starting from the right-hand side of its head represents the sky with stars and Zodiac symbols (Aries, Scorpio and Taurus). On the left, a convex surface represents the sky with a star, the Zodiac sign of Aquarius and the planet Saturn. 8.5x3.8cm.
  Marked Pʃ © in a lozenge © - AA231123.
  Identification of the manufacturer, to whom the trademark refers or finding information about Stanley MacNeil (a British citizen living in New York) has proved to be an impossible task.

  Gold-plated metal brooch, with enamel in various colors, of a boy playing a fiddle. 8x6cm.
  Unmarked.
  In Goebel's catalog an identical figurine is called "Little Fiddler".

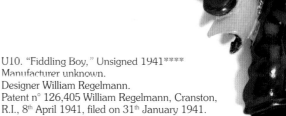

**U10.** *"Fiddling Boy,"* Unsigned 1941\*\*\*\*
Manufacturer unknown.
Designer William Regelmann.
Patent n° 126,405 William Regelmann, Cranston, R.I., 8th April 1941, filed on 31th January 1941.

U11. "Dog Hunting a Boy," Unsigned
1941****
Manufacturer unknown.
Designer William Regelmann.
Patent n° 126,917 William
Regelmann, Cranston, R.I., 29th
April 1941, filed on 17th February
1941.

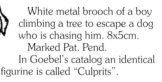

White metal brooch of a boy
climbing a tree to escape a dog
who is chasing him. 8x5cm.
Marked Pat. Pend.
In Goebel's catalog an identical
figurine is called "Culprits".

White metal brooch with enamel of various colors, of a boy holding a travel bag and
an umbrella. 6.5x4cm
Marked Pat.Pend.
This item can also be found with the trademark Silson.
In Goebel's catalog an identical figurine is called "Merry Wanderer".
A fourth design, of a peasant girl, was patented in William Regelmann's
name. (Des. n° 126,916).
William Regelmann's patented and unpatented designs, which were also used
by Silson Inc., were inspired by or directly copied from drawings by Schwester
Maria Innocentia Hummel, secular name Berta Hummel, who was born in
Massing, Bavaria, in 1909, and died on 6th November 1946 in the convent of
Siessen, where she had been living since 1931. From childhood Berta Hummel
had shown a great talent for drawing. Her favorite subjects where scenes from
Bavarian peasant and village life. On 9th January 1935 an agreement was signed
between Berta Hummel and Franz Goebel, the owner of W. Goebel Porzellanfabrik
GmbH & Co., KG, Germany, for the manufacture of porcelain statuettes based on the
designs of Schwester Maria Innocentia. The copyright proceeds were to be transferred to the
Siessen convent. This new line of statuettes was presented at the Leipzig fair in the spring of
1935 and obtained immediate success not only in Europe, but also in America, which accounts for Regelmann and Silson's idea to make costume jewelry on the same designs.
These statuettes are still manufactured today, based on the original designs by Berta Hummel and on new designs in the same style.

U12. "Traveling Boy," Unsigned 1941****
Manufacturer unknown.
Designer William Regelmann.
Patent n° 126,915 William Regelmann, Cranston, R.I.,
29th April 1941, filed on 17th February 1941.

U13. 'Oriental Mask', Unsigned 1940**
Manufacturer and designer unknown.
    Gold-plated metal brooch, red and sky-blue crystals, of an Oriental mask. 6x5.5cm.
    Unmarked.

U14. "Cannibal King," Unsigned 1940***
Manufacturer and designer unknown.
    Gold-plated metal brooch, with black and red enamel and rhinestones, depicting the crowned head of a black cannibal king, with two dangling earrings with human bones. 4.8x3.8cm.
    Unmarked.

U15. "Zulu," Unsigned 1940****
Manufacturer and designer unknown.

*The Miami Herald*, March 21, 1940.

    White metal and gold-plated metal brooch with red and white enamel and rhinestones, of a Zulu warrior with tremblant shield and spear. 8x5cm.
    Unmarked.
    This brooch, together with an identical one, appeared in an advertisement published in the "Miami Herald," on 21st March 1940. Sale price: $ 1.

Gold-plated sterling brooch of an Arabian man with a turban and a scimitar. 4.5x4.3cm.
Marked Sterling.
Louis Goldstein and Harry Lustig are the authors of some patented designs, the manufacturer of which is unknown.

U16. "Arabian Man," Unsigned 1946***
Manufacturer unknown.
Designers Louis H. Goldstein and Harry Lustig.
Patent n° 144,052 Louis H. Goldstein, Providence, R.I., and Harry Lustig, New York, 5th March 1946, filed on 5th September 1945.

U17. "Blackamoor Head," Unsigned 1937-39**.
Manufacturer and designer unknown.

*Harper's Bazaar*, April 1937: "Esclave Noir" by Cartier.

Gold-plated metal pin clip, with cream colored, black and red enamel, two red stones and a pearl, of a Moor's head with a turban. 3.1x1.5cm.
Unmarked.
This is an accurate costume jewelry version (except for the fact that pearls were used instead of a plume at the center of the turban) of a brooch called "Esclave Noir" manufactured by Cartier in 1936, and inspired, according to an advertisement in *Harper's Bazaar* of April 1937, by antique Venetian cufflinks. The original was made of silver or turquoise with black and cream colored enamel, decorated with diamonds or other precious stones, pearls and turquoises. Many firms, including Trifari and Coro, made costume jewelry versions of this Cartier brooch.

CARTIER OF PARIS

One of the jeweled Moor's heads that Cartier of Paris reproduced from old Venetian cuff-links.

*WWD*, February 17, 1939: "Glitter Glass" at Saks.
Gold-plated metal brooch, with brown, pink, white and black enamel, blue baguettes and large ruby red crystal, of a dog house with a man looking out of it. 4.5x4cm.
Unmarked.
This item appeared with this name in an advertisement by Saks Fifth Avenue in *WWD*, 17th February 1939," as part of a collection called "Glitter Glass." The brooch was on sale for $ 5.00.

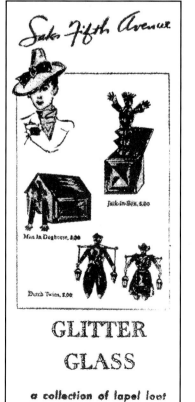

GLITTER
GLASS

*a collection of lapel loot*

U18. "Man in Doghouse," Unsigned 1939****
Manufacturer and designer unknown.

U19. "Female Head,"
Unsigned 1941***
Manufacturer and
designer unknown.

*A hand-modelled* PLATINUM HEAD; *crowned with flowing 14kt gold bands, diamonds and rubies; makes this distinctive clip. Actual size $1,400.*

# BLACK, STARR & GORHAM

FIFTH AVENUE AT 48TH ST. • CENTRAL AVENUE, EAST ORANGE

U20. "Playing Harlequin,"
Unsigned 1947***
Manufacturer unknown.
Designer Morris Paschman.
Patent n° 146,871 Morris Pas-
chman, New Jersey, 3th June 1947,
filed 19th June 1946.

*Vogue,* October 1, 1941: "Platinum Head" by Black, Starr & Gorham.
   Two color, gold and rhodium plated brooch with red, blue and white stones, of a long-haired woman's head with an elaborate hairdo. 8x5.2cm.
   Unmarked.
   Other versions of this brooch featured an enamel or a lucite face. There are also matching earrings to this brooch.
   This brooch is a costume jewelry copy of a precious piece of jewelry by Black, Starr & Gorham made of platinum, low carat gold, diamonds and rubies, which was advertised in *Vogue,* 1st October 1941, and was on sale for $ 1,400.

Relief gold-plated sterling brooch
with red, green and pink stones, topaz
colored faceted stone and rhinestones,
of Harlequin playing the mandolin.
7.7x4.6cm.
   Marked Sterling.
   No information is available about
Morris Paschman, the owner of two other
patents, n° 146,870 of 3rd June 1947 (a
harp) and 147,142 of 15th July 1947 (a
traffic light), respectively.

U21. "Willow Tree," Unsigned 1942-1945**
Manufacturer and designer unknown.
Rhodium plated sterling brooch, with green cabochons
with a rhinestone at the center and rhinestone pavé, of
a willow tree. 7x5.2cm.
Marked Sterling.

U22. "Elephant with Cornack," Unsigned 1947***
Manufacturer unknown.
Designer Frank J. Gargano.
Patent n° 146,651 Frank J. Gargano, Providence,
R.I., 22nd April 1947, filed 13th May 1946.

Gold-plated sterling brooch, with black and white enamel, small red and aqua green stones, of an elephant and its cornack (rider). 5x5cm.
Marked Sterling Pat. Pend.
The brooch was inspired by a design by the Duke of Verdura.
Nothing is known about Gargano. Some items made following his designs were marked Carman, a company (or trademark) about which there is no available information.

U23. "Caged Bird," Unsigned 1947***
Manufacturer unknown.
Designer Frank J. Gargano.
Patent n° 146,564 Frank J. Gargano, Providence,
R.I., 22nd April 1947, filed 13th May 1946.

Gold-plated sterling brooch with rhinestones, of a bird in a cage dangling from a bow. 7x4cm.
Marked Sterling Pat.Pend.
The piece is sometimes marked Carman.

U24. "Sailboat," Unsigned 1947***
Manufacturer unknown.
Designer Frank J. Gargano
Patent n° 147,267 Frank J. Gargano, Providence, R.I., 12th August 1947, filed 8th July 1946.

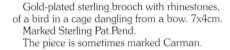

Gold-plated sterling brooch, sky-blue, white and red rhinestones, in the shape of a sailing boat. 6x4.5cm.
Marked Sterling.

**UNSIGNED**

U25. "Cuban Dancers," Unsigned 1948****
Manufacturer unknown.
Designer Grayce Norato.
Patent (woman) n° 150,027 Grayce Norato, Providence, R.I., 22nd June 1948, filed 25th October 1946.

Earrings clip patent n° 1,967,965 Eugene Morehouse and Melvin W. Moore, East Providence, R.I., 24th July 1934, filed 30th March 1934, assignor to B. A. Ballou & Co., Inc.

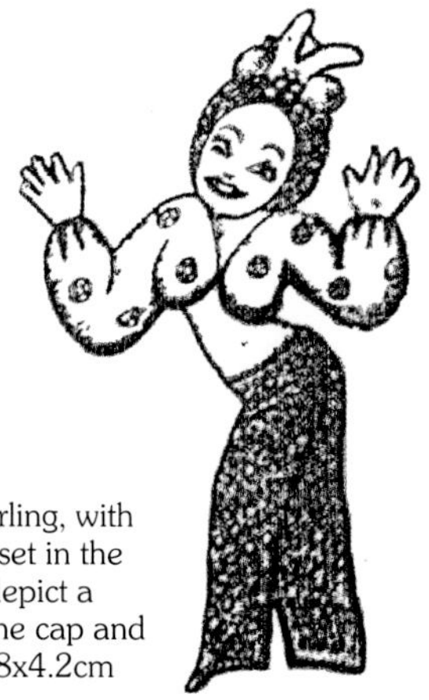

Set made up of two brooches and clip earrings made of gold and rhodium plated sterling, with brown, red, black, white, yellow, orange and green enamel, green, red and blue stones set in the man's shirt, while the woman's bodice is covered with rhinestone pavé. The brooches depict a dancer playing the maracas and a woman dancer with a headdress made of a rhinestone cap and fruit. The earrings replicate the head of the woman dancer. 5.9x3.8cm; man dancer: 6.8x4.2cm woman dancer; 2x1.1cm earrings.

The man dancer is marked Sterling. The woman dancer is marked Sterling Pat. Pend.. The earrings are marked Sterling Pat. 1967965.

Nothing is known about Grayce Norato who owned only this patent which was issued one and a half years after the application. The items definitely date from 1946.

The earrings are fitted with the famous Ballou clips, used by many manufacturers of the time. (Coro, Réja, De Rosa, etc.).

U26. "Palm Trees," Unsigned 1940***
Manufacturer Unknown.
Designer Marie Petit.
Patent n° 131,226 Marie Petit, New York, 27th January 1942, filed on 22nd November 1941.

Gold-plated metal brooch with green and red enamel, of two palm trees with coconuts. 8.2x6.3cm.

Marked Pat. Apl'd For Pat. 131226.

There is no information available about Marie Petit, a British citizen living in New York, who patented another design with a single palm tree (n° 131,225). Nothing is known either about the company that made the items using her designs.

U27. "Viking Ship," Unsigned 1946**
Manufacturer unknown.
Designer John Caianiello.
Patent n° 144,480 John Caianiello, New York, 23nd
April 1946, filed on 10th November 1945.

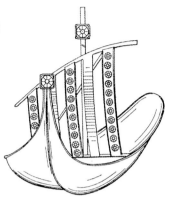

Pink gold-plated sterling brooch,
with a green stone and rhinestones, of
a Viking ship. 5x4.5cm.
Marked Sterling.

U28. "Farmers," Unsigned 1943***
Manufacturer and designer unknown.
Rhodium-plated sterling brooches, blue, red and
yellow enamel, of two farmers; a man and a woman.
5x2cm (both).
Marked Sterling.

U29. 'Parrot', Unsigned 1940**
Manufacturer unknown.
Designer José Rodriguez.
Patent n° 120,453 José Rodriguez, New York, 7th
May 1940, filed on 29th March 1940.

Pot metal brooch, red, yellow and green enamel,
rhinestones, of a parrot on a branch. 8x4.3cm.
Marked Maps USA intertwined with a symbol in the
shape of a star.
There is no information about the mark.
José Rodriguez was a Cuban citizen resident in New
York. Four designs are patented in his name, the three
presented here and another one of a fish (Des. n°
120,839).

U30. 'Fish', Unsigned 1940***
Manufacturer unknown.
Designer José Rodriguez.
Patent n° 120,454 José Rodriguez, New York,
7th May 1940, filed on 29th March 1940.

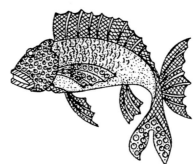

Rhodium-plated metal brooch, sky-
blue and green enamel, rhinestones,
in the shape of a fish. 6.5x7.5cm.
Unmarked.

Rhodium-plated metal brooch,
pink, yellow and green enamel, rhinestones, of a toucan. 7.5x4cm.
Unmarked.

U31. 'Toucan', unsigned 1940***
Manufacturer unknown.
Designer José Rodriguez.
Patent n°120,452 José Rodriguez, New York,
7th May 1940, filed on 29th March 1940.

U32. "Singing Bird," Unsigned 1940*
Manufacturer and designer unknown.
  Gold-plated metal brooch, with
white and black enamel, large lozenge
shaped blue stone and rhinestones,
depicting an anthropomorphic bird in
the act of singing. 6.2x5.2cm.
Unmarked.

U33. "Ara Parrot," Unsigned 1941**
Manufacturer and designer unknown.
  Large gold-plated metal brooch, with yellow, brown, blue,
white and black enamel and rhinestones, shaped like a parrot (American ara) perching on a branch with outspread wings.
13.5x7.9cm.
Unmarked.

U34. "Swallow," Unsigned 1939**
Manufacturer and designer unknown.
   Rhodium-plated metal brooch, with red and blue enamel and rhinestones, shaped like a flying swallow. 5x6.5cm.
   Marked Pat. Pend.
   The marking and style of the brooch mean that it could be a Trifari item designed by Alfred Philippe, in which case the Pat. Pend. mark could refer to the "Flying Swallow" design of 1937 (T18.). However, since this design is unpatented and since copying was common at that time, the item has been necessarily classified as unsigned.

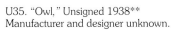

U35. "Owl," Unsigned 1938**
Manufacturer and designer unknown.
   Rhodium-plated metal brooch, with black, gray and yellow enamel and rhinestone pave, depicting a flying owl. The head is assembled to the body by means of a mobile screw, in order to produce a quivering effect. 6.9x5.9cm.
   Unmarked.
   This is a contemporary, non-identical, copy of the owl designed by Geissmann for Coro (C9.).

U36: "Pelican," Unsigned 1939*
Manufacturer and designer unknown.
   Rhodium-plated metal brooch, with black and violet enamel, a green stone and rhinestone pave, of a pelican. 8.4x7.6cm.
   Marked MADE IN USA underneath a star; circle made of dots on the tail.

U37. "Fish," Unsigned 1941****
Manufacturer and designer unknown.
   Two color gold and rhodium plated metal brooch of a fish with fins and tail studded with large lilac and aqua green marquise cut faux tourmalines. 7.8x8.2cm.
   Unmarked.

U38. "Lobster," Unsigned 1940-41***
Manufacturer and designer unknown.
    Gold-plated metal brooch, with matte pale green enamel and
rhinestones, of a lobster with tremblant claws. 10.5x6cm.
    Unmarked.
        A red enamel version of this brooch also exists. At the time
    this subject was much imitated in flat items without the
    tremblant effect.

U39. "Wishing Well," Unsigned 1939***
Manufacturer unknown.
Designer Larry Winters.
Patent n° 113,585 Larry Winters, Brooklyn, N.Y., 28th February 1939, filed on
20th January 1939.

Rhodium-plated metal pin clip, brown
and black enamel, small red, green and
blue cabochons, rhinestones, depicting a
wishing well. 4.5x2.5cm.
    Unmarked.

U40. "The Joker," Unsigned 1941***
Manufacturer and designer unknown.
    Two color gold and rhodium plated metal brooch with
green and red rhinestones, of a joker with a mobile stick.
    12.5x5.5cm.
        Unmarked.

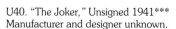

U41. "Hand with Flower," Unsigned 1940-41****
    Manufacturer and designer unknown.
    Rhodium-plated metal brooch
shaped like a hand clutching an orchid.
The hand has red enameled nails, rhinestones and black enamel cuffs, pink enamel
flowers. The orchid has a green enamel stalk,
blue and shaded blue enamel corolla with
central pearl. The corolla is mounted
to a spring to produce a tremblant
effect. 10x6.8cm.
    Unmarked.
    There is also a lucite version of this model
(JB105.).

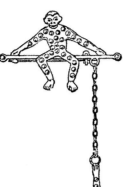

U42. 'Monkeys', Unsigned 1938***
Manufacturer unknown.
Designer Louis Ditchik.
Patent n°109,610 Louis Ditchik, New York,
10th May 1938, filed on 21st January 1938.

Rhodium-plated metal brooch,
rhinestone pavé, red rhinestones, of
a monkey sitting on a bar which has
another monkey hanging from it by a
little chain. 8x3.7cm.
Unmarked.

U43. "Dutch Twins," Unsigned 1939***
Manufacturer and designer unknown.
   Pair of rhodium-plated metal pin clips with pigeon's blood red and blue
moonstones, blue baguettes and white and red rhinestones, depicting
two water bearers, a man and a woman, wearing traditional Dutch folk
costumes; the woman's face is a pearl, the man's is a faceted white stone.
4x2.8cm (man); 4x2cm (woman).
   Unmarked.
   The pins are a contemporary imitation of two designs by Jacques H. Leff
for Dujay (n° 114,027 and 114,028 of 28th March 1939), presented as the
"Dutch Twins" by Saks Fifth Avenue in a *WWD* advertisement, 17th February 1939 ("Glitter Glass" collection) and were on sale for $ 5.00.
   The problem of copying and the need to protect designs exploded in
1939, when the greatest costume jewelry manufacturers (among them
Dujay) made plans to form an association to protect their products from
this so-called "style piracy". These items are good examples of how, with
just a few changes, it was possible to avoid the risk of being accused of
patent breach. It was not just by chance that Dujay began to mark its items
in 1939 and that, in the following year, won its case against Déja for the
similarity between their trademark names.

U44. "Nibs," Unsigned 1939-40****
Manufacturer and designer unknown.
   Couple of pin clips in gold and rhodium
plated metal and black enamel, in the shape of
a nib.
   5x2.7cm (both).
   Unmarked.

U45. "King and Queen Cards," Unsigned 1939****
Manufacturer unknown.
Designer Jeanne Toussaint.
Patent King 113,979, Queen 113,980 Jeanne Toussaint,
Paris, France, 28th March 1939, filed on 25th May 1938,
assignor to Cartier, Societé Anonyme Paris, France.

Set of two pin clips in gold-plated metal, red, white and black
enamel, depicting the King and Queen of Hearts. 4x3.5cm.
Unmarked.
   These pieces are copies of a set of two precious jewelry items designed by Jeanne Toussaint for Cartier. The items were made for Sacks
by an unknown producer and were published in *WWD*, 17th February
1939, and were on sale for $2 each. Costume jewelry copies of Cartier
pieces were fairly frequent at the time.
   Jeanne Toussaint (1887-1978) had joined Cartier in the early 1920s.
Initially she directed the creation of a range of accessories and from
1933 she was put in charge of high jewelry.

# JELLY BELLIES

Strictly speaking Jelly Bellies or Clear Bellies are animal-shaped brooches, made of sterling or metal with the animal's body made of a Lucite center. Yet the term is also used in a broader sense, and Jelly Bellies have become the term used for all jewelry items in which Lucite is a primary component of the design or ornamental motif. Apparently both terms were coined recently, since at the time these items were simply called Lucite jewels. Lucite is the characteristic feature of these items which nowadays are almost all collector's items.

Lucite – a trade name registered in 1937 by Du Pont Plastics, a division of E.I. Du Pont de Nemours & Co., Inc., Arlington, New Jersey – is a thermoplastic acrylic resin, a synthetic product that can be molded under the combined action of heat and pressure. It was a plastic material invented and manufactured by Du Pont. Its creation was announced with two advertisements extolling its properties published in June and August 1937 in the magazine *Modern Plastic*. It was described as being as transparent as crystal, flexible, shatter-proof, light, resistant to chemical agents and to oxidization, anti-fogging, and easy to process both for technical and ornamental purposes. In addition, it was available in all colors, glossy, transparent or matte, and in pastel shades.

Lucite was used in jewelry from the end of the 1930s and more or less continuously thereafter, as a substitute for other plastic materials for the creation of items entirely made of Lucite without any metal components, apart from a few details or supporting frames. Nowadays this jewelry is simply called "Lucite" and from a costume jewelry collecting point of view, belongs to the category of "plastic jewelry."

Jelly Bellies, on the other hand, are metal or sterling jewelry items with a substantial, but by no means only, Lucite component, instead of colored stones or large rhinestone pavés.

The first Jelly Bellies were manufactured in 1938-39, though they reached peak diffusion in the period between 1943 and 1945. There were many different reasons for this success, mainly related to the particular historical moment when they appeared on the market. Lucite was almost as good as rock crystal and allowed for the creation of designs that were both fanciful and refined. It was a novelty and as such, appealed to the public. Moreover, it was relatively inexpensive and easy to find, whereas crystals and rhinestones were scarce, due to the interruption of imports from Europe. Finally it allowed for the manufacturing of large, flashy jewelry which was very much in keeping with the taste of the time. Its use also meant that the use of sterling – which was rationed and expensive at the time – could be limited.

The Lucite variety mainly used in jewelry was the white transparent kind. However there are a few examples of colored Lucite, although the overall effect was less appealing, since it lacked the brightness and transparence of the white variety. Lucite was also marginally used to manufacture small white and colored cabochons which were used instead of glass stones.

At the time the press exhaustively documented a rich production of Lucite jewelry, especially in the first half of the 1940s, thereby providing important information on many companies, some of them still known nowadays, though others remain unknown, which offered entire Jelly Belly collections. This demonstrates how fashionable Lucite jewelry was, but, at the same time, it was very common, manufactured in large quantities and in a great number of models. Therefore the best production can be traced back to 1941-46. Thereafter use of Lucite continued, though discontinuously, according to the dictates of fashion.

In the period under review Trifari, Coro, Leo Glass, Sandor Goldberger, Fred A. Block, Lisner, Schreiner, A. Aquilino (Anthony Creations), and Norma all manufactured Jelly Bellies as single pieces or entire collections, as did many other less famous or completely unidentifiable manufacturers, who did not mark their pieces. In fact, a conspicuous part of Jelly Belly production consisted of unmarked pieces, some made of sterling (and therefore traceable back to 1942-47) and some made of various metal alloys (therefore possibly from the 1941-42 period, or the end of the 1940s). Many unsigned pieces are highly appreciated on the collectors' market nowadays.

Among the manufacturers who did not mark their pieces and for this reason were difficult to trace, was Ben Felsenthal & Co., Inc., a New York company located at 1 East 33rd Street. This company was established in 1914, and the designers Catherine Cleary (1934) and Mary Lynn Woodley collaborated with this company. Woodley had first worked for Leo Glass, then, in 1937, she was hired as a designer by Monocraft Products Inc. A Ben Felsenthal line of jewelry, the "Mary Lynn Jewelry" was named after her and, beginning in the fall of 1941, a series of Lucite collections was presented under this line. In June 1944 a series of brooches was made, with animal and floral motifs made of sterling and Lucite. The subjects included an alligator with a curled tail (possibly reproduced in Schiffer's, *Fun Jewelry*, p.15), a flying horse, cats with arched backs, a running greyhound and large daisy-like flowers with rhinestones and gold-plated stems and leaves.

Brody Designs Inc., a company established by A. Brody in 1938 with offices at 560 7th Avenue, began making Lucite jewelry because it was running out of sterling in the spring of 1945. Among these items, which were marked just sterling, a fairy (JB149.) and a sterling siren with a Lucite fish are worthy of mention.

In 1945 Alfred Herz Co. presented a sterling and Lucite collection including a Lucite bowknot with a black jet center. This firm also manufactured wood, ceramic, and cataline jewelry and, in 1945, produced a line of ceramic heads with fabric hats and a line of animals with ebony and Lucite heads.

All this production was unsigned and, due to lack of patent documentation, advertisements of the time are the only way to attribute it, and even attribution based on advertising information is seldom possible.

Sandor Goldberger was one of the first to make significant use of Lucite in November 1940 for necklaces, bracelets, and earrings. Among these pieces there was a remarkable cuff-bracelet, which, although it had the appearance of being heavy, was actually very light. It was featured in *Women's Wear Daily*, 29th November 1940. The bracelet featured a Lucite component set in a golden metal frame with blue zircon inserts and white enamel leaves. In those years Lucite remained a constant of the Sandor designs, and, for the spring 1941 collection, he presented two floral subject brooches made of gold-plated metal with Lucite petals and a tremblant center of colored stones that were matched by similar stones in the earrings in the same set. In the spring of 1942, Sandor designed a collection of brooches shaped like underwater creatures, such as a siren with a moving tail and a dolphin, bunches of flowers and animals, including frogs and owls. The collection included also the so-called "Balinese Heads," metal and black-enamel masks with banana leaf headdresses made of Lucite (S1., S3., S4.). Only a few of these items are available today.

In the spring of 1942, D. Lisner & Co manufactured a series of Lucite and rhinestone brooches portraying deer, dogs, and fish, which were designed by Martha Sleeper, who had been with the company from 1938. The collection was featured in *Women's Wear Daily,* which praised its remarkably beautiful designs, and informed its readership that it belonged to the medium-high price range. The firm, established in 1904 by David Lisner, and managed by Sidney Lisner and Saul Ganz, was located in New York, 303 Fifth Avenue. The company engaged in both manufacturing and importing jewelry. In 1926 it was the exclusive importer of Lanvin jewelry and in 1938 it became the importer and distributor of Schiaparelli (Sch.1) jewelry. Its own production was aimed mainly at the low-price market segment. However in 1933, in an attempt to relaunch the company which had been in difficulty for some time, the quality standard of its production improved remarkably. In this framework the 1947 "Cinderella Pumpkin" line, inspired by the Walt Disney movie of the same name, which was based on partly patented designs by Paul Flato (*Harper's Bazaar*, October 1947) is worthy of mention.

The company also had showrooms in Los Angeles and Chicago and advertised nationwide.

As regards the Jelly Belly production of Anthony Creations (designed by Antonio Aquilino), Fred A. Block (designed and manufactured by Sandor Goldberger), Leo Glass, Elzac, Kreisler (based on designs by William Diehl), Norma Jewelry Co., reference is made to the company monographs and/or item descriptions.

As far as is known, none of the other major companies, such as Boucher, Eisenberg, Hobé, Pennino, Réja, ever manufactured any Jelly Bellies.

The most famous Jelly Belly products, all of which are worthy of being collector items, are made by Trifari. The collection featured animals, floral motifs and figurative subjects, and included brooches, earrings and necklaces. Most designs were by Alfred Philippe (61 patents), two were by Norman Bel Geddes (JB1. and JB4.), and one was by David Mir (JB8.). Several versions were made of some designs. Other designs were used for production, at a later time, for jewelry items of different materials and with different dimensions. There were also some unpatented pieces: the "Crab" (JB23.), the "Horse Shoe Earrings" (JB28.), an alligator mentioned by *WWD* in spring 1944, a reindeer, and two birds on a branch in a Lucite full moon.

The first 1941 brooches were made of base metal or gold-plated metal: "Cleo" (JB2.), "Sailfish" (JB1.), "Bel Geddes Swan" (JB4.), "Double Flower" (JB3., also in single and triple flower versions), as well as the magnificent "Eagle" (JB8.). In 1942 other extraordinary pieces were made, which were of unique beauty and size, using rhodium-plated metal and rhinestones; "Big Poodle" (JB7.), "Airedale" (JB10.), "Pekinese" (JB6.), "Frog on a Leaf" (JB11.), "Parrot" (JB9.), "Big Elephant" (JB12.). The first series of twelve sterling animals, with the addition of "Sail Boat" (JB25.) and "Ball Earrings" (JB30.), date from the spring of 1943. The second series of animal and floral motifs dates back to the spring and fall of 1944. Only two designs are dated 1945: "Carnation" (JB42.), and a small bird, while, in 1946, four brooches were made; "Bird Head" (JB45), "Parrot Head," "Peacock Head" (JB47.), and "Rooster Head" (JB46.). All the production of this period was made of sterling.

The last series, which was made entirely of Trifanium, dated from the spring of 1949 and consisted of fifteen designs with figurative and abstract subjects on which the whole range of jewelry was based: items included brooches, clips, necklaces and earrings. Finally, in 1952, three brooch designs were created – a leaf, "Beetle" (JB62. & 63), and "Heart" (JB64.) – also made of golden Trifanium.

In 1965 Trifari reproduced some models made of Lucite and glazed gold-plated metal. These pieces cannot possibly be mistaken for the originals on account of the different materials, weight, and manufacturing technique used.

Coro manufactured some very beautiful Jelly Bellies designed by Adolph Katz, but only 24 designs were patented, all of which were brooches and Duettes, and it is therefore difficult to pinpoint with certainty which pieces made up the complete series.

The first patented design was dated 1942, the "Angel Fish" (JB72.), and it was made of sterling. The best collections are dated 1944, spring (series of enamel animals) and fall (some top pieces, such as "Pegasus," JB74.) and spring 1945. *Women's Wear Daily*, 29th June 1944, mentioned series of fun animal brooches made of colored enamel with crystal-like Lucite cabochons and again, on 22nd January 1945, animal brooches with Lucite. All items from this period were made of sterling, sometimes with rhinestones set in Lucite, including the

Duettes of animals with matching earrings. Thereafter, only three fish-shaped brooches were patented: "Fish Duette" in 1948 (JB90.), "Small Fish" in 1949 (JB96.) and "Fish" in 1950 (JB94.).

Coro used colored Lucite cabochons instead of stones. In spring 1942 (*WWD*, 20th March 1942), for example, it presented a series of sterling brooches with colored Lucite cabochons. The brooches were mainly of floral subjects and are particularly interesting because they were a first limited experiment in sterling jewelry, possibly made to test the public's reaction.

Coro Jelly Bellies are not as well known and valued as Trifari's, although they are often as remarkable for their quality and design sophistication. At times, they were even more imaginative.

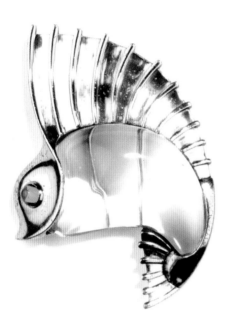

JB1. "Sailfish," Trifari 1941****
Manufacturer Trifari, Krussman & Fishel.
Designer Norman Bel Geddes.
Patent n° 129,165 Norman Bel Geddes, New York,
26th August 1941, filed on 22nd July 1941.

Gold-plated metal pin clip with lucite and rhinestones, depicting a dolphin. Three variants of the same design were made: "Sailfish" with two-toned ribbed gold-plated fin, 8.5x6.5cm; "Strass Sailfish" with rhinestone-studded ribbed gold-plated fin, 8.5x6.5cm; "Small Sailfish" made of gold-plated sterling with ribbed fin and rhinestone-studded snout, 7x5.5cm. The latter is a revisitation of the original design made in 1943, when Trifari produced its most important lucite and sterling animal collection.
Marked "Sailfish" Trifari Pat. Pend. "Strass Sailfish" Des. Pat. No. 129165. "Small Sailfish" Trifari Sterling Des. Pat. No. 129165.
The patent refers to "Strass Sailfish".
A new version of the "Small Sailfish" was made in 1965 using glazed gold-plated metal with lucite or a baroque white pearl.

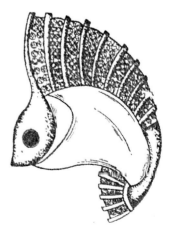

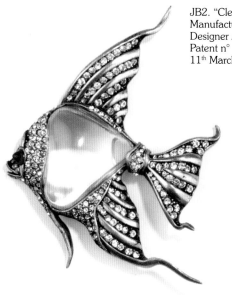

JB2. "Cleo," Trifari 1941****
Manufacturer Trifari, Krussman & Fishel.
Designer Alfred Philippe.
Patent n° 125,822 Alfred Philippe, New York,
11th March 1941, filed on 6th February 1941.

White metal alloy brooch (originally a pin clip) with lucite, a small red cabochon and rhinestones, depicting a fish. 7.5x6cm.
    Marked D. Pat. 125822.
    This was Trifari's first Jelly Belly. Another version of this model featured a faceted colored stone.
    The name given to this item is a fantasy name. The design seems to have been inspired by Cleo, Pinocchio's goldfish, from the Walt Disney film produced in 1940.

JB3. "Double Flower," Trifari 1941*****
Manufacturer Trifari, Krussman & Fishel.
Designer Alfred Philippe.
Patent n° 126,483 Alfred Philippe, New York,
8th April 1941, filed on 27th February 1941.

Gold-plated metal pin clip, lucite, blue cabochon, red stones and rhinestones, in the shape of a double flower. The leaves are made of red stones set using the invisible setting technique. 10x7.5cm.
    Marked Trifari.
    Two other brooches were patented, one with a single flower (Des. n° 126,482) and another with three flowers (Des. n° 126,484).

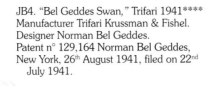

JB4. "Bel Geddes Swan," Trifari 1941****
Manufacturer Trifari Krussman & Fishel.
Designer Norman Bel Geddes.
Patent n° 129,164 Norman Bel Geddes,
New York, 26th August 1941, filed on 22nd
   July 1941.

White metal alloy brooch (originally a
pin clip) with contoured lucite, blue cabochon and rhinestones, depicting a swan
with a rhinestone studded head and neck.
5.5x6.5cm.
   Marked Des. Pat. No. 129164.
   Norman Bel Geddes only designed
two Jelly Belly brooches for Trifari.

Gold-plated sterling brooch with lucite,
small red cabochon and rhinestones
depicting a swan. 6x5cm.
   Marked Trifari Sterling Des. Pat. No.
137201.

JB5. "Swan," Trifari 1944****
Manufacturer Trifari, Krussman & Fishel.
Designer Alfred Philippe.
Patent n° 137,201 Alfred Philippe, Provi-
dence, R.I., 8th February 1944, filed on 20th
December 1943.

JB6. "Pekinese", Trifari 1942*****
Manufacturer Trifari, Krussman & Fishel.
Designer Alfred Philippe.
Patent n° 131,871 Alfred Philippe, New York, 31st
March 1942, filed on 25th January 1942.

Rhodium plated metal brooch, lucite, black
enamel and rhinestones, in the shape of a
Pekinese dog. 5x7.5cm.
Marked Trifari Pat. Pend.
In the early months of 1942 Alfred
Philippe designed (December 1941 –
February 1942) and patented (February
1942 – April 1942) six outstanding brooches,
in rhodium plated metal, lucite, enameling and
rhinestones: "Pekinese," "Big Poodle" (JB7.),
"Airedale" (JB10), "Parrot" (JB9.), "Frog on a
Leaf" (JB11.), "Big Elephant" (JB12.). Probably,
only a relatively small number of these items were
made.

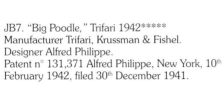

Rhodium plated metal pin clip with lucite, black enamel and rhinestones,
depicting a French poodle with rhinestone studded muzzle and paws. 6x7cm.
Marked Trifari Pat. Pend.
The "Big Poodle" was featured in the "Ladies' Home Journal," April 1942.
Another version of the "Poodle" was made in 1944. This version was a
smaller version than the original and was made of sterling (JB26.).

JB7. "Big Poodle," Trifari 1942*****
Manufacturer Trifari, Krussman & Fishel.
Designer Alfred Philippe.
Patent n° 131,371 Alfred Philippe, New York, 10th
February 1942, filed 30th December 1941.

JB8. "Eagle," Trifari 1941*****
Manufacturer Trifari, Krussman & Fishel.
Designer David Mir.
Patent n° 130,096 David Mir, New York, 21st
October 1941, filed on 15th September 1941.

Gold plated metal brooch with
lucite, blue enamel with gold and
red accents, white baroque pearl
and rhinestones depicting an eagle
with contoured lucite wings, perched
on a rock. 11.5x8cm.
Marked Trifari Des. Pat. No 130096.

JB9. "Parrot," Trifari 1942*****
Manufacturer Trifari, Krussman & Fishel.
Designer Alfred Philippe.
Patent n° 131,962 Alfred Philippe, New
York, 7th April 1942, filed on 14th February
1942.

Rhodium plated metal pin clip, lucite, yellow,
black and red enamel, rhinestones, depicting a
parrot with spread lucite wings, perched on a
perch. 10x6.5cm.
Marked Trifari Pat. Pend.

JB10. "Airedale", Trifari 1942*****
Manufacturer Trifari, Krussman & Fishel.
Designer Alfred Philippe.
Patent n° 131,785 Alfred Philippe, New
York, 24th March 1942, filed on 20th
January 1942.

Rhodium plated metal pin clip, lucite,
black enamel and rhinestones in the
shape of an Airedale. 7x5cm.
Marked Trifari Pat. Pend.

Rhodium plated metal brooch
with lucite, green and light green
enamel, red cabochons for the eyes
and rhinestones, depicting a frog
sitting on a contoured lucite water
lily leaf. 6.5x6cm.
Marked Trifari Pat. Pend.

JB11. "Frog on a Leaf," Trifari 1942*****
Manufacturer Trifari, Krussman & Fishel.
Designer Alfred Philippe.
Patent n° 131,867 Alfred Philippe, New York,
31st March 1942, filed on 29th January 1942.

Rhodium plated metal pin clip, lucite,
black and red enamel, rhinestones, in
the shape of an elephant. 8.5x4.5cm.
Marked Trifari.

JB12. "Big Elephant," Trifari 1942*****
Manufacturer Trifari, Krussman & Fishel.
Designer Alfred Philippe.
Patent n° 132,001 Alfred Philippe, New York, 7th
April 1942, filed on 14th February 1942.

Gold-plated sterling brooch with lucite, red cabochon, green marquise cut stones and rhinestones,
depicting a rabbit chewing on a twig held in its
paws. 4.8x4.5cm.
   Marked Trifari Sterling Des. Pat. No. 135169.
   In 1945 Coro made a similar model from a
design by Adolph Katz (JB82.).

JB13. "Rabbit," Trifari 1943****
Manufacturer Trifari, Krussman & Fishel.
Designer Alfred Philippe.
Patent n° 135,169 Alfred Philippe, Cranston,
R.I., 2nd March 1943, filed on 3rd February 1943.

Gold-plated sterling brooch with
lucite, small green stones for eyes and
rhinestones. The brooch is of a turtle.
6x4cm.
   Marked Trifari Sterling Des. Pat.
No. 135170.

JB14. "Turtle," Trifari 1943***
Manufacturer Trifari, Krussman & Fishel.
Designer Alfred Philippe.
Patent n° 135,170 Alfred Philippe, Cranston,
R.I., 2nd March 1943, filed on 3rd February 1943.

JB15. "Hummingbird," Trifari 1943***
Manufacturer Trifari, Krussman & Fishel.
Designer Alfred Philippe.
Patent n° 135,171 Alfred Philippe, Cranston,
R.I., 2nd March 1943, filed on 3rd February
1943.

Gold-plated sterling brooch with lucite, small red
stone and rhinestones, depicting a "Black-Chinned"
hummingbird, a species found in the west and
south-west of the USA. Its scientific name is "Ar-
chilocus". 5.8x7.3cm.
   Marked Trifari Sterling Pat. Pend.
   Another version of this model was made in 1965.
The new brooch was made of glazed gold-plated
metal with a central pearl.

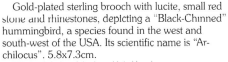

Gold-plated sterling brooch with lucite, green cabochon and rhinestones, depicting a frog with bulging eyes and stretched out legs in the act of jumping. 7x4.7cm.
Marked Trifari Sterling Des. Pat. No. 135172.

JB16. "Frog," Trifari 1943****
Manufacturer Trifari, Krussman & Fishel.
Designer Alfred Philippe.
Patent n° 135,172 Alfred Philippe, Cranston, R.I., 2nd March 1943, filed on 3rd February 1943.

JB17. "Pig," Trifari 1943****
Manufacturer Trifari, Krussman & Fishel.
Designer Alfred Philippe.
Patent n° 135,173 Alfred Philippe, Cranston, R.I., 2nd March 1943, filed on 3rd February 1943.

Gold-plated sterling brooch with lucite, representing a piglet with rhinestones on its snout and legs, a tiny red stone for its eye and round lucite body. 4x5.5cm.
Marked Trifari Sterling Des. Pat. No. 135173.

Gold-plated sterling brooch with lucite and rhinestones depicting a duckling peeking out from a hatched egg. 5.3x4cm.
Marked Trifari Sterling Des. Pat. No. 135176.

JB18. "Duckling in an Egg," Trifari 1943****
Manufacturer Trifari, Krussman & Fishel.
Designer Alfred Philippe.
Patent n° 135,176 Alfred Philippe, Cranston, R.I., 2nd March 1943, filed on 3rd February 1943.

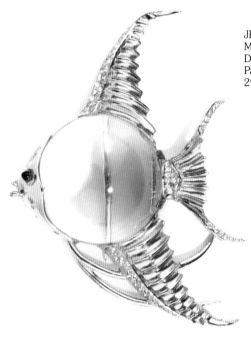

JB19. *"Angel Fish,"* Trifari 1943\*\*\*\*
Manufacturer Trifari, Krussman & Fishel.
Designer Alfred Philippe.
Patent n° 135,177 Alfred Philippe, Cranston, R.I.,
2nd March 1943, filed on 3rd February 1943.

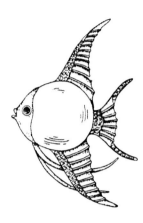

 Gold-plated sterling pin clip with lucite, small red stone and rhinestones depicting an angel fish. 9x6.5cm.
 Marked Trifari Sterling Des. Pat. No. 135177.
 Both the "Angel Fish" and "Horse-Shoe" earrings appeared together in Women's Wear Daily, on 3rd September 1943.
 This is a different, more refined version of a subject already created by Coro in 1942 based on a design by Adolph Katz (JB72.).

JB20. *"Great Blue Heron,"* Trifari
1943\*\*\*\*\*
Manufacturer Trifari, Krussman & Fishel.
Designer Alfred Philippe.
Patent n° 135,175 Alfred Philippe, Cranston, R.I., 2nd March 1943, filed on 3rd February 1943.

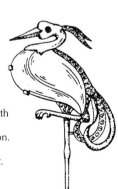

 Gold-plated sterling brooch, with lucite, red cabochon and rhinestones depicting a great blue heron. 10x6.5cm.
 Marked Trifari Sterling Des. Pat. No. 135175.

JB21. "Penguin," Trifari 1943****
Manufacturer Trifari, Krussman & Fishel.
Designer Alfred Philippe.
Patent n° 135,189 Alfred Philippe, Cranston, R.I.,
9th March 1943, filed on 3rd February 1943.

Gold-plated sterling brooch depicting a
penguin with a lucite body, a green stone
for its eye and rhinestone pavé on its beak
and legs. 5.8x3.5cm.
Marked Trifari Sterling Des. Pat. No.
135189.

JB22. "Sea Lion," Trifari 1943***
Manufacturer Trifari, Krussman & Fishel.
Designer Alfred Philippe.
Patent n° 135,188 Alfred Philippe, Cr-
anston, R.I., 9th March 1943, filed on 3rd
February 1943.

Gold-plated sterling brooch, with lucite,
small blue stone and rhinestones, depicting a
sea lion holding a fake pearl on its nose (or, a
colored stone in other versions). 6x4.4cm.
Marked Trifari Sterling Des. Pat. No. 135188.

JB23. "Crab," Trifari 1943-44****
Manufacturer Trifari, Krussman & Fishel.
Designer Alfred Philippe.
Not patented.
Gold-plated sterling brooch, with lucite, small red stones and rhine-
stones, depicting a crab. 4.5x7cm.
Marked Trifari Sterling Pat. Pend.
The design is unpatented, although the item bears a Pat. Pend. mark.
Another "Crab" version exists, with central faceted stone in various
colors.

JB24. "Spider," Trifari 1943****
Manufacturer Trifari, Krussman & Fishel.
Designer Alfred Philippe.
Patent n° 135,190 Alfred Philippe, Cranston, R.I., 9th March 1943, filed on 3rd February 1943.

Gold-plated sterling pin clip with lucite, baguettes and rhinestones, depicting a spider. 5x4.5cm.
Marked Trifari Sterling Des. Pat. No. 135190.
The spider appeared in *Vogue* on 1st December 1943, priced $18.50, and again in *Vogue*, 1st June 1944 together with the "Big Fly".

JB25. "Sail Boat," Trifari 1943*****
Manufacturer Trifari, Krussman & Fishel.
Designer Alfred Philippe.
Patent n° 135,174 Alfred Philippe, Cranston, R.I., 2nd March 1943, filed on 3rd February 1943.

Gold-plated sterling brooch with lucite, depicting a sailboat with lucite and rhinestone sail. 6.5x4cm.
Marked Trifari Sterling Des. Pat. No. 135174.
This is the only non animal subject of the 1943 Jelly Belly collection. It is a very rare piece with a refined and true-to-life design.

JB26. "Poodle," Trifari 1944****
Manufacturer Trifari, Krussman & Fishel.
Designer Alfred Philippe.
Not patented but see JB7.
Gold-plated sterling brooch with lucite and rhinestones, depicting a poodle. 5.5x4.5cm.
Marked Trifari Sterling Pat. Pend.
Another version of this model had colored square stones instead of the lucite and rhinestones.
The Patent Pending mark does not tally with the existing patent. However, it is possible that the "Poodle" was in the process of being independently patented, although the procedure was never completed.

JB27. "Eastern Screech Owl," Trifari 1943****
Manufacturer Trifari, Krussman & Fishel.
Designer Alfred Philippe.
Patent n° 135,191 Alfred Philippe, Cranston, R.I., 9th March 1943, filed on 3rd February 1943.

Gold-plated sterling pin clip, with lucite and rhinestones, depicting an owl perched on a branch. The owl has large eyes with two small green cabochons for the pupils. The design was inspired by the Eastern Screech owl, a common species of owl in the USA. 6x3cm.
Marked Trifari Sterling Pat. Pend.
This pin clip and the "Ball" earrings appeared in an advertisement by Trifari published in *Vogue*, 1st April 1943, where it stated that the "Screech Owl" was selling at Gerlou for $16.50 and the "Ball Earrings" for $12.50.

*JELLY BELLIES*

JB28. "Horse-Shoe Earrings," Trifari 1943*
Manufacturer Trifari, Krussman & Fishel.
Designer Alfred Philippe.
Not patented.
   Gold-plated sterling clip earrings with small lucite ball surrounded by rhinestones. 2cm.
   Marked Trifari Sterling.
   Universal model. In Trifari's Jelly Belly collections, the company tended to create earrings that could be matched with a series of items, whereas Coro favored creating brooch and earrings sets (same design, only smaller).
   These earrings were featured in WWD, 3rd September 1943 together with "Angel Fish".

JB29. "Flies Set," Trifari 1944***
Manufacturer Trifari, Krussman & Fishel.
Designer Alfred Philippe.
Patent n° 137,200 Alfred Philippe, Cranston, R.I., 8th February 1944, filed on 20th December 1943.

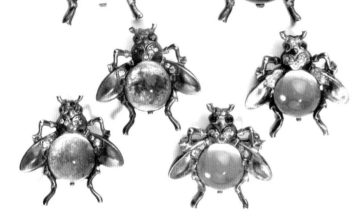

A line composed of gold-plated sterling brooches and earrings with lucite and rhinestones, shaped like flies and based on a single design with size and color variants, "Big Fly," 5x5cm, corresponds to the patented design. Pair of "Flies," 4x4.2cm, in two lucite color variants; clear and violet, with a flat profile. Pair of "Small Flies," 3x3cm, both with clear lucite and flat profile. "Fly" clip earrings, 3cm, with clear lucite and a flat profile.
   Marked Trifari Sterling Des. Pat. No. 137200.
   The "Big Fly" is the most common item, whereas the violet lucite "Fly" and the earrings are rather rare. There was also a contemporary copy of the "Big Fly" manufactured by Dalsheim Accessories in 1945 (Mademoiselle, March 1945).
   The "Big Fly" appeared in Vogue, 1st June 1944, together with the Jelly Belly "Spider". The complete set – "Big Fly," "Fly," "Small Fly" and earrings appeared in a full-page color advertisement by Trifari in Vogue, 1st March 1945.

Gold-plated sterling clip earrings with lucite half-spheres and rhinestones. 2.5cm.
   Marked Trifari Sterling Des. Pat. No. 136594.
   This model can be matched with all the Jelly Bellies.

JB30. "Ball Earrings," Trifari 1943**
Manufacturer Trifari, Krussman & Fishel.
Designer Alfred Philippe.
Patent n° 136,594 Alfred Philippe, Cranston, R.I., 2nd November 1943, filed on 24th September 1943.

Gold-plated sterling brooch, lucite,
green stone and rhinestones, in the shape
of a kiwi. 4.5x4.5cm.
Marked Trifari Sterling.

JB31. "Kiwi," Trifari 1944****
Manufacturer Trifari, Krussman & Fishel.
Designer Alfred Philippe.
Patent n° 137,322 Alfred Philippe, Provi-
dence, R.I., 22nd February 1944, filed on 13th
January 1944.

JB32. "Lizard," Trifari 1944****
Manufacturer Trifari, Krussman & Fishel.
Designer Alfred Philippe.
Patent n° 137,323 Alfred Philippe, Providence, R.I., 22nd
February 1944, filed on 13th January 1944.

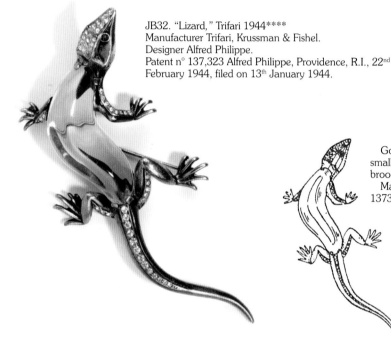

Gold-plated sterling brooch, with lucite,
small red stone and rhinestones. The
brooch is of a lizard. 4.3x10cm.
Marked Trifari Sterling Des. Pat. No.
137323.

JB33. "Chanticleer," Trifari 1944****
Manufacturer Trifari, Krussman & Fishel.
Designer Alfred Philippe.
Patent n° 137,324 Alfred Philippe, Provi-
dence, R.I., 22nd February 1944, filed on
13th January 1944.

Gold-plated sterling brooch, with lucite, small red
stones and rhinestones. The brooch is of a
rooster. 6.5x5cm.
Marked Trifari Sterling Pat. Pend.
In a *WWD* article of 10th March 1944
the item was called "Chanticleer". In
1965 Trifari made another version of this
brooch, using glazed gold-plated metal and
a pearl.

Gold-plated sterling brooch, with lucite, red crystals and rhinestones, depicting a peony with lucite petals and a heart of red crystals. 6.5x5.3cm.
Marked Trifari Sterling Des. Pat. No. 139255.

JB34. "Peony," Trifari 1944****
Manufacturer Trifari, Krussman & Fishel.
Designer Alfred Philippe.
Patent n° 139,255 Alfred Philippe, Providence, R.I., 24th October 1944, filed on 29th August 1944.

Gold-plated sterling pin clip, with lucite, small red cabochon and rhinestones, depicting a horse's head with a lucite neck. 5.5x4.5cm.
Marked Trifari Sterling Des. Pat. No. 138353.
Coro made a similar unpatented model, probably in 1942, with a less graceful line, which is nowadays rarer than Trifari's model. (JB67.).
The brooch, together with the "Horse Shoe" earrings, appeared in *Vogue*, 1st June 1944, in an advertisement by Gerlou – an elegant New York store, 501 Fifth Avenue – in which the prices of brooch ($20) and earrings ($12,50) were indicated.
Almost two years later, the model was copied by S. Packales & Company – a New York company with offices at 307 Fifth Avenue – which was advertised (*WWD* 19th February 1946) under the name "Horse Head Pin" on sale for $2. The item by Packales was slightly larger, made of molded sterling and lucite, very light and rather badly finished.

JB35. "Horse Head," Trifari 1944****
Manufacturer Trifari, Krussman & Fishel.
Designer Alfred Philippe.
Patent n° 138,353 Alfred Philippe, Providence, R.I., 18th July 1944, filed on 12th February 1944.

JB36. "Sparrow," Trifari 1944****
Manufacturer Trifari, Krussman & Fishel.
Designer Alfred Philippe.
Patent n° 137,573 Alfred Philippe, Providence, R.I., 28th March, 1944. filed on 12th February 1944.

Gold-plated sterling brooch, with lucite, red baguettes and rhinestones depicting a nestling sparrow. Its tail, wings and breast are studded with rhinestones, and the tail tip is ornamented with red baguettes, its eye is a tiny blue stone. 4x6.5cm.
Marked Trifari Sterling Des. Pat. No. 137573.
The brooch was remade in 1965 using glazed gold-plated metal.

JB37. "Small Turtle," Trifari 1944***
Manufacturer Trifari, Krussman & Fishel.
Designer Alfred Philippe.
Patent n° 138,695 Alfred Philippe, Providence, R.I., 5th
September 1944, filed on 20th July 1944.

Small, flat gold-plated sterling brooch with lucite and
rhinestones, depicting a turtle. 4x3cm.
   Marked Trifari Sterling.
   This model was remade in 1965 using glazed gold-
plated metal and a center pearl.

Gold-plated sterling brooch, contoured lucite,
red, blue, white, yellow and brown enamel, small
red cabochon for its eye, and rhinestones. The
brooch is of an eagle. 5x4.8cm.
   Marked Trifari Sterling Pat. Pend.

JB38. "Patriotic Eagle," Trifari 1944****
Manufacturer Trifari, Krussman & Fishel.
Designer Alfred Philippe.
Patent n° 137,572 Alfred Philippe, Providence, R.I., 28th
March 1944, filed on 12th February 1944.

JB39. "Moghul Turtle," Trifari 1949***
Manufacturer Trifari, Krussman & Fishel.
Designer Alfred Philippe.
Golden Trifanium brooch, lucite, small red cabochons
and rhinestones. The brooch is of a turtle. 4x3cm.
Marked Trifari Pat. Pend,
This is the lucite version of the "Moghul Turtle" (T220.).

Gold-plated sterling brooch in the shape
of a rose with lucite petals. 6.5x4.2cm.
Marked Trifari Sterling Pat. Pend.

JB40. "Rose," Trifari 1944****
Manufacturer Trifari, Krussman & Fishel.
Designer Alfred Philippe.
Patent n° 138,696 Alfred Philippe, Providence,
R.I., 5th September 1944, filed on 20th July
1944.

JB41. "Orchid," Trifari 1944*****
Manufacturer Trifari, Krussman & Fishel.
Designer Alfred Philippe.
Patent n° 138,652 Alfred Philippe, Providence, R.I.,
29th August 1944, filed on 20th July 1944.

Gold-plated sterling brooch, lucite and rhinestones, depicting an
orchid with lucite petals. 8.7x6.2cm.
Marked Trifari Sterling Des. Pat. No. 139256.
The patent number punched on the brooch is incorrect and
refers to another brooch in the shape of a daisy with a lucite
heart, the patent for which was assigned to Alfred Philippe on
24th October 1944, in response to an application filed on 29th August 1944. It is possible that a punching mistake was made, and
this may have occurred because the designs were very alike,
belonged to the same collection (fall-winter 1944) and were
manufactured in the same period.

JB42. "Carnation," Trifari 1945****
Manufacturer Trifari, Krussman & Fishel.
Designer Alfred Philippe.
Patent n° 139,945 Alfred Philippe, Providence,
R.I., 2nd January 1945, filed on 1st November
1944.

Gold-plated sterling brooch, lucite
and rhinestones, in the shape of a carnation. 10x5.4cm.
Marked Trifari Sterling Des. Pat.
No.
Strangely the patent number
was omitted.

Gold-plated sterling brooch, with lucite, red drop-shaped cabochons and rhinestones. The brooch is of a trumpeting elephant with lucite saddle cloth. 7x6.8cm. Marked Trifari Sterling Des. Pat. No. 138202.

JB43. "Elephant," Trifari 1944*****
Manufacturer Trifari. Krussman & Fishel.
Designer Alfred Philippe.
Patent n° 138,202 Alfred Philippe, Providence, R.I., 4th July 1944, filed on 12th February 1944.

Gold-plated sterling brooch, lucite and rhinestones, depicting a lily of the valley, with large lucite leaf and rhinestone-studded stalk and branches. 8.5x4.7cm. Marked Trifari Sterling Des. Pat. No. 139254.

JB44. "Lily of the Valley," Trifari 1944****
Manufacturer Trifari, Krussman & Fishel.
Designer Alfred Philippe.
Patent n° 139,254 Alfred Philippe, Providence, R.I., 24th October 1944, filed on 29th August 1944.

JB45. "Bird Head," Trifari 1946****
Manufacturer Trifari, Krussman & Fishel.
Designer Alfred Philippe.
Patent n° 145,260 Alfred Philippe, Scarsdale,
NY., 22nd July 1946, filed on 24th January 1946.

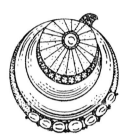

Gold-plated sterling brooch, with
contoured round lucite, blue cabochons
and rhinestones, depicting a bird's head.
4.5x4cm.
    Marked Trifari Sterling Pat. Pend. "61".

JB46. "Rooster Head," Trifari 1946****
Manufacturer Trifari, Krussman & Fishel.
Designer Alfred Philippe.
Patent n° 145,272 Alfred Philippe, Scarsdale, NY., 23rd
July 1946, filed on 24th January 1946.

Gold-plated sterling pin clip, lucite,
red stones and rhinestones, depicting a
rooster's head. 7x3.5cm.
    Marked Trifari Sterling Pat. Pend.

Gold-plated sterling pin clip, lucite, red,
green and blue stones, rhinestones, in the
shape of a peacock's head. 5x4cm.
    Marked Trifari Sterling Pat. Pend. "19".

JB47. "Peacock Head," Trifari 1946****
Manufacturer Trifari, Krussman & Fishel.
Designer Alfred Philippe.
Patent n° 145,271 Alfred Philippe, Scarsdale,
NY., 23rd July 1946, filed on 24th January 1946.

JB48. "Fairyland Clips," Trifari 1949***
Manufacturer Trifari, Krussman & Fishel.
Designer Alfred Philippe.
Patent n° 153,630 Alfred Philippe, Scarsdale,
NY., 3rd May 1949, filed on 15th January 1949,
assignor to Trifari, Krussman & Fishel.

Golden Trifanium clip pair, with
half-moon lucite, white baguettes and
rhinestones. 4x3cm.
Marked Trifari Pat. Pend.
The clips are part of the "Fairyland"
series which featured half-moon lucite, as
mentioned by *WWD*, 4th March 1949.

JB49. "Retro Pin," Trifari 1949***
Manufacturer Trifari, Krussman & Fishel.
Designer Alfred Philippe.
Patent n° 153,029 Alfred Philippe, Scarsdale, NY., 8th
March 1949, filed on 4th January 1949, assignor to
Trifari, Krussman & Fishel. The patent is for a necklace,
which has a pendant that is similar to the pin.

Retro style golden Trifanium pin clip with lucite
"curl," baguettes and rhinestones. The pin is fitted with
a safety clasp. 4x5.5cm.
Marked Trifari Pat. Pend.
This item belongs to a jewelry series which featured
"curled" lucite

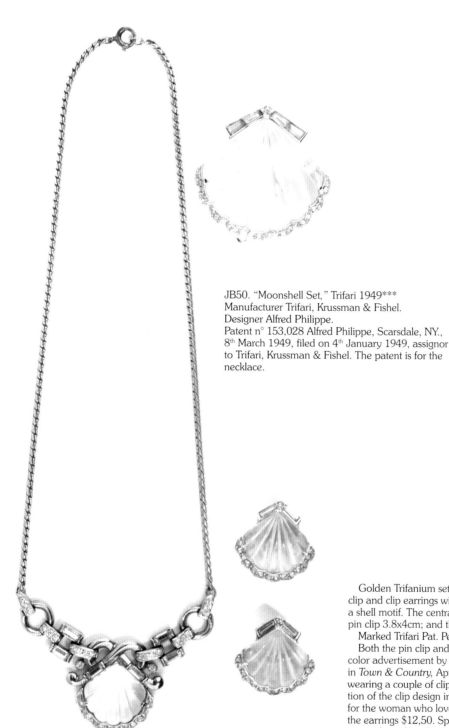

JB50. "Moonshell Set," Trifari 1949***
Manufacturer Trifari, Krussman & Fishel.
Designer Alfred Philippe.
Patent n° 153,028 Alfred Philippe, Scarsdale, NY.,
8th March 1949, filed on 4th January 1949, assignor
to Trifari, Krussman & Fishel. The patent is for the
necklace.

Golden Trifanium set made up of a necklace with a fine chain, a pin clip and clip earrings with lucite, baguettes and rhinestones. The set has a shell motif. The central part of the necklace measures 6.5x2.5cm; the pin clip 3.8x4cm; and the earrings 2cm.
Marked Trifari Pat. Pend.
Both the pin clip and the earrings featured in a picture in a full page color advertisement by Trifari in *Harper's Bazaar,* February 1949, and in *Town & Country,* April 1949. The advertisement shows a model wearing a couple of clips and matching earrings. There is a reproduction of the clip design inset, with the slogan "Individually designed for the woman who loves romantic jewels". The pin clip cost $10 and the earrings $12,50. Special attention was paid to claim and defend copyright in the advertisement: a caption appears under the Trifari logo declaring that jewelry items are genuine only if they bear the Trifari mark stamped at the back. Underneath the design there is a caption specifying that there is a "Patent Pending". The name "Moonshell" is original.

JB51. "Butterfly," Trifari 1949****
Manufacturer Trifari, Krussman &
Fishel.
Designer Alfred Philippe.
Patent n° 153,379 Alfred Philippe,
Scarsdale, NY., 12ᵗʰ April 1949,
filed on 4ᵗʰ January 1949, assignor to
Trifari, Krussman & Fishel.

Golden Trifanium brooch, with lucite, baguettes
and rhinestones, depicting a butterfly with lucite
wings and a rhomboid ruby red stone for its head.
3x5.5cm.
Marked Trifari Pat. Pend.

JB52., JB53., JB59. "Crown set", Trifari 1949****
Manufacturer Trifari, Krussman & Fishel.
Designer Alfred Philippe.
Patent earrings n° 153,020, 8ᵗʰ March 1949, filed 16ᵗʰ
December 1948, brooch n° 153,078, 15ᵗʰ March 1949,
filed on 10ᵗʰ December 1948, necklace n° 153,386, 12ᵗʰ
April 1949, filed on 22ⁿᵈ January 1949, Alfred Philippe,
Scarsdale, NY., assignor to Trifari, Krussman & Fishel.

A necklace, earrings and brooch set made of golden Trifanium, lucite,
baguettes and rhinestones. Earrings 2.6x2cm, brooch 4.2x4cm, necklace
with a central motif measuring 3x8cm. All marked Trifari Pat. Pend.
   The crown and earrings design was recreated in 1953 for the crown and
earrings that were part of the "Coronation Gems" line, created on the occasion of Queen Elisabeth II of Britain's coronation (T225).

JB54. "Curl Pin," Trifari 1949**
Manufacturer Trifari, Krussman & Fishel.
Designer Alfred Philippe.
Patent n° 153,624 Alfred Philippe,
Scarsdale, NY., 3rd May 1949, filed on 4th
January 1949, assignor to Trifari, Krussman
& Fishel.

Golden Trifanium clip, with lucite, baguettes
and rhinestones, complete with safety clasp.
3.8x2.5cm.
  Marked Trifari Pat. Pend.
  The patent application was filed for the
lucite design, i.e. the "curl" motif, which was
used in several sets, designed and partly patented in 1949 (JB55., JB56., JB61.)

Golden Trifanium clip earrings,
with lucite, baguettes and rhinestones.
2.5cm.
  Marked Pat. Pend.

JB55. "Curl Earrings," Trifari 1949**
Manufacturer Trifari, Krussman & Fishel.
Designer Alfred Philippe.
Patent n° 154,211 Alfred Philippe, Scarsdale,
NY., 21st June 1949, filed on 22nd January
1949, assignor to Trifari, Krussman & Fishel.

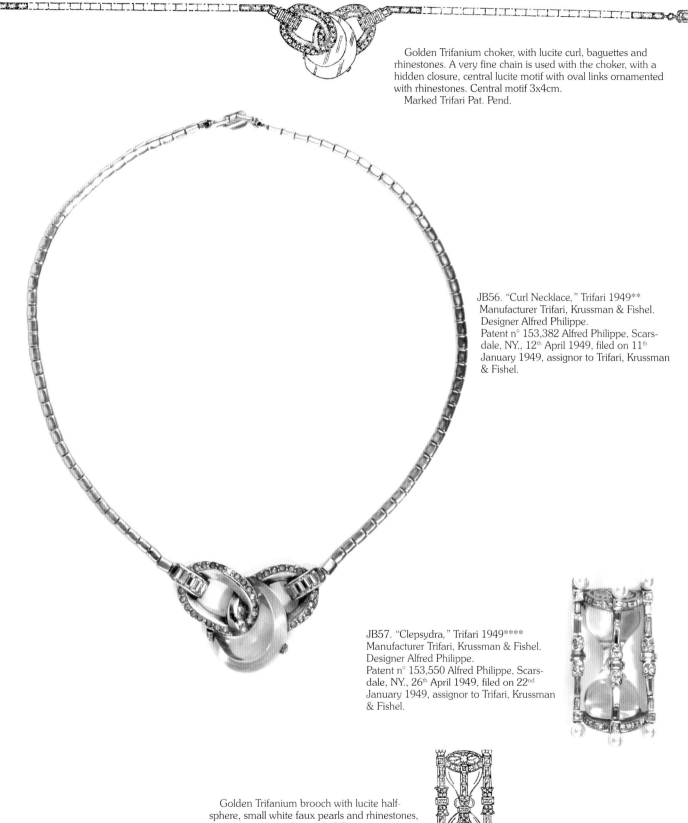

Golden Trifanium choker, with lucite curl, baguettes and rhinestones. A very fine chain is used with the choker, with a hidden closure, central lucite motif with oval links ornamented with rhinestones. Central motif 3x4cm.
Marked Trifari Pat. Pend.

JB56. "Curl Necklace," Trifari 1949**
Manufacturer Trifari, Krussman & Fishel.
Designer Alfred Philippe.
Patent n° 153,382 Alfred Philippe, Scarsdale, NY., 12th April 1949, filed on 11th January 1949, assignor to Trifari, Krussman & Fishel.

JB57. "Clepsydra," Trifari 1949****
Manufacturer Trifari, Krussman & Fishel.
Designer Alfred Philippe.
Patent n° 153,550 Alfred Philippe, Scarsdale, NY., 26th April 1949, filed on 22nd January 1949, assignor to Trifari, Krussman & Fishel.

Golden Trifanium brooch with lucite half-sphere, small white faux pearls and rhinestones, depicting an hourglass. 4.5x2.5cm.
Marked Trifari Pat. Pend.

JB58. "Fairyland Rooster," Trifari 1949****
Manufacturer Trifari, Krussman & Fishel.
Designer Alfred Philippe.
Patent n° 153,446 Alfred Philippe, Scarsdale,
NY., 19th April 1949, filed on 4th January 1949,
assignor to Trifari, Krussman & Fishel.

Golden Trifanium brooch of a crowing
rooster. Lucite body, small red cabochon
and rhinestones. 5x4.6cm.
Marked Trifari Pat. Pend.

JB60. "Fairyland Snail," Trifari 1949****
Manufacturer Trifari, Krussman & Fishel.
Designer Alfred Philippe.
Patent n° 153,453 Alfred Philippe, Scarsdale,
NY., 19th April, 1949, filed on 15th January
1949, assignor to Trifari, Krussman & Fishel.

Golden Trifanium brooch, with lucite, baguettes and
rhinestones, depicting a snail with a lucite shell. 4.5x5.5cm.
Trifari Pat. Pend.
This item is part of the "Fairyland" line of the 1949 spring
collection, which *Women's Wear Daily* (4th March 1949) described as being full of fantasy. The line included clear lucite
snails, hearts and crowns (JB52.).

JB61. "Curl Bracelet," Trifari 1949***
Manufacturer Trifari, Krussman & Fishel.
Designer Alfred Philippe.
Not patented.
   Golden Trifanium bracelet, lucite and rhinestone. h 1.5cm.
   Marked Trifari Pat. Pend.
   Reference to the patent regards the design of a lucite "Curl" motif (JB54., JB55., JB56.).

JB62 & 63. "Beetles," Trifari 1952***
Manufacturer Trifari, Krussman & Fishel.
Designer Alfred Philippe.
Patent n° 166,631 Alfred Philippe, Scarsdale, NY., 29th
April 1952, filed on 21st January 1952, assignor to Trifari,
Krussman & Fishel.

   Pair of golden Trifanium brooches with lucite,
green and red stones and rhinestones. The design
is of a beetle with a lucite body inserted into a
metal structure ornamented with stones. The design
was made in two sizes: large 6x5.3cm and small
3.5x2.7cm.
   Marked Trifari.
   There is also a bright green lucite version.

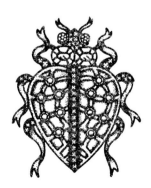

JB64. "Heart," Trifari 1952**
Manufacturer Trifari, Krussman & Fishel.
Designer Alfred Philippe.
Patent n° 166,627 Alfred Philippe, Scarsdale, NY.,
19th April 1952, filed on 17th January 1952, assignor
to Trifari, Krussman & Fishel.

Golden Trifanium brooch, with
lucite, drop-shaped green cabochons
and rhinestones, shaped like a heart.
The lucite component is inserted
into a stone studded metal structure.
5.5x5cm.
Marked Trifari Pat. Pend.

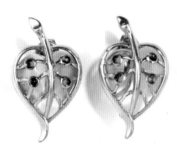

JB65. "Leaf earrings," Trifari 1952**
Manufacturer Trifari, Krussman & Fishel.
Designer Alfred Philippe.
Not patented.
   Golden Trifanium clip earrings with lucite and green stones. The earrings
are of two leaves. 3.3x2cm.
   Marked Trifari Design Pat. Pend.
   The earrings design is unpatented, whereas a leaf-shaped – heart-
pierced-by-an-arrow - brooch was patented. (des. n° 166,628 29th April
1952).

JB66. "Ara Parrot," Coro 1944***
Manufacturer Coro, Inc.
Designer Adolph Katz.
Patent n° 137,350 Adolph Katz, Provi-
dence, R.I., 22nd February 1944, filed
on 26th January 1944, assignor to
Coro Inc., New York.

   A brooch of an Ara parrot perched on a branch. Its body
is made of lucite, its head and crest are enameled in red and
black, its tail in yellow-orange and brown, and the leaves
in green. The parrot's body is silhouetted by a rhinestone
outline. 9x5.3cm.
   Marked CoroCraft Sterling.
   Adolph Katz designed a series of Jelly Belly brooches with
animal, floral and vegetable subjects for the spring 1944 collection. The brooches were made of gold-plated sterling with
enamel and rhinestone accents and colored stones. Some
of these designs were patented, whilst others were not. The
combination of lucite and colored enamel is a classic Coro
trademark.

JB67. "Horse Head," Coro 1942*****
Manufacturer Cohn & Rosenberger, Inc.
Designer Adolph Katz.
Not patented.
    Gold-plated sterling pin clip of a horse's head, with lucite, a green stone for its eye, red and black enamel and rhinestones. The horse's neck and mane are made of lucite. 5.8x5cm.
    Marked Sterling CoroCraft.

JB68. "Squirrel," Coro 1944*****
Manufacturer Coro, Inc.
Designer Adolph Katz.
Not patented.
    Gold-plated sterling brooch of a squirrel with a large lucite tail. Lucite, shaded green enamel and rhinestones. 5.5x6.2cm.
    Marked CoroCraft Sterling.
    A picture of this brooch appeared in the spring-summer 1944 Sears catalog, in a page with a series of sterling Coro brooches, advertised as "Heirloom Quality" and sold at prices ranging from $13.50 to $42. The "Squirrel" is the only Jelly Belly, shown under the letter "C" and was priced $13,75. The enamel colors and enameling technique used are the same as those used for the "Elephant" and the "Gazelle" which were patented on 11th January 1944 (C111. and C112.).

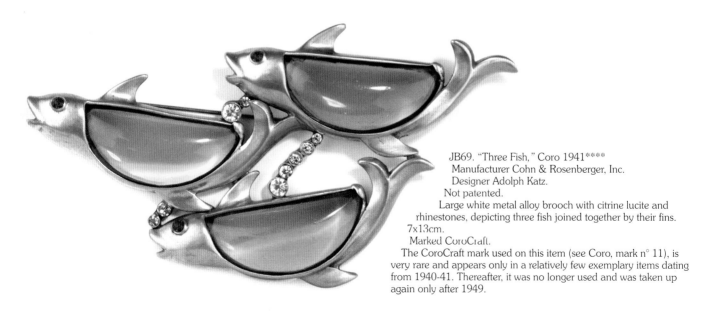

JB69. "Three Fish," Coro 1941****
Manufacturer Cohn & Rosenberger, Inc.
Designer Adolph Katz.
    Not patented.
    Large white metal alloy brooch with citrine lucite and rhinestones, depicting three fish joined together by their fins. 7x13cm.
    Marked CoroCraft.
    The CoroCraft mark used on this item (see Coro, mark n° 11), is very rare and appears only in a relatively few exemplary items dating from 1940-41. Thereafter, it was no longer used and was taken up again only after 1949.

Gold-plated sterling brooch, with lucite, yellow and green enamel and rhinestones, depicting a flying mallard. 5x6cm.
Marked CoroCraft Sterling.
There is also another variant with ruby red lucite.

JB70. "Mallard," Coro 1944***
Manufacturer Coro, Inc.
Designer Adolph Katz.
Patent n° 137,356 Adolph Katz, Providence, R.I., 22nd February 1944, filed on 26th January 1944, assignor to Coro, Inc., New York.

JB71. "Grouse," Coro 1944****
Manufacturer Coro, Inc.
Designer Adolph Katz.
Not patented.
Gold-plated sterling brooch, with lucite, yellow with red and black shades and rhinestones, depicting a grouse, a bird species with a large neck with a colored collar, large tail and small crest. 6.7x8cm.
Marked CoroCraft Sterling.

Gold-plated sterling brooch, with lucite and rhinestones, depicting a fish. 6.8x6.6cm.
There is also another version of this brooch with blue enamel fins and a version with a mother-of-pearl imitation central stone and blue enamel fins, which is part of a set with earrings that reproduce the same design in a smaller version.
Marked CoroCraft Sterling.
The subject was developed by Trifari based on a design by Alfred Philippe of March 1943 (JB19.).

JB72. "Angel Fish," Coro 1942***
Manufacturer Cohn & Rosenberger, Inc.
Designer Adolph Katz.
Patent n° 133,470 Adolph Katz, Providence, R.I., 18th August 1942, filed on 15th July 1942, assignor to Cohn & Rosenberger, Inc. New York.

JB73. "Pheasant," Coro 1944*****
Manufacturer Coro, Inc.
Designer Adolph Katz.
Patent n° 138,957 Adolph Katz, Providence, R.I.,
3rd October, 1944, filed on 19th July 1944, assignor
to Coro, Inc., New York.

Pink gold-plated sterling brooch, with lucite
and rhinestones, depicting a pheasant on a
branch. The pheasant's body is made of lucite
and its long tail is ornamented with rhinestones.
6.5x10cm.
Marked CoroCraft Sterling.
Series of three brooches – "Pheasant," "Pegasus"
and "Antelope" – designed and patented by Adolph Katz in July
– October 1944. The brooches were similar in design, style, and size.
They were all made of sterling and were very good quality. "Pheasant" and "Pegasus" have the CoroCraft mark and have a pink gilding,
"Antelope" is marked Coro, has a yellow gilding and is less bulky. The
"Pheasant" appeared in an advertisement together with other Jelly Bel-
lies of the CoroCraft line, in "Harper's Bazaar, February 1945.

JB74. "Pegasus" Coro 1944*****
Manufacturer Coro, Inc.
Designer Adolph Katz.
Patent n° 139,072 Adolph Katz, Providence,
R.I., 10th October, 1944, filed on 29th July 1944,
assignor to Coro, Inc., New York.

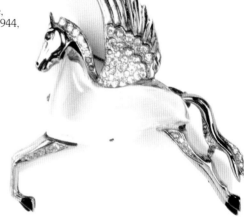

Pink gold-plated sterling brooch with lucite,
black and red enamel and rhinestones. The
brooch is of Pegasus. 7.5x7cm.
Marked CoroCraft Sterling.
Pegasus is one of the company trademarks,
which was mainly used for the CoroCraft line.

JB75. "Cornucopia," Coro 1944*****
Manufacturer Coro, Inc.
Designer Adolph Katz.
Not patented.
Gold-plated sterling brooch of a cornucopia with fruit and a
parrot perched on top of it. The cornucopia is made of lucite,
the fruit and parrot are made of enamel in various colors.
6.5x4.7cm.
Marked CoroCraft Sterling.
A smaller, recent imitation, marked Boucher, is being sold at
high prices, but is a fake.

JB76. "Orchid," Coro 1944-45***
Manufacturer Coro, Inc.
Designer Adolph Katz.
Not patented.
  Pink gold-plated sterling brooch with lucite and rhinestones, depicting an orchid with two lucite flowers. 9x6.3cm.
  Marked Sterling CoroCraft.

JB77. "Fruit Basket," Coro 1944****
Manufacturer Coro, Inc.
Designer Adolph Katz.
Not patented.
  Gold-plated sterling pin clip, with lucite, yellow, red, green, blue and orange enamel, red baguettes and rhinestones, depicting a fruit basket. A lucite basket and colored enamel fruit. 5.8x4.8cm.
  Marked CoroCraft Sterling.

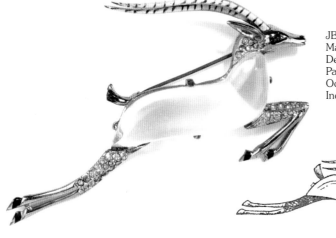

JB78. "Antelope," Coro 1944****
Manufacturer Coro, Inc.
Designer Adolph Katz.
Patent n° 139,073 Adolph Katz, Providence, R.I., 10th October 1944, filed on 29th July 1944, assignor to Coro, Inc., New York.

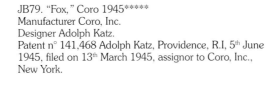

Gold-plated sterling brooch, with lucite, black and cream white enamel and rhinestones, depicting a running antelope. 5.5x9.5cm.
  Marked Coro Sterling.

JB79. "Fox," Coro 1945*****
Manufacturer Coro, Inc.
Designer Adolph Katz.
Patent n° 141,468 Adolph Katz, Providence, R.I, 5th June 1945, filed on 13th March 1945, assignor to Coro, Inc., New York.

Gold-plated sterling brooch, with lucite and rhinestones, depicting a fox looking backwards. Lucite body, and rhinestone pavé on its tail, paws, nails and ear, and a small red stone for its eye. 4x8cm.
  Marked CoroCraft Sterling.
  This item appeared in an advertisement published in *Vogue*, in June 1945.

JB80. "Cat," Coro 1945**
Manufacturer Coro, Inc.
Designer Adolph Katz.
Patent n° 140,608 Adolph Katz, Providence, R.I., 20th
March 1945, filed on 9th January 1945, assignor to
Coro, Inc., New York.

Gold-plated metal brooch of a cat with an arched back. Its
body is made of lucite, its legs and tail are rhinestone-studded,
its eyes are green stones and its whiskers are made of very fine
metal filaments inserted into a slot in the nose. 3.5x4.5cm.
    Marked Coro.
    The original model – reproduced in an advertisement pub-
lished in *Mademoiselle*, March 1945, with the slogan "Feline
Beauty by Coro" – has colored stones around the cat's neck, is made
of sterling and is marked CoroCraft. The brooch cost $22 plus taxes.
    The metal model, in both versions, with or without colored stones
around its neck, was probably manufactured in 1949, when Katz designed some new
Jelly Bellies and reused some previous designs.

JB81. "Small Swan," Coro 1945*
Manufacturer Coro Inc.
Designer Adolph Katz.
Patent n° 140,945 Adolph Katz, Providence, R.I.,
    24th April 1945, filed on 12th February 1945, as-
    signor to Coro, Inc., New York.

Gold-plated sterling brooch,
with lucite and rhinestones,
depicting a swan. 3.5x4cm.
    Marked Coro Sterling.

JB82. "Rabbit," Coro 1945**
Manufacturer Coro, Inc.
Designer Adolph Katz.
Patent n° 141,119 Adolph Katz, Providence, R.I.,
8th May 1945, filed on 20th February 1945, as-
signor to Coro, Inc., New York.

Gold-plated sterling pin clip, with lucite, green and
blue faceted stones and rhinestones. The brooch is of a
rabbit chewing on a twig. 3x4cm.
    Marked CoroCraft Sterling.
    This model is similar to Trifari's Jelly Belly "Rabbit,"
designed by Alfred Philippe on 2nd March 1943 (JB13.).

JB83. "Twinkling Twins," Coro 1944****
Manufacturer Coro, Inc.
Designer Adolph Katz.
Patent n° 137,511 Adolph Katz, Providence, R.I., 21st March 1944, filed on
12th February 1944, assignor to Coro, Inc., New York.
    The patent is for a single pin, which can be found on the market, and the
design was also used for the Duette brooches and earrings.

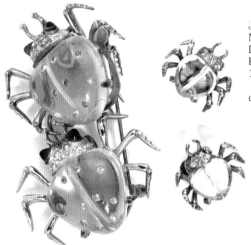

A set composed of Duette brooch and earrings, made of gold
plated sterling, lucite studded with rhinestones, green cabochons
and rhinestones, depicting scarabs. Duette 4x6.7cm; screwback
earrings 2cm.
    Marked Duette clip Coro Sterling. Sterling mechanism. Sterling
earrings. The pair of brooches appeared in an advertisement–
*Harper's Bazaar*, March 1944 – with the name "Twinkling Twins"
by Coro, priced $18 the pair. The advertisement also informs
readers that the brooches are made of sterling and real lucite.
    This is one of the first examples of rhinestone-studded lucite,
which is a trademark of Coro's Jelly Bellies.

JB84. "Spider," Coro 1945**
Manufacturer Coro, Inc.
Designer Adolph Katz.
Patent n° 141,637 Adolph Katz, Providence, R.I.,
19th June 1945, filed 29th March 1945, assignor to
Coro, Inc., New York.

    Gold-plated sterling brooch, rhinestone-studded lucite, red baguettes and rhinestones, depicting a spider. 4.5x4.5cm.
    Marked Coro Sterling.
    The brooch appeared together with other Jelly Belly models in an advertisement published in *Harper's Bazaar*, February 1945.

JB85. "Frog Duette," Coro 1944****
Manufacturer Coro, Inc., Toronto, Canada.
Designer Adolph Katz.
Patent n° 138,958 Adolph Katz, Providence, R.I.,
3rd October 1944, filed on 19th July 1944, assignor
to Coro Inc., New York.

    Gold-plated sterling Duette brooch with rhinestone-studded lucite, depicting two leaping frogs with rhinestones on their legs and faces, and protruding eyes made of green stones. 5.4x5.4cm.
    The mechanism was marked CORODUETTE Sterling Made in Canada. The clips were marked Coro Sterling.
    This item, as emphasized by the marking of the mechanism, was made by Coro Canada in the Toronto plant, and this also accounts for the mark on the clips, written in block letters, which is different from those used for the American products of those years.
    The model appeared, together with other Jelly Bellies, in an advertisement published in *Harper's Bazaar*, February 1945.

JB86 "Fighting Birds," Coro 1945****
Manufacturer Coro, Inc.
Designer Adolph Katz.
Patent n° 141,180 Adolph Katz, Providence, R.I.,
8th May, 1945, filed on 14th February 1945, as-
signor to Coro, Inc., New York.

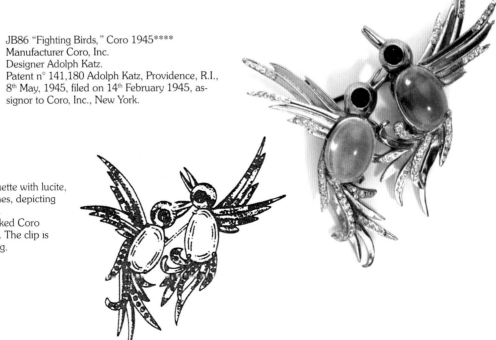

    Gold-plated sterling Duette with lucite, blue stones and rhinestones, depicting fighting birds. 6.5x6.5cm.
    The mechanism is marked Coro Duette Pat. No. 1798867. The clip is marked CoroCraft Sterling.

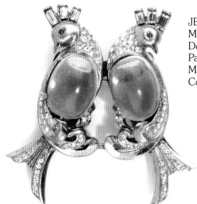

JB87. *"Lovebirds Duette,"* Coro 1945****
Manufacturer Coro, Inc.
Designer Adolph Katz.
Patent n° 141,120 Adolph Katz, Providence, R.I., 8th
May 1945, filed on 20th February 1945, assignor to
Coro, Inc., New York.

Gold-plated sterling Duette with lucite, baguettes and rhinestones representing a Pileated Woodpecker, a species of woodpecker. The name "Lovebirds" comes from the position of the birds, who are side by side and "in love". 5.5x5.2cm.
Mechanism marked Sterling. Clip marked Sterling CoroCraft.

JB88. *"Fish Duette,"* Coro 1944***
Manufacturer Coro, Inc.
Designer Adolph Katz.
Patent n° 139,405 Adolph Katz, Providence, R.I., 14th
November 1944, filed on 21st September 1944, assignor
to Coro, Inc., New York.

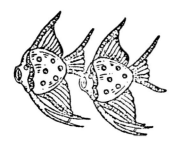

Gold-plated sterling Duette, with rhinestone-studded lucite, red and blue stones and rhinestones. The Duette depicts two fish. 5x6.5cm. The set also includes earrings shaped like miniature fish.
The mechanism is marked Coro Duette Sterling Pat. No. 1798867. The clip is marked Sterling. This item appeared with other Jelly Bellies in an advertisement published in *Harper's Bazaar*, February 1945. The trademark is CoroCraft with Pegasus.

JB89. "Strass Earrings," Coro 1945**
Manufacturer Coro, Inc.
Designer Adolph Katz.
Not patented.
   Gold-plated metal screwback earrings with rhinestone-studded lucite half-spheres. 2cm.
   Marked Coro. The earrings appeared together with other models of the CoroCraft line in an advertisement published in *Harper's Bazaar*, February 1945. The original model was made of sterling, whereas the metal version dates from the end of the 1940s. It is a universal model that can be matched to all Jelly Bellies with rhinestone-studded lucite.

JB90. "Fish Duette," Coro 1948****
Manufacturer Coro, Inc.
Designer Adolph Katz.
Patent n° 149,189 Adolph Katz, Providence, R.I., 6th April 1948, filed on 13th March 1947, assignor to Coro, Inc., New York.

   Gold-plated sterling Duette, lucite, red enamel, red and white rhinestones, depicting two fish. 3.8x6.5cm.
   Marked mechanism Coro Duette Sterling Pat. No. 1798867, clips Coro Sterling.

JB91. "Carp," Coro 1945****
Manufacturer Coro, Inc.
Designer Adolph Katz.
Patent n° 141,467 Adolph Katz, Providence, R.I. 5th June 1945, filed on 13th March 1945, assignor to Coro, Inc., New York.

   Gold-plated sterling and lucite brooch of a carp. Lucite body, a red stone for its eye, tail and nose ornamented with rhinestones. 4.8x8cm.
   Marked CoroCraft Sterling.

JB92. "Marlin," Coro 1945***
Manufacturer Coro, Inc.
Designer Adolph Katz.
Patent n° 141,470 Adolph Katz, Providence,
R.I., 5th June 1945, filed on 13th March 1945,
assignor to Coro, Inc., New York.

Gold-plated sterling and lucite brooch of a marlin. Lucite body, fins with marquise-cut blue stones, nose and tail with rhinestone pavé, small red stone for its eye. 5x5.5cm.
Marked Sterling CoroCraft.
This item featured together with the earrings with the same subject in a CoroCraft line advertisement with the slogan "Masterpieces of Fashion Jewelry" in *Vogue*, June 1945. The design was used again by Coro in 1949 – 50, when Katz designed some new Jelly Bellies and reused some of his older designs. The last model was made of gold-plated metal with pale yellow gilding, was slightly larger and had a less arched tail.

JB93. "Turtle Duette & Earrings," Coro 1945***
Manufacturer Coro, Inc.
Designer Adolph Katz.
Patent n° 141,073 Adolph Katz, Providence,
R.I., 1st May 1945, filed on 20th January 1945,
assignor to Coro, Inc., New York.

Gold-plated sterling Duette with rhinestone-studded lucite, small green stones and rhinestones, of a turtle. 4x6cm. Gold-plated metal earrings with rhinestones, each depicting a turtle. 2.3x1cm.
Mechanism marked Coro Duette Pat. No. 1798867. Clip marked Sterling.
Earrings marked Coro.
The Duette featured, together with other Jelly Bellies, in an advertisement of the CoroCraft line published in *Harper's Bazaar*, 20th February 1945.

JB94. "Fish," Coro 1950**
Manufacturer Coro, Inc.
Designer Adolph Katz.
Patent n° 158,755 Adolph Katz, Providence, R.I., 30th May 1950, filed on 2nd February 1950, assignor to Coro, Inc., New York.

Gold-plated metal and lucite brooch of a fish, with a lucite body inserted into a structure made of thin metal bars with black enamel. 4.5x4.8cm.
Marked Coro.

JB95. "Genie," Coro 1945****
Manufacturer Coro, Inc.
Designer Adolph Katz.
Patent n° 140,607 Adolph Katz, Providence, R.I., 20th March 1945, filed on 9th January 1945, assignor to Coro, Inc., New York.

Gold-plated sterling brooch , with lucite, enamel, red cabochons, drop-shaped blue stones and rhinestones. The brooch is of a crouching genie with a large lucite sphere between his legs. 5.7x4cm.
Marked CoroCraft Sterling.
This is the only known example of a Jelly Belly with a human subject, in the whole Coro and Trifari line. With the slogan "Enchantment by Coro," the brooch appeared in an advertisement in *Mademoiselle*, March 1945, with a sale price of $25 plus taxes. There is also a later version of this brooch, probably dating from 1949, made of gold-plated metal, in which the genie is holding a lucite bottle instead of a sphere. This version was advertised as "Ali Baba by Coro" with the indication that the bottle had been tested as a perfume container. The brooch sold for $11 plus taxes.

JB96. "Small Fish," Coro 1949*
Manufacturer Coro, Inc.
Designer Adolph Katz.
Patent n° 153,696 Adolph Katz, Providence, R.I., 10th May 1949, filed on 19th January 1949, assignor to Coro, Inc., New York.

Gold-plated metal brooch of a fish. Its body was made of rhinestone studded lucite, and its tail, fins and nose were ornamented with rhinestones, while its open mouth was made more evident with red enamel. 2.8x4cm.
Marked Coro.
The patent refers to two previous designs by Katz ("Angel Fish," JB72. and "Carp," JB91.) and to two designs by Alfred Philippe ("Fan Tail Fish," T103. and "Fish," T196.). Thereafter, reference was made to previously patented designs with the same theme, even though they were not identical to the patent subject. At first this use took place sporadically, but later became common practice. The "Fish" appeared together with other fish in a 1949 advertisement with the slogan "Sea Imps by Coro" and sold for about $5.
It is an interesting example of minor, late, cheap Jelly Belly production.

JB97. "Sea Horse," Leo Glass 1941*****
Manufacturer Leo Glass & Co.
Designer David Mir.
Not patented.
    Gold-plated and rhodium plated metal brooch, carved lucite, pink enamel and rhinestones, of a sea-horse on a sea anemone with a small coral tree. 8.5x6cm.
Marked Leo Glass (on a polygonal plate).
    *WWD*, March 14th 1941, presented Leo Glass's spring collection with the title: "Purple Jewelry; deep sea motifs" and wrote: "Among the newer pins designed by David Mir are a number in deep sea motifs".

JB98. "Pond Lily," Fred A. Block 1941*****
Manufacturer Sandor Goldberger for Fred A. Block Jewelry, Inc.
Designer Sandor Goldberger
Not patented
    Gold-plated metal and lucite brooch of a pond lily with lucite petals, pistils with small pink stones and a small enameled frog in the center. The frog is attached to a small spring to produce a tremblant effect. 9x9cm.
    Marked Fred A. Block Jewelry.
    This design is identical to one by Sandor, also made of lucite and gold-plated metal, which appeared in *Women's Wear Daily*, 21st March 1941. The only variant is represented by the center of the brooch which, in Sandor's version, consisted of faceted stones mounted on small springs to achieve a tremblant effect. It is therefore plausible that Sandor made part of Fred A. Block's production

JB99. "Snowman," Fred A. Block 1941*****
    Manufacturer Sandor Goldberger for Fred A. Block Jewelry, Inc.
    Designer Sandor Goldberger.
    Not patented.
    Gold-plated metal pin clip, lucite, lilac ceramic, yellow cabochons and rhinestones, depicting a snowman. 7.5x6.2cm.
    Marked Fred A. Block Jewelry.
    There are two versions of the same identical design, the one catalogued marked Fred A. Block, and the other marked Sandor. This confirms the fact that Fred A. Block had his jewelry designed and manufactured by Sandor Goldberger.

JB100. *"Ram Heads Set,"* Unsigned
1940-41*****
Manufacturer and designer unknown.

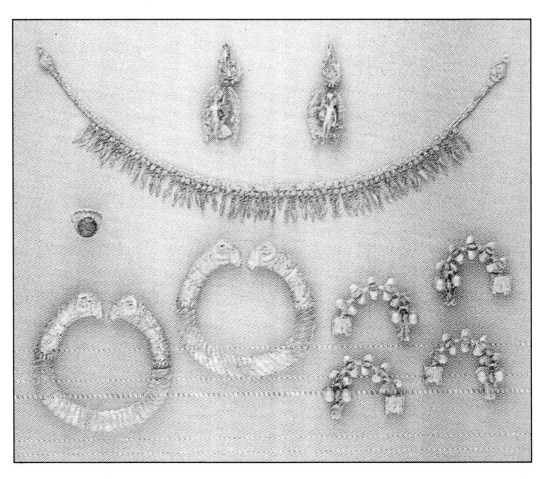

JB101. "Flowers," Unsigned
1941-42*****
Manufacturer and designer unknown.
   Gold-plated metal brooch, lucite, green
enamel and rhinestones, depicting two
flowers with leaves. 12x7.5cm.
   Unmarked.

**Opposite page, bottom:**
The Metropolitan Museum of Art Guide: "Ganymede's Jewels". Harris
Brisbane Dick Fund.

   Gold-plated metal and lucite brooch, bangle and earrings. Barrette
brooch with central part made of retorted lucite with two ram heads at the
extremities, 3x11cm. Round bangle open at the top made of retorted lucite
with two ram heads at the extremities. One of the ram heads has a spring
for the opening of the bangle; ram head motif size: 5cm. Gold-plated metal
clip earrings, each shaped like a ram head, 3cm.
   Model inspired by Hellenistic jewelry. The bangle in particular, is a
faithful copy of a couple of crystal rock bangles with golden ram protomes,
finely chiseled with motifs of leaves and fruit. The original Thracian or
Persian style bangles were discovered before 1913, in the Salonika area
and dated from 330-300 B.C approx.
   The Salonika treasure, known as the "Ganymede's group," also included
a necklace, two pairs of fibulae, a ring and a pair of earrings depicting
Ganymede's abduction, thus the set's name.
   After their discovery, these items appeared on the antique market and
were purchased by the German Von Gans family which, in 1921, sold
them to the Bachstitz gallery from where they were purchased by the Harris
Brisbane Dick Fund in 1937 for the Metropolitan Museum of New York,
where they still are today.
   The Salonika treasure was on display as early as 1938, as reported
in an article in the *Jewelers' Circular Keystone,* November 1938, which
included a picture of the treasure. Afterwards, on 20th November 1940, the
items were displayed in the "The Art of the Jeweler" exhibition, organized
by the Metropolitan Museum and dedicated to Egyptian, Mesopotamian,
Etruscan, Roman, Chinese, Indian and European jewelry art. It can be
reasonably conceived that the "Ram Heads" were exhibited at the same
time at this exhibition. According to *WWD,* 22nd August 1941, Ralph De
Rosa was inspired by the same exhibition for his own "Ram's Head" which
was part of his fall 1941 collection, and included brooches, bracelets and
earrings with ram heads. A few years later Nettie Rosenstein created a
faithful reproduction in a gold-plated sterling brooch (p. 21, *The Golden
Age of Design*, Joanne Dubbs Ball) of the design of the earrings depicting Ganymede being abducted by Zeus transformed into an eagle. The
Salonika treasure, including the bangles, was again displayed (1994-95)
in the itinerant exhibition "Greek Gold, Jewellery of the Classical World,"
organized in collaboration by the British Museum, the Hermitage and the
Metropolitan Museum. The entire Ganymede set was described in the
exhibition catalog, by Dyfri Williams and Jack Ogden and published by the
British Museum, on pages 74-79.

JB102. "Flower," Unsigned
1941-42****
Manufacturer and designer unknown.
   Gold-plated metal brooch, lucite,
red cabochon and rhinestones, in the
shape of a flower. 12x7.5cm.
   Unmarked.
   The item is sometimes incorrectly
attributed to Coro on the basis of "Jewels
of Fantasy," p. 178-179, however there is
no documented reference. On the contrary,
there is a matching necklace made of a
chain with three flowers attached, which is
also unsigned.

JB103. "Flower Spray," Unsigned 1944-45***
Manufacturer and designer unknown.
    Gold-plated sterling brooch, lucite, green stones and
rhinestones, in the shape of a flower spray. 7.5x6.5cm.
Marked Sterling.

JB104. "Rose," Unsigned 1944-45***
Manufacturer and designer unknown.
    Gold-plated sterling brooch, carved lucite,
red stones, in the shape of a rose. 7.8x5cm.
    Marked Sterling.

JB105. "Hand with Flower," Unsigned 1941*****
Manufacturer and designer unknown.
    Gold-plated metal brooch of a lucite hand with varnished
nails, holding an orchid with a pearl in the center. 11x8cm.
Unmarked.
    For the metal and enamel version *see* U41.

JB106. "Oyster Valve," Unsigned 1944-45**
Manufacturer and designer unknown.
   Gold-plated sterling brooch with carved lucite in
the shape of an oyster valve. 5.5x5.7cm.
   Marked Sterling.

JB107. "Acorns," Mazer 1941****
Manufacturer Mazer Bros., Inc.
   Designer unknown.
   Not patented.
      Gold-plated metal brooch, carved lucite
and rhinestones, of a branch with three
acorns. 9x6cm.
      Marked Mazer "K".

JB108. "Snail Shell," Unsigned 1944-45***
Manufacturer and designer unknown.
   Gold-plated sterling brooch and carved Lucite,
in the shape of a snail shell. 4.7x5cm.
   Marked Sterling.

JB109. "Pear," Unsigned 1944-45****
Manufacturer and designer unknown.
    Gold-plated sterling brooch of a pear. The fruit is
made of heavy contoured lucite, and the leaves are
made of gold-plated sterling with rhinestones. 7.3x5cm.
    Marked Sterling.

JB110. "Shell," Unsigned 1944-45**
Manufacturer and designer unknown.
    Gold-plated sterling brooch with carved Lucite, in the
shape of a shell. 5x6cm.
    Marked Sterling.

JB111. "Dolphin," Unsigned 1941***
Manufacturer and designer unknown.

*Mademoiselle*, September 1941: "Dolphin".

    Gold plated metal brooch, lucite and small pink coral
pearl, of a dolphin. 4.5x10cm.
    Unmarked.
    The item was advertised in *Mademoiselle*, September
1941, and was on sale at Bloomingdale's for $2.98.

JB112. "Angel Fish," Unsigned 1941-42***
Manufacturer and designer unknown.
    Gold-plated metal and lucite brooch of an angel fish, with oval lucite body studded with iridescent rhinestones and a pink iridescent stone for its eye. 6.5x8cm.
    Unmarked.

JB113. "Fishing Swan," Unsigned 1941-42***
Manufacturer and designer unknown.
    Gold-plated metal and lucite brooch of a swan, with a contoured lucite body, a small red stone for its eye, and a red enamelled fish in its bill. 5.5x7cm.
    Unmarked.

JB114. "Lobster," Unsigned 1941****
Manufacturer and designer unknown.
    Gold-plated metal brooch, with engraved lucite and small red cabochons, depicting a lobster with tremblant claws. 8x5.3cm.
    Unmarked.

JB115. "Penguin," Unsigned
1941-42***
Manufacturer and designer unknown.
Gold-plated metal brooch, lucite
and red cabochon, in the shape of a
penguin. 7.5x3cm.
Unmarked.

JB116. "Frog", Kreisler 1946****
Manufacturer Jacques Kreisler Manufacturing Co.
Designer William Diehl.
Patent n° 143,956 William Diehl, Summit, NJ., 26th
February 1946, filed on 6th October 1945, assignor to
Jacques Kreisler Manufacturing Corporation, North
Bergen, NJ.

Gold-plated sterling pin clip, lucite,
blue cabochons, rhinestones, in the
shape of a frog. 5.6x3.5cm.
Marked Sterling.

*Mademoiselle,* March 1945: "Leap Frog".

   Gold-plated sterling brooch, lucite and red
cabochons, in the shape of a frog. 6x6cm.
Marked Sterling.
   The brooch was reproduced in *Mademoiselle,* March 1945, under the name "Leap
Frog," and was on sale at Richter's, New York,
589 Fifth Avenue, for $5.95 plus tax. This
reproduction was made of marble turquoise
instead of lucite.

JB117. "Leap Frog," Unsigned 1945***
Manufacturer and designer unknown.

JB118. "Jumping Frog," Unsigned 1944-45***
Manufacturer and designer unknown.
   Gold-plated sterling brooch, lucite and green cabochons, in the shape of a frog. 5.5x6cm.
   Marked Sterling.

JB119. "Small leaping frog," Unsigned 1941*
Manufacturer and designer unknown.
   Gold-plated metal brooch with lucite, black enamel and two green cabochons, depicting a leaping frog. 2.5x3cm.
   Unmarked.

JB120. "Crab," Unsigned 1944-45****
Manufacturer and designer unknown.
   Gold-plated sterling and lucite brooch of a crab. 5.2x8cm.
   Marked Sterling.
   The "Crab" bears only the Sterling mark; however an identical brooch, belonging to a set with earrings, was manufactured by Karu (Kaufmann & Ruderman Co., Inc., 411 Fifth Avenue New York) and advertised with the name "The Crab" in *Mademoiselle*, June 1945.

JB121. "Carved Turtle", Unsigned 1941-42***
Manufacturer and designer unknown.
   Gold-plated metal brooch, carved lucite, enamel and red stones, in the shape of a turtle. 7x5cm.
   Unmarked.

JB122. "Dangling Earrings," Unsigned 1944-45***
Manufacturer and designer unknown.
  Gold-plated sterling earrings with rhinestone-studded lucite. 5cm.
  Marked Sterling.

JB123. "Flying Swan," Unsigned 1944-45**
Manufacturer and designer unknown.
  Gold-plated sterling brooch, lucite and red stone, depicting a swan in mid-flight. 6.5x5.2cm.
  Marked Sterling.

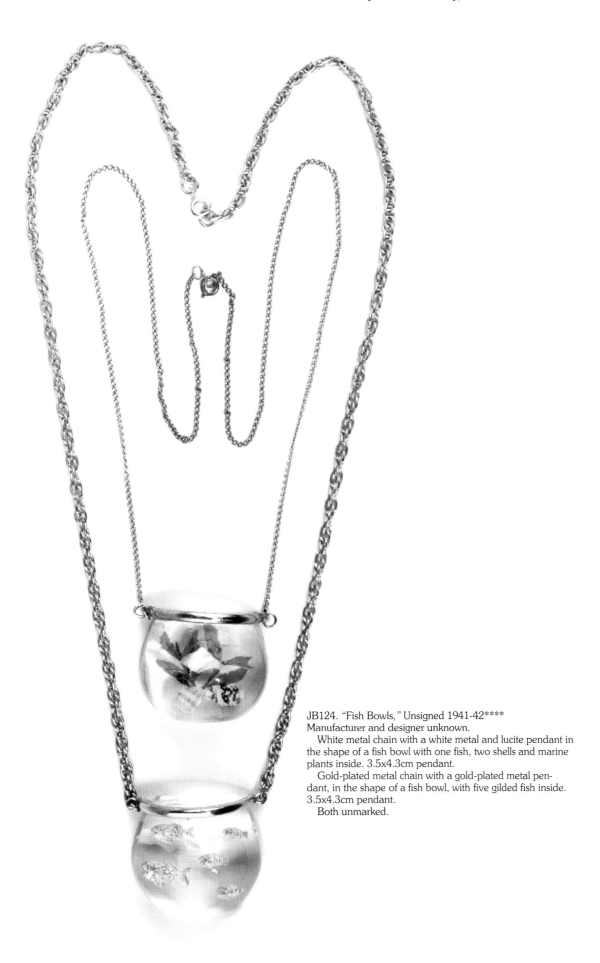

JB124. "Fish Bowls," Unsigned 1941-42****
Manufacturer and designer unknown.
    White metal chain with a white metal and lucite pendant in
the shape of a fish bowl with one fish, two shells and marine
plants inside. 3.5x4.3cm pendant.
    Gold-plated metal chain with a gold-plated metal pen-
dant, in the shape of a fish bowl, with five gilded fish inside.
3.5x4.3cm pendant.
    Both unmarked.

JB125. "Rooster," Unsigned 1944-45***
Manufacturer and designer unknown.
   Gold-plated sterling and lucite brooch of a
crowing rooster. 8.5x5cm.
   Marked Sterling.

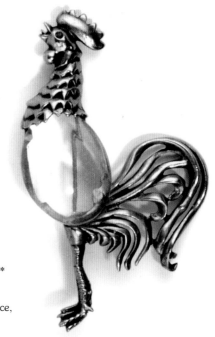

JB126. "Cat Fishing in a Bowl," Unsigned 1948*****
Manufacturer Anthony Creations Inc.
Designer Antonio Aquilino.
   Patent n° 149,925 Antonio Aquilino, Providence,
R.I., 15th January 1948, filed on 13th May
1946.

Gold-plated sterling brooch, with lucite, red carrè cut
stones and rhinestones. The brooch is of a cat trying
to fish a goldfish from its lucite bowl. The fish is
back-engraved in red in the lucite. 4.3x6.8cm.
   Marked Sterling.
   The patent registration date has been indicated as usual, however, due to both the amount
of time that elapsed between the application
and the registration of the patent, and the
use of sterling, it is possible that the brooch
was manufactured during the second half
of 1946.
   Antonio Aquilino, clearly of Italian descent,
albeit an American citizen, first worked for Coro and then
founded his own firm with the name of Anthony Creations Inc.
(Ball & Torem Masterpieces of Costume Jewelry, p. 71). According to Rainwater (American Jewelry Manufacturers, p. 27), the
president of Anthony Creations Inc. of Providence was Joseph
M. Aquilino, who was most probably one of Antonio's relatives.
   The company advertised on a national scale, using the slogan
"Originals by Anthony". In 1947, a brooch and earrings set
called "Cascade" appeared in an advertisement in Harper's
Bazaar. The design of these items was patented by Antonio Aq-
uilino on 8th April 1947 (des. n° 146,552, filed on 3rd May 1946).

JB127. "Fat Cat," Unsigned 1941-42***
Manufacturer and designer unknown.
   Gold-plated metal brooch of a seated cat with a round
lucite body and a long tail, and a red stone for its nose. The
cat has its eyes closed. 9 (tail included) x 4cm.
   Unmarked.

JB128. "Gazelle," Unsigned 1944-45****
Manufacturer and designer unknown.
    Gold-plated sterling brooch of a gazelle
with a lucite body and a green stone for
its eye. 4.5x9cm.
    Marked Sterling.

JB129. "Bassethound," Unsigned 1944-45***
Manufacturer and designer unknown.
    Gold-plated sterling brooch, with lucite and
red cabochon, depicting a dachshund. 7.5x4cm.
    Marked Sterling.

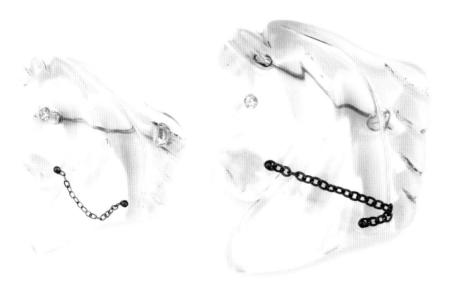

JB130. "Horse heads" Unsigned 1940-42***
Manufacturer and designer unknown.
    Pair of different sized lucite brooches, each
of a horse's head, with gold-plated metal
reins. 5.5x4.5cm and 4.5x4.5cm.
    Unmarked.

JB131. *"Unicorn,"* Unsigned 1944-45***
Manufacturer and designer unknown.
    Gold-plated sterling and lucite brooch of a unicorn head, with contoured and engraved lucite muzzle and neck, gold-plated sterling mane and a horn with rhinestones. 6.5x4.5cm.
    Marked Sterling.

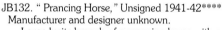

JB132. *" Prancing Horse,"* Unsigned 1941-42****
Manufacturer and designer unknown.
    Large lucite brooch of a prancing horse with a saddle, reins and stirrups made of gold-plated metal. 11x7cm. The brooch contains no metal structure except at the back, to which it is fastened only in three points – muzzle, saddle and tail –using the ornamental elements without any glue or staples. The design is made entirely of contoured lucite and the brooch is therefore different from the usual Jelly Bellies whereby the design is made of sterling or metal, and Lucite is only used as an ornamental center piece. A black plastic variant of this brooch also exists.

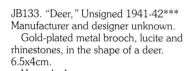

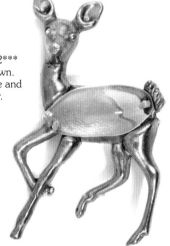

JB133. *"Deer,"* Unsigned 1941-42***
Manufacturer and designer unknown.
    Gold-plated metal brooch, lucite and rhinestones, in the shape of a deer. 6.5x4cm.
    Unmarked.

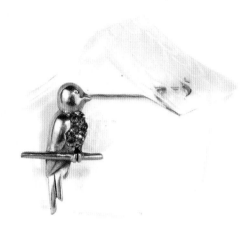

JB.134 "Birdhouse," Unsigned 1941*****
Manufacturer and designer unknown.
    Gold-plated metal brooch with lucite and blue rhinestones, depicting a lucite birdhouse with engravings, with a gold-plated metal bird perched beside it. 6.8x5.2cm.
    Unmarked.

JB135. "Bird on a branch," Unsigned 1940-42**
Manufacturer and designer unknown.
    Gold-plated metal brooch with lucite and rhinestones, depicting a lucite bird on a gold-plated metal branch, about to fly off. 7.5x7.5cm.
    Unmarked.

JB136. "Cricket," Unsigned 1941-42**
Manufacturer and designer unknown.
    Gold-plated metal brooch of a cricket, with an oval lucite cabochon for its body, red enameled antennae and black enameled legs. 5.5x3.5cm.
    Unmarked.

JB137. "Swallow," Unsigned 1941*****
Manufacturer and designer unknown.
    Gold-plated metal brooch with lucite,
rhinestones and a green cabochon, depicting
a swallow in flight. 11x7.1cm.
    Unmarked.
    Other enameled versions of this item exist,
in different colors.

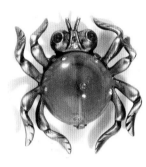

JB138. "Spider," Unsigned 1944-45***
Manufacturer and designer unknown.
    Gold-plated sterling brooch with rhinestone-studded lucite
and pink cabochons, shaped like a spider. 3x4cm.
    Marked Sterling.

JB139. "Rabbit," Norma 1944-45***
Manufacturer Norma Jewelry Corp., New York.
Designer unknown.
Not patented.
    Gold-plated sterling brooch, with lucite, red cabochon and rhinestones,
depicting a rabbit taking off his top hat in a sign of greeting and holding a cane
under its left paw. 5.3x4.1cm.
    Marked Norma Sterling Pat. Pend.
    Norma Jewelry Corp. was most probably set up in 1944, by Alfred Benjamin
Shawl who was the holder of three patents deposited on 19th July 1944 and
registered on 1st January and 19th June 1945 respectively. These designs were of
a "Water Girl" (Des. No. 140,147); an "Accordionist" (Des. No. 140,148) and a
"Cow Girl" (Des. No. 140,149). These items were made of gold-plated sterling
while the faces were made of colored Lucite. Male counterparts were created
of these designs but these were not patented. Shawl was also the holder of two
copyrights of 16th December 1952 for a "Jeweled Crown" brooch and of 27th
September 1954 for "Combination twisted link bracelet and choker," respectively.
After this date no further information is available about Norma Jewelry and it is
likely that the company folded by the end of the 1950s.

JB140. "Grandma Duck," Norma 1944-45**
Manufacturer Norma Jewelry Corp., New York.
Designer unknown.
Not patented.
    Gold-plated sterling brooch with Lucite, of a duck wearing a hat.
4.5x4.5cm.
    Marked Sterling.
    Another version marked Norma Sterling also exists.

JB141. "Duck," Norma 1944-45**
Manufacturer Norma Jewelry Corp., New York.
Designer unknown.
Not patented.
   Gold-plated sterling brooch with Lucite, of a duck with an umbrella. 4.5x2cm.
   Marked Norma Sterling Pat. Pend.
   Despite the mark "Patent Pending" this item was not patented.

JB142. "Hunting Dog," Norma 1944-45**
Manufacturer Norma Jewelry Corp., New York
Designer unknown
Not patented
Gold-plated sterling brooch and lucite, depicting a dog wearing a hunter's hat and holding a rifle. 4x4.5cm.
Marked Norma Sterling Pat. Pend.
Despite the mark "Patent Pending" this item was not patented.

JB143. "Little pig," Unsigned 1941*
Manufacturer and designer unknown.
Gold-plated metal brooch with lucite and two green cabochons, depicting a pig. 3.9x2cm.
Unmarked.

JB144. "Pig," Unsigned 1944-45***
Manufacturer and designer unknown.
   Gold-plated sterling and lucite brooch of a piglet with a corkscrew tail. The body is made of lucite and the ears are rhinestone-studded. 4x6.5cm.
   Marked Sterling.
   In the year between the fall of 1944 and the fall of 1945, partly due to the difficulty of finding sterling and possibly due to the success of Trifari and Coro's Jelly Belly lines, there was a good quality and plentiful production of animal sterling brooches with lucite bodies. Some manufacturers produced whole lines of animal brooches. Among them, Ben Felsenthal & Co., Inc., was the most important in terms of quantity and originality of designs. There are no elements allowing for specific attribution of these items to a given manufacturer. The technique used in the manufacturing and setting of lucite with prongs, allows only for the hypothesis that a group of brooches with similar features had been manufactured by the same company.

JB145. "Owl," Elzac 1945****
Manufacturer Elzac California Jewelry & Gift Ware.
Designer unknown.
Not patented.
   Gold-plated sterling brooch, carved lucite and green cabochons, depicting an owl on a branch. 6x4.2cm.
   Marked Sterling.

JB146. "Monkey," Unsigned 1944-45***
Manufacturer and designer unknown.
   Gold-plated sterling brooch, sky blue lucite, red stones and rhinestones, depicting a monkey. 6x5cm.
   Marked Sterling.

JB147. "Freshie," Elzac 1945***
Manufacturer Elzac California Jewelry & Gift Ware.
Designer unknown.
Not patented.

*"Freshie"*
(COPYRIGHTED)
THE COLLEGE BOY PENGUIN

He's a jaunty freshman that's lovable in his outlandish collegiate get-up. Sparkling blue rhinestone eyes, rakishly tilted cap, and large bow tie make him a devil with the co-eds. His glasses seem designed more to curry favor with the profs than serve as an aid to eyesight. He struts his stuff with a puffed out Plexiglas front—
— PLEXIGLAS BODY framed in HEAVY GOLD PLATED STERLING with RHINE STONE EYES—finished in exquisite detail —$4.50 each.

This is typical of the many clever jewelry creations in Elzac's new quality line to delight discriminating customers.

**Elzac**
California Jewelry & Gift Ware

NEW YORK: 047 Fifth Avenue (Jewelry)
LOS ANGELES: 607 South Hill Street
CHICAGO: 1512 Merchandise Mart
DETROIT: 206 East Grand River Avenue
ATLANTA: Chamber of Commerce Building
TORONTO, CANADA: 7 Wellington West
VANCOUVER, CANADA: 144 Water Street

*WWD*, November 9, 1945: "Freshie" by Elzac.

   Gold-plated sterling brooch, lucite and blue rhinestones eyes, depicting a penguin wearing a beret, bow tie and spectacles. 5.5x3.5cm.
   Marked Sterling.
   The item was reproduced in *WWD*, 9th November 1945, in an advertisement by Elzac, under the name "Freshie The College Boy Penguin" and was on sale for $4.50. A miniature version with a Plexiglas black body also exists. (*WWD*, 10th January 1947).

JB148. "Trembling Butterfly," Unsigned
1944-45****
Manufacturer and designer unknown.
Gold-plated sterling brooch, carved lucite
and rhinestones, represents a butterfly with
trembling wings. 8.5x5cm.
Marked Sterling.

JB149. "Fairy," Brody Designs, Inc.
1945*****
Manufacturer Brody Designs Inc.,
New York.
Designer unknown.
Not patented.

Using lucite, gold-plated sterling
and rhinestone Brody Designs,
Inc., introduces this ethereal figure with wings of lucite, body of
sterling, and headgear and wand
of rhinestone.

WWD, April 7, 1945: "Fairy" by Brody Designs Inc.

Gold-plated sterling brooch, with lucite and rhinestones, depicting
a flying fairy with lucite wings, holding a magic wand with a star at
the tip. 10.5x8cm.
Marked Sterling.
The fairy is described as one of the most interesting items of the
spring 1945 collection by Brody Designs Inc., and its picture was
published in WWD, 7th April 1945.

JB150. "Windmill," Unsigned 1944-45***
Manufacturer and designer unknown.
   Gold-plated sterling brooch, lucite, blue cabochon, in the shape of a windmill. 5.5x2.5cm.
   Marked Sterling.

JB151. "Banjo," Unsigned 1940-42***
Manufacturer and designer unknown.
   Brooch of a banjo with engraved black bakelite neck assembled to a round back-engraved box and gold plastic coated strings. 10x4cm.
   Unmarked.

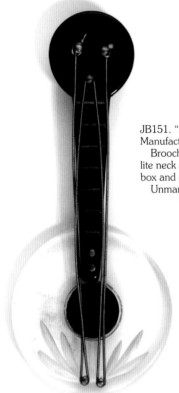

JB152. "Balalaika," Unsigned 1940-42***
Manufacturer and designer unknown.
   Lucite brooch of a balalaika with a black painted neck, back-engraved box and natural strings. 8.5x4.5cm.
   Unmarked.

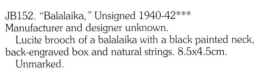
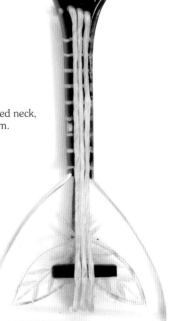

# PATRIOTIC JEWELRY

*Town & Country*, January 1943: Veronica Lake wearing a Lili Daché ermine beret and holding up a Josef bag which has 26 emblems from the Allied Nations pinned onto it.

World War I: Navy Recruiting Poster by Howard Chandler Christy

Patriotic jewelry is the name given to items that are inspired by symbols of the Nation. In the case of the US, these symbols include: The flag (Old Glory) and its colours, the Eagle, Uncle Sam's hat, the Liberty Bell, the Liberty Torch and – particularly during the war – emblems and badges of various military divisions, the V for Victory, and the so-called sentimental jewelry that reminded people of loved-ones who were at the front, such as "lockets" with photographs and "in-service pins." Jewelry can also be defined as being patriotic even when it is not directly symbolic but displays the patriotic colours of white, blue and red with enamel and stones.

Large-scale production of this type of jewelry began with the First World War, first in Europe and, from 1917 1918, in the United States. However, it reached its peak in quality and quantity during the Second World War. Since then, patriotic jewelry has been produced to be worn on special occasions, but mainly in difficult times such as during the Korean War, the Vietnam War, the Gulf War, and most recently, terrorist attacks. It is mainly low-cost jewelry, to be worn by everybody, although there are a number of precious items.

During the Second World War the items were initially made with gold-plated or rhodium-plated base metal, with stones or enamel. Then, after the second half of 1942, they were made with sterling or alternative materials such as Bakelite or Lucite, plastic, ceramic, wood, and cloth due to the rationing of base metals.

In the case of jewelry produced to support the Allied forces during the War (Great Britain, Belgium, France, Greece, etc.), a large proportion of profits were put back into the companies or public bodies that worked to this end. Among these it is appropriate to mention the British War Relief Society Inc. and the Bundles for Britain Inc., the American Committee for French War Relief, the Greek War Relief Society, and the Belgium War Relief Society.

All of the costume jewelry companies, from the most important, such as Coro, Trifari, Mazer, Eisenberg, Chanel/Reinad, Staret, Leo Glass, Sandor, and Ciner, to the less well-known such as Accessocraft, Albert Mfg. Co., Kaufmann & Ruderman (Karu), Rice-Weiner,

Silson, E.K.Wertheimer & Sons, and Bowman Foster & Wurzburger, produced patriotic jewelry.

Already on 10th February 1939 when *WWD* presented "Regimental Crests," which was probably the first collection by Sandor Goldberger, it noted that: "The war abroad is stimulating fashion interest in military themes, not only in Paris but here as well."

Nevertheless until America joined the War, the country was divided between two ideals, one which was against direct intervention by America in the conflict and one which was in favour of it. An example of this is seen in two cases where the American Eagle is represented; once as a symbol of peace without an olive branch and arrows, (s. PT5.) or just with olive branch (s. PSi23.). The other with an aggressive approach, in flight, depicted like an aeroplane with its claws outstretched (s. PT4. and PGP19.) or clutching a bundle of arrows between its claws as if they were a bomb. (s. PRW21.).

The American Eagle. Air Corps U.S Army poster.

The American Eagle. Civilian Defense poster.

On 14th June 1940 *WWD*, reported with reference to costume jewelry: "Wave of Patriotism brings sudden demand for American Flag Lapel Pins, Patriotic Jewelry" and continued "within the past 10 days a new lapel pin has suddenly become one of the biggest wholesale sellers, with buyers clamoring for supplies and manufacturers rapidly developing new designs. This is the Flag lapel pin – the American flag in particular, but the British and French flags as well. Manufacturers say consumers started this demand, which originated with the recent acute turn of events in the European war and the consequent wave of patriotism sweeping this country. This same demand developed during the 1917-1918 period, when many jewelry houses worked day and night shifts to supply the market with such pins. The forerunner of this interest was the French cockade lapel pin clip (s. PSi 26.) which during the past month has sold in enormous quantities over the country. Retailing for $3.50, it is sponsored by the American Friends of France, who get a percentage of the returns. A survey of New York shops indicates that these pins are retailing chiefly at $1, $1.95, $2.95, and $ 3.95. The shops report that other patriotic jewelry is selling too, such as the gold-finished "God bless America" bracelet, retailing for $1, and red-white and blue enamel and rhinestone bowknots. Both buyers and manufacturers expect a new spurt of interest in all jewelry in red-white-blue combinations, with a carry over of the patriotic theme into fall sales."

Remember Pearl Harbor: "Avenge December 7," poster by Perlin Bernard, 1942.

The home front: "Rosie the Riveter" wears proudly her production award "E" and keeps her feet on Hitler's "Mein Kampf". *The Saturday Evening Post* cover. Norman Rockwell, 1943 © Curtis Publishing Co.

After the Japanese attack on Pearl Harbor on 7th December 1941 and America's subsequent entry into war, nobody spoke about isolationism anymore and the whole nation concentrated on helping with the War effort. Women took on an important role, especially in substituting on the so-called "Home front," in fields, factories and in other civil work, for men who were at war. Propaganda posters displayed announcements such as "Rosie the Riveter" and "Jenny on the job," which were symbols of working women, and the affirmative message that "We can do it" or, for those who were more hesitant, "Longing won't bring him back sooner... GET A WAR JOB!"

The home front: "Rosie to the Rescue." *The Saturday Evening Post* cover. Norman Rockwell 1943 © Curtis Publishing Co.

"Willie Gillis in Blackout." *The Saturday Evening Post* cover. Norman Rockwell 1942 © Curtis Publishing Co.

The home front: "Jenny on the Job," poster by Kula, 1944.

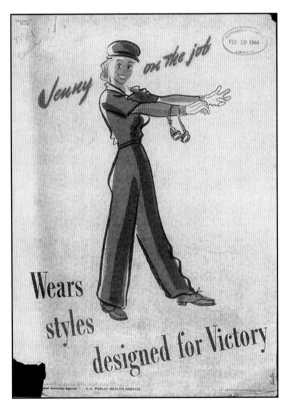

The home front: "Jenny on the Job," poster by Kula, 1944.

The home front: "We can do it!" Poster by J. Howard Miller, 1943.

World War II: "Get a war job!" Poster for the U.S. Employment Service by Lawrence Wilbur, 1944.

Another national heroine was "Commando Mary," who did for the Armed Services wha Rosie the Riveter did for the defense industry.

World War two: "Commando Mary," WAAC (Women's Army Auxiliary Corps) recruiting poster, 1943.

In addition to working in factories, many American women also joined the armed services. They worked in supply areas as well as in the more traditional nursing corps: Women Air force Service Pilots (WASP), Women's Army Auxiliary Corps (WAAC), WAVES (Navy), Marine Corps Women's Reserve (MCWR), SPARS (Semper paratus - always ready, the motto of the coast guard), the Army Nurse Corps (ANC) and Navy Nurse Corps (NNC).

World War II: Wave and Spar. Recruiting poster by McClelland Barclay, 1942.

World War II: MCWR (Marine Corps Women Reserve). Recruiting poster by McClelland Barclay, 1942.

World War II: "Join the Waves." Design for a recruiting poster by McClelland Barclay.

Women at home were proud of wearing patriotic jewelry on their overcoats, coat collars and blouses. A particular comment was made with reference to the "Remember Pearl Harbour" brooches in *WWD* on 23rd January 1942:

Starting early in December, stores displayed renewed interest in collections of authentic military and naval emblem jewelry. In general, aside from individual promotion pieces such as the various "Remember Pearl Harbour" pins and a few flag pieces, *WWD* has noticed a reaction from some sources that as yet no manufacturer of jewelry has produced a patriotic pin which has had the immediate appeal of certain of the propaganda emblems. The British War Relief shield (s. PAC37.) is a particularly outstanding instance of the pin, which, it must be admitted, sold as much for the charm of the design as for the charity behind it. The torch of liberty emblem of Fight for Freedom (PSt 14.) is another such example.

Many women do not care to wear a flag: some feel it cheapens the emblems, others want a little more distinction. There seems to be a definite place for some emblem motif, signifying the American spirit. Which has a charming design and colour, a moderate size, and jet a little individuality. The current success of identification jewelry (recent retail advertising devoted space by no less than five important New York stores in one newspaper to such pieces) has a basic foundation. It is a wartime interpretation of the monogram fashion - women love to identify their personality - and the identification jewelry responds to this psychology while at the same time recognising precaution of wartime.

World War II: "Be a Cadet Nurse." Recruiting poster for the Cadet Nurse corps by John Withcomb, 1944.

PT1. "Sailor," Trifari 1942*****
Manufacturer Trifari, Krussman & Fishel.
Designer Alfred Spaney.
Patent n° 131,246 Alfred Spaney, New
York, 27th January 1942, filed on 23rd
December 1941.

Rhodium-plated metal brooch, white, pink,
black, blue and red enamel, depicting a sailor
who is walking, holding a world map in his
left hand, where The Americas can be seen.
6x4.5cm.
Marked Trifari.

PC2. "Emblem of the Americas," Coro 1941**
Manufacturer Cohn & Rosenberger, Inc.
Designer Lester Gaba.
Patent n° 130,836 Lester Gaba, New York, 23rd
December 1941, filed on 17th November 1941,
assignor to Cohn & Rosenberger, Inc.

Gold-plated metal brooch with various color
enamel depicting the 21 flags of the Union
of American Republics. The flagpoles are
wrapped in a white enamel painted ribbon
with "Amigos Siempre" written on it. The US
flag is in the middle, and from left to right, in
alphabetical order, are the flags of Argentina,
Brazil, Bolivia, Chile, Colombia, Costa Rica,
Cuba, The Dominican Republic, Ecuador,
Guatemala, Haiti, Honduras, Mexico, Nica-
ragua, Panama, Paraguay, Peru, Salvador,
Uruguay and Venezuela. These form the 21
nations that founded the Union, which was
reaffirmed at the conference of Lima in 1938.
6.5x6cm.
Marked Coro Pat. No. 130836.
As reported in *Women's Wear Daily* of 23rd
January 1942, this brooch was designed as a
symbol of the unity of the western hemisphere
and exhibits the flags of all 21 American
Republics. The initiative was promoted by
"Ladies' Home Journal" which chose Lester
Gaba to be the designer and Coro to be the
manufacturer. The royalties (the brooch was
on sale for $3,95) went to the Interamerican
Scholarship Fund, an organization which
was founded to promote student exchanges
between American countries. The brooch was
presented for the first time, in New York that
very same day, 23rd January, and in Washington on 26th January during a luncheon
especially organized for the occasion. The First
Lady, Mrs. Eleanor Roosevelt, who probably
backed the initiative, wore the brooch in support of the fund. The brooch was presented
by "Ladies' Home Journal" in February 1942
under the name "Emblem of the Americas".

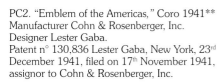

Lester Gaba. Photo by Frederick Bradley from Weekly Magazine Section, November 27, 1935.

Lester Gaba, designer, sculptor and window-dresser,
was born in Hannibal, Missouri, in 1907 and started his
career in the 1920's by making sculptures made of soap.
These were figurines and miniatures so impressive that
they were used in advertising campaigns, photographed
for book covers and Christmas cards, exhibited in store
windows and museums and shown at the 1933-34
Chicago World Fair. In the 1930s he started to create
window-display mannequins, which at the time were
heavy sculptures made of plaster. One of these mannequins was a female figure that Gaba named Cynthia and
which he always took with him to parties despite the fact
that five men were needed to carry her, given that the sculp-
ture weighed more than 100lbs. One day, at a party, Cynthia
fell over and smashed into pieces.

Mannequins by Lester Gaba. Photo by Frederick Bradley from Weekly Magazine Section, November 27, 1935.

As a jewelry designer, in 1938 Gaba worked for Albert Mfg. Co. which belonged to Albert Weiner. While working for this company, he designed a series of small rhinestone pavé brooches called "Yankee Doodlers" (s. AM1. AM2). In 1939 Gaba designed for Albert Mfg. Co. a series called "Alice in Wonderland," which was presented by Altman. Gaba worked with Coro again in 1948 preparing a large presentation of Duettes.

PT3. "Newspaper man," Trifari 1942*****
Manufacturer Trifari, Krussman & Fishel.
Designer Alfred Spaney.
Patent n° 131,248 Alfred Spaney, New York, 27th January 1942, filed on 23rd December 1941.

Rhodium-plated metal brooch, black, white, blue and red enamel and rhinestones, depicting a black American newspaperman holding a pile of newspapers. The man is running and holding up a newspaper showing the front-page headlines with a red V for victory on it. 5.3 x 5.3cm.
Marked Trifari Des. Pat. No. 131248.

Rhodium-plated metal brooch, red and blue enamel, rhinestones, depicting the American Eagle in flight and diving like a fighter plane. 2.5x10cm.
Marked Trifari Pat. Pend.

PT4. "Flying Eagle," Trifari 1941**
Manufacturer Trifari, Krussman & Fishel.
Designer Alfred Philippe.
Patent n° 126,799 Alfred Philippe, New York, 22nd April 1941, filed on 19th March 1941.

PT5. "American Eagle," Trifari 1940****
Manufacturer Trifari, Krussman & Fishel.
Designer Alfred Philippe.
Patent n° 122,220 Alfred Philippe, New York,
27th August 1940, filed on 26th July 1940.

Gold-plated metal brooch, large
blue centre stone, rhinestones and red
and white baguettes, depicting the
American Eagle with spread wings.
4.5x4.5cm.
Marked Trifari.

PT6. "Twin Birds," Trifari 1942****
Manufacturer Trifari, Krussman & Fishel.
Designer Alfred Philippe.
Patent n° 131,235 Alfred Philippe, New York, 27th
January 1942, filed on 17th December 1941.

Rhodium-plated metal brooch, red and blue enamel, depicting two birds in flight together. Their heads are made from
cabochons: one is red, the other blue, with a little rhinestone
set in the center, while their beaks are yellow enamel. The tip
of their wings and tails are red and blue enamel with a pavé
rhinestone border. 5x6cm.
Marked Trifari Pat. Pend.
This is a classic example of patriotic jewelry, not because of
the subject matter but due to the choice of colors used which
are those of the American flag.

PT7. "Flying Bird, Trifari 1941**
Manufacturer Trifari, Krussman & Fishel.
Designer Alfred Philippe.
Patent n° 125,819 Alfred Philippe, New York, 11th
March 1941, filed on 6th February 1941.

Rhodium-plated metal pin clip, red and
blue enamel, rhinestones, cabochons and
baguettes, depicting a bird with outspread
wings. 5x5.6cm.
Marked Trifari Des. Pat. No. 125819.

PT8. "Faith, Hope, Charity," Trifari 1940*
Manufacturer Trifari, Krussman & Fishel.
Designer Alfred Philippe.
Patent n° 121,821 Alfred Philippe, New York,
6th August 1940, filed on 29th June 1940.

Gold-plated metal brooch, red and blue enamel and rhinestones, depicting an anchor with 'Faith, Hope, Charity' written on it and two circles with respectively a cross on red enamel and a heart on blue enamel in the middle. 3.8x3cm.
Marked Trifari Pat. Pend.
The colors red, white and blue have both a patriotic and a religious meaning. The former because they are the colors of the flag and red indicates courage, white hope and blue pureness of aim. The religious connotations derive from the fact that red represents faith, white hope and blue charity. Moreover the anchor symbolizes hope, the heart charity and the cross faith.

PT9. "Lion of Victory," Trifari 1941**
Manufacturer Trifari, Krussman & Fishel.
Designer Alfred Philippe.
Patent n° 129,440 Alfred Philippe, New York, 9th
September 1941, filed on 29th January 1941.

Rhodium-plated metal brooch, rhinestones, blue stones and red baguettes in the shape of a V for Victory with the British Lion in the centre. 5x3.5cm.
Marked Trifari Pat. Pend.
This brooch probably celebrates the Victory of the British in the Battle of Britain (a series of air-force operations took place from August to October 1940, in the skies over England, between German aviation troops who had 3000 airplanes at their disposal and the British Air-Force which had only one thousand fighter planes). Germany consequently withdrew its troops and gave up plans to invade British territory.
There were two other brooches patented in the same period. One with a stemma representing both the American and British flags that featured both the American Eagle and the British Lion (PT10). The other is the same as the one catalogued here, with the eagle's head placed in the centre of the V but replacing the Lion.

PT10. "Allies," Trifari 1941***
Manufacturer Trifari, Krussman & Fishel.
Designer Alfred Philippe.
Patent n° 129,314 Alfred Philippe, New York, 2nd
September 1941, filed on 25th July 1941.

Gold-plated metal brooch with red, blue and white enamel and rhinestones, depicting the American eagle and the British lion facing each other over their respective flags. 4.5x4.9cm.
Marked Trifari Pat. Pend.
The brooch emphasized the alliance between the United States and Great Britain at a time when the United Kingdom was under attack from Germany, which culminated in the so-called "Battle of Britain" between the "Luftwaffe" and the "RAF" (PT9.).
A brooch depicting the lion alone, without the flag also exists.

PB11. *"Sailors,"* Boucher 1942****
Manufacturer Marcel Boucher Ltd.
Designer Marcel Boucher.
  Not patented. Marcel Boucher had designed and patented a brooch depicting a sailor who is leaning on a hatchway, which was similar both in design and materials used (PB12.).
  Rhodium-plated metal brooch, black enamel, rhinestones and white pearls, depicting the back of two sailors walking together. 5.5x3.8cm.
  Marked MB.
  There was a very similar brooch reproduced in 'Life', 18th November 1940, and in 'Glamour', March 1941, without any indication of a mark.

PB12. *"Sailor in a Hatch,"* Boucher 1942****
Manufacturer Marcel Boucher Ltd.
Designer Marcel Boucher.
Patent n° 131,416 Marcel Boucher, New York, 17th February 1942, filed on 12th January 1942.

  Two-toned gold and rhodium plated pin clip with rhinestones and a pearl, depicting a sailor emerging from a hatch. 6x4.5cm.
  Marked Pat. Pend. B.

PLG13. *"Anchors Away!,"* Leo Glass 1941****
  Manufacturer Leo Glass & Co.
  Designer Anne Glass.
  Patent n° 124,817 Anne Glass, New York, 28th January 1941, filed 16th December 1940.

  Rhodium plated metal brooch with red, blue, white and black enamel, a pearl for the face and rhinestones, depicting a sailor standing on an anchor. 5.5x4cm.
  Marked Leo Glass.

PSt14. *"Remember Pearl Harbor,"* Staret 1942\*\*\*\*\*
Manufacturer Staret Jewelry Co., Inc.
Not patented.
 Gold-plated metal brooch, red, white and blue enamel, rhinestones, red and blue stones, with a white pearl in the center, depicting an American Eagle with "Remember Pearl Harbor" written on it, the pearl substitutes the word 'pearl'. 6.2x6.7cm.
 Marked Staret.
 Brooches such as this one swept the market after the Japanese attack on Pearl Harbor Naval Base in Hawaii on December 7th 1941. Sometimes the inscription is complete; sometimes the word 'pearl' is substituted by a pearl. Among the most significant designs are one by Adolph Katz for Coro which depicts the battleship Arizona with 'Remember Pearl Harbor' written on the bow (Des. 131,769, 24th March 1942) and one by Walter Lampl for Walter Lampl Inc. (PWL18.).

The Liberty Torch. Poster 1942.

 Metal base brooch, pink, red and violet enamel, rhinestone pavé and blue stones, depicting a woman's hand holding a lit torch, which is similar to that of the Statue of Liberty. 11x3.5cm.
 Marked Staret.

PSt15. *"Liberty Torch,"* Staret 1942\*\*\*\*\*
Manufacturer Staret Jewelry Co., Inc.
Not patented.

PSt16. *"Thanksgiving Turkey,"* Staret 1941\*\*\*\*\*
Manufacturer Staret Jewelry Co., Inc.
Not Patented.
 Metal base brooch, red and black enamel, rhinestones, red and blue stones, of a turkey. 6x6.5cm.
 Marked Staret.

PU17. "Remember Pearl Harbor," Unsigned 1942****
Manufacturer and designer unknown.
  Rhodium-plated metal brooch, blue and green enamel, depicts
Pearl Harbor bay with two palm trees on each side, the anchored
battleship Arizona and a Japanese fighter 'Zero' that is diving
downwards, Remember Pearl Harbor 12-7-41 is inscribed on
the base. 5.5x6.5cm.
  Unmarked.
  The brooch was promoted by the Honolulu Community Chest
in order to raise funds. There is also a gold-plated version.

PWL18. "Remember Pearl Harbor," Lampl 1942****
Manufacturer Walter Lampl.
Designer Walter Lampl.
Patent n° 131,401 Walter Lampl, New York, 10th February 1942, filed on 29th December 1941.

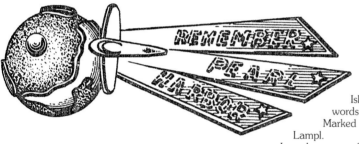

Gold-plated metal brooch with blue, white and red enamel, depicting
the globe with, at the center, a cultured pearl standing out on the blue
enamel of the Pacific Ocean with the Hawaii Islands made of gold-
plated metal. A Japanese "Zero" fighter plane hovers over the Hawaii
Islands. Three flames coming from the globe are surmounted by the
words REMEMBER PEARL HARBOR. 7.6x2.6cm.
  Marked For Aid To The Honolulu Community Chest Des. Pat. App. For By
Lampl.
  Lampl was one of the first to apply for a patent for a Remember Pearl Harbor brooch,
which he intensively promoted nationwide with an advertisement showing a woman wearing it. The
advertisement was published in five hundred national papers. Sixty-five radio stations broadcasted infor-
mation on this item, which was also advertised in *Mademoiselle*, March 1942 and presented in editorial
articles by "Harper's Bazar," *Vogue, Glamour*, "Esquire" and "Bride Magazine".
  The brooch was on sale for $ 1 and 10% of the proceeds was earmarked for the "Pearl Harbor Relief
Fund," at the Honolulu Community Chest. In the month of January 1942 alone, Lampl paid a contribu-
tion of $ 1630.80 into the fund which means that it sold 16,380 brooches in one month.
  Lampl also made patriotic jewelry for the British War Relief Fund which received 40% of the wholesale
price. *WWD*, 5th May 1941, mentions a brooch representing the British lion and a series of charms, including one shaped like a box that could be opened to reveal a fine silk English flag. On the box lid was written "Britain Can Take It". Another heart-shaped charm had the words "My Heart Belongs to England".

Rhodium-plated metal brooch with
rhinestone pavé, depicting an eagle in
flight. 6.7x6.7cm.
  Unmarked.
  No other information about
Goldstein-Poland is available.

PGP19. "Eagle," Unsigned 1941**
Manufacturer Goldstein-Poland Co., Inc.
Designer James J. Poland.
Patent n° 126,635 James J. Poland, Providence, R.I., assignor
to Goldstein-Poland Co., Inc., Providence, R.I., a corporation
of Rhode Island, 15th April 1941, filed on 8th February 1941.

PCh20. *"Old Glory,"* Chanel 1941 *****
Manufacturer Chanel Novelty Co.
   Gold-plated metal brooch, white and
red stones, blue rhinestones, depicting the
American flag. 5.5x5cm.
   Marked *Chanel*.

PRW21. *"American Eagle,"* Rice-Weiner 1940**
Manufacturer Rice-Weiner & Co., Providence,
Rhode Island.
Designer Louis C. Mark.
Patent n° 121,913 Louis C. Mark, Providence, R.I.,
13th August 1940, filed on 26th June 1940, assignor
to Rice-Weiner & Co., Providence, R.I.

   Silver-plated metal brooch of the American Eagle
in an aggressive position with a bundle of arrows
like a bomb held within its claws. The notches and
the tips of the arrows are enameled in the patriotic
colors. 6.5x6.5cm.
   Unmarked.
   This is the first design patented by Louis Mark.
The item was described by *WWD*, 21st June 1940,
where it specified that it came either in
white metal or gold-plated metal.

*Mademoiselle,* September 1941.

   Gold-plated and white metal brooch, in the shape of
overlapping wings. 3.8x12cm.
   Marked Barclay©
   The brooch was published in *Mademoiselle*, September 1941, where it specifies that it was made in various
different sizes. The catalogued brooch is the biggest and
was on sale for $3.

*Fashion Takes to Wings*

DESIGNED
BY
McCLELLAND BARCLAY

   With a flair for the air, America's
leading illustrator creates in metal a
smartly new, winged motif for costume jewelry to streamline your fall
wardrobe.
   Barclay's newest creations—wings of
gold and silver plate—reach a new
high in jewelry designed exclusively
for Rice-Weiner.
   The enchanting pin, pictured here,
retails at $2.00, a larger size, $3.00;
clips, $3.00 a pair; earrings, $2.00,
bracelet, $3.00. Comes also in a
combination of pale pink and pale
green gold. Ask for Barclay jewelry
at leading stores everywhere.

RICE-WEINER & COMPANY
*Makers of America's Beauty Fashion Jewelry*
366 Fifth Avenue                New York, N.Y.

PRW22. *"Wings,"* Rice-Weiner 1941*****
Manufacturer Rice-Weiner & Co., Providence, Rhode Island.
Designer McClelland Barclay.
Not Patented.

PSi23. "American Eagle," Silson 1940***
Manufacturer Silson Inc.
Designer Victor Silson.
Patent n° 121,403 Victor Silson, New York, 9th July 1940, filed on 8th June 1940.

Gold-plated metal brooch, red, white and blue enamel, depicting the American Eagle perched on an olive branch which is wrapped in a ribbon that symbolizes the flag. 5.5x7.8cm.
Marked Silson PAT.PEND.
The ribbon flag-print and the olive branch are also patented separately. (Des. 121,402).

PSi24. "American Cockade," Silson 1940***
Manufacturer Silson Inc., New York.
Designer Victor Silson.
Patent n° 121,352 Victor Silson, New York, 2nd July 1940, filed on 4th June 1940.

Gold-plated metal pin clip with red, white and blue enamel, shaped like a cockade with the colors and stars of the American flag. 6x4cm.
Marked Silson Pat. Pend.
The center of the cockade was patented as a pin clip (des. n° 121,734 of 30th July 1940).

Gold-plated pin clip and earrings, white, blue and red enamel, in the shape of a shield with the symbols of the British and American Ambulance Corps, the British Crown and flag, and an anchor with two wings. Brooch 5.5x5.2cm, earrings. 2.5x2.5cm.
Marked Silson PAT.D. 122211.
The brooch was made in order to contribute to the financing of the Ambulance Corps who were in charge of rescuing the injured, and was published on the cover of *Town & Country*, January 1943, with Veronica Lake, wearing a Lily Daché ermine beret and holding up a Josef bag (not to be confused with Joseff, the jewelry designer) on which are pinned 26 emblems from the Allied Nations.

PSi25. "British and American Ambulance Corps," Silson 1940***
Manufacturer Silson Inc.
Designer Victor Silson.
Patent n° 122,211 Victor Silson, New York, 27th August 1940, filed on 27th July 1940.

PSi26. "French Cockade," Silson 1940***
Manufacturer Silson Inc.
Designer Victor Silson.
Patent n° 120,967 Victor Silson, New York, 4th June 1940, filed on 3rd May 1940.

Gold-plated metal brooch, white, red and blue enamel, in the shape of a cockade with the colors of the French flag and three ribbons with the motto "Liberté Egalité Fraternité" written on them. 7x4.3cm.
Marked Silson Pat. 120967.
*WWD*, June 14th 1940, referred to this brooch as "the French Cockade lapel pin which during the past month has sold in enormous quantities over the country". It was promoted by the Americas Friends of France, which received some of the profits. The brooch was also advertised in Vogue and it cost $3.95.

PSi27. "R.A.F. Pin," Silson 1941***
Manufacturer Silson Inc.
Designer Victor Silson.
Patent n° 125,294 Victor Silson, New York, 18th February 1941, filed on 28th December 1940.

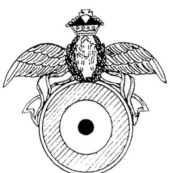

Gold-plated metal brooch, white, red and blue enamel, with the R.A.F. emblem over a circle that is a target, with the colors of the British flag. 4x4cm.
Marked Silson.
According to *WWD*, 7th March 1941, this brooch, depicted as a gentleman's lapel button in this article, and another similar one (Des. 125,293) were made and sold to support the British-American Ambulance Corps.

PSi28. "Long Live Belgium," Silson 1940****
Manufacturer Silson Inc.
Designer Victor Silson.
Earrings: Patent n° 121,341 Victor Silson, New York, 2nd July 1940, filed on 29th May 1940.
Pin: Patent n° 121,640 Victor Silson, New York, 23rd July 1940, filed on 20th June 1940.

Gold-plated metal pin clip and earrings, red, yellow and black enamel. The earrings are in the shape of ribbons. The brooch depicts a lion, the symbol of Belgium, which is standing on a ribbon with 'Long Live Belgium' written on it. It has the Belgian flag, which is black, yellow and red. Earrings: 2.5x1.5cm, pin clip: 9.3x4cm.
Marked Silson PAT.D 93186 (application number).
The earrings are unmarked.

PSi29. "Young Women's Christian Association," Silson 1940***
Manufacturer Silson Inc.
Designer Victor Silson.
Patent n° 124,395 Victor Silson, New York, 31st December 1940, filed on 27th November 1940.

Gold-plated metal brooch, white and blue enamel, depicting the emblem of the association; an upside-down triangle, repeated three times, linked together by a ribbon with a bow. 4.5x4.8cm.
Marked Silson PAT.PEND. YWCA.

The Young Women's Christian Association is a Christian organization whose mission is "to advance the physical, social, intellectual, moral and spiritual interest of young women". This motto is symbolized in its insignia, a blue triangle whose three sides stand for body, mind and spirit. The first YWCA was founded in England in 1855 by Lady Kinnaird. In the US the first group was organized in New York in 1858 by Mrs. Marshal O. Roberts. Another group, the first to officially call themselves YWCA, was founded in Boston in 1866. In 1906 the National Association of YWCA in the US was founded with its head office held in New York from 1912 and, in 1894, the World YWCA was established, with its headquarters in Geneva, Switzerland. During the Second World War, the YWCA along with the Young Men's Christian Association (YMCA) and other organizations, formed united service organizations for recreation and welfare activities. The association was in charge of assisting Japanese-American women who were kept at so-called relocation centers. Today the association has about two million members.

PSi30. "A.F.O.B.," Silson 1940****
Manufacturer Silson Inc.
Designer Howard Chandler Christy.
Not Patented.

Gold-plated metal brooch, red, white and blue enamel, depicting the American stemma with two hands locked in a hand-shake surmounted by the British Lion and the American Eagle which have an olive branch between them. At the base are the initials A.F.O.B. (Allied Forces of Britain?). 3x4.5cm.
Marked Silson Designed by Howard Chandler Christy.

Howard Chandler Christy.

Howard Chandler Christy ca. 1935: "Self- portrait with Model".

World War I. Howard Chandler Christy: recruiting poster for the Navy 1917.

Howard Chandler Christy (1873-1952) was a famous illustrator and painter. He was born in Duncan Falls, Ohio, to Francis Marion Christy and Mary Matilda Chandler. As an illustrator he designed books and magazine covers and also patriotic posters. As a painter he was famous for his portraits of movie stars and of other important figures of the time such as Benito Mussolini, Umberto the prince of Italy, the presidents of the United States, Franklin D. Roosevelt, Calvin Coolidge, Herbert C. Hoover, James Knox Polk, Martin Van Buren and James A. Garfield. Another famous painting painted by this artist, is "The signing of the Constitution" which is in the Capitol rotunda in Washington D.C.

PSi31. "Question Mark," Silson 1940****
Manufacturer Silson Inc., New York.
Designer Victor Silson.
Patent n° 120,174 Victor Silson, New York,
23rd April 1940, filed on 23rd February 1940.

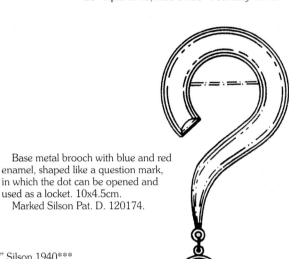

Base metal brooch with blue and red
enamel, shaped like a question mark,
in which the dot can be opened and
used as a locket. 10x4.5cm.
Marked Silson Pat. D. 120174.

PSi32. "Euzone," Silson 1940***
Manufacturer Silson Inc.
Designer Victor Silson.
Patent n° 124,401 Victor Silson,
New York, 31st December 1940,
filed on 7th December 1940.

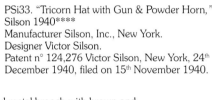

Gold-plated metal pin clip, white blue, red and sky-blue enamel, depicts
a 'euzone' in front of two Greek flags. 5x3.5cm.
Marked Silson PATENTED G.W.W.R. (Greek World War Relief).
The euzone – from the Greek Euzonos, light, ready, literally "he who
has a nice waist" – with his characteristic white uniform, skirt and embroi-
dered waistcoat, is the symbol of the Greek Army. Today the euzones
form the Head-of-State Guards, and also guard the monument dedicated
to soldiers who died in the War which stands in front of the Parliament building in Athens. The brooch was promoted by The Greek War Relief Association
to support the effort made by Greece during the War.

PSi33. "Tricorn Hat with Gun & Powder Horn,"
Silson 1940****
Manufacturer Silson, Inc., New York.
Designer Victor Silson.
Patent n° 124,276 Victor Silson, New York, 24th
December 1940, filed on 15th November 1940.

Gold-plated metal brooch with brown and
blue enamel, depicting a tricorn hat, a gun with
attached bayonet and a horn for gun powder hung
on a chain. 10x5.5cm.
Marked Silson Patented.
This is the first of a series of designs patented by
Victor Silson and dedicated to subjects from the
American War of Independence, on the surge of
patriotic feeling inspired by the war in Europe. In
addition to this item, the series includes the "Boston
Tea Party" (PSi34.), the "Declaration of Independence" (des. n° 124,416 of 31st December 1940), a
town crier (des. n° 124,417 of 31st December 1940), a cannon (des.
n° 124,984 of 4th February 1941), a "Sakem" (des. n° 125,044 of
4th February 1941).

PSi34. "Boston Tea Party," Silson 1940*****
Manufacturer Silson Inc. New York
Designer Victor Silson.
Patent n° 124,277 Victor Silson, New York, 24th
December 1940, filed on 15th November 1940.

Gold-plated metal pin clip, with black, white and red enamel, depicting the head of a staring Mohawk redskin, with a three-master and a box with TEA written on it hanging on chains. 7.8x4.3cm.
Marked Silson Patented.
The decision taken by the British Parliament to tax the American colonies (Stamp Act of 1765 and Thompson Act of 1767) had caused protests and disorders culminating on 5th March 1770 in the so-called "Boston Massacre," when British troops shot at a protesting crowd, killing five Americans.
Taxes were subsequently reduced, however the tax on tea remained and, moreover, in 1773, the British Parliament assigned the exclusive right to import and sell tea in the colonies to the British East India Company, causing a further price increase. In November 1773 some ships arrived in the Boston harbor loaded with tea and Governor Huntchinson put pressure on the local merchants to buy it but they refused to purchase it. On the night of 16th December, about seven thousand rebels, met together at Samuel Adams' invitation and moved towards the harbor declaring "Tonight Boston Harbor is a tea-pot". Fifty men dressed up as Mohawks, boarded the ships and threw 342 chests of tea into the sea. The episode became immediately famous as the "Boston Tea Party".

PSi35. "Panoplia," Silson 1940***
Manufacturer Silson Inc., New York.
Designer Victor Silson.
Patent n° 124,116 Victor Silson, New York, 17th
December 1940, filed on 13th November 1940.

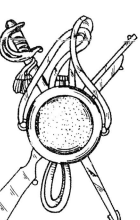

Gold-plated metal brooch with black, red and brown enamel, depicting panoply including a sword, a gun and a sash. The center of the brooch can be opened to hold a picture. 6.5x4.5cm.
Marked Silson Patented.

PSi36. "Propeller," Silson 1940***
Manufacturer Silson, Inc., New York.
Designer Victor Silson.
Patent n° 124,115 Victor Silson, New York, 17th
December 1940, filed on 13th November 1940.

Gold-plated metal brooch, with black and red enamel, of an airplane propeller. The center can be opened to hold a picture. 9.8x3.3cm.
Marked Silson Patented.

PAC37. "British War Relief," Accessocraft 1940 ****
Manufacturer Accessocraft Products Corp.
Designer Robert R. Appleby.
Patent n° 123,071 Robert R. Appleby, Pelham, NY., assignor
for one-half to The British War Relief Society, Inc., New York,
NY., a corporation of District of Columbia, and one-half to
Bundles for Britain, New York, NY., a corporation of New
York, 15th October, 1940, filed on 11th July 1940.

Gold-plated metal badge (brooch), red, white and blue enamel, depicting a shield with the British Crown and Lion and the motto "Dieu et
mon Droit," laid on a double-ribbon with the colors of the British
flag. 4.5x4cm.
Marked Official B.W.R.S. and BB by Accessocraft U.S.
Patent no. 123071.
WWD, 28th June 1940, featured the brooch, inform-
ing its readers that the British War Relief Society, Inc.,
and Bundles for Britain Inc., would receive 40% of the
sales profits. The brooch was also printed on the cover
of Town & Country, January 1943, (s. Psi25.). The
same design was used for many other objects made by
B.W.R.S. and B.B. such as tie-pins, plates and glasses
made by Copeland Spode of London, letter openers,
thanksgiving cards, boxes of matches, compacts and
cigarette cases etc.
The same design but with a red crown, and the white
Greek Cross, symbolizing the white and blue of the Greek flag,
was used by Accessocraft for the brooch made by the Greek
War Relief Association, Inc.

PU38. "Production Award," 1942**
Manufacturer unknown for US Army & Navy.
Patent n° 134,959 William S. Knudsen, USA Army, Washington, D.C.,
2nd February 1943, filed on 11th November 1942, assignor to the USA of
America as represented by the secretary of war.

Rhodium-plated sterling barrette brooch with red, blue and white enamel,
depicting the American flag with the letter E inscribed in the center, in a laurel
wreath. 3x1.2cm.
Marked Army – Navy Production Award Sterling.
In 1942, to reward companies and workers (especially women) engaged in
war production, this badge with an E for "Excellence" was created. The design
was conceived, and might have been designed, by William Signius Knudsen,
the Director of War Production for the Department of War with the rank of
Lieutenant General.
The badge rewarded excellence in production and was highly coveted by
companies, which advertised this award in the press, and by workers, who proudly wore it on their
work- and everyday clothes. An example is offered in the most famous portrait of "Rosie the Riveter," the one designed
by Norman Rockwell for the cover of the Saturday Evening Post of 20th May 1943. In this picture Rosie is wearing the
production award on her coveralls.
The badge was sent in an envelope with its picture on it and the recommendation "don't open this envelope 'til…" the
day of the official awarding ceremony. A certificate stating the reason for the award was also enclosed. Companies were
also awarded a flag with the symbol, that they could raise on their plant.
William Signius Knudsen (25/3/1879-27/4/1948) was born in Denmark and emigrated to the United States in 1900.
There he made a brilliant career in industry, which culminated with his appointment as president of General Motors in
1937.
In 1940, upon President Roosevelt's request, he joined the "Advisory Commission to the Council of National Defense". In 1941 he was appointed General Manager of the Production Management Office and, in 1943, he became
Director of War Production in the Department of War, with the rank of lieutenant general. In 1944 he became responsible for the Air Technical Service Commission.
In 1945, since production was proceeding smoothly, Knudsen gave up his appointment and went back to the Board
of Directors of General Motors. He died on 27th April 1948.

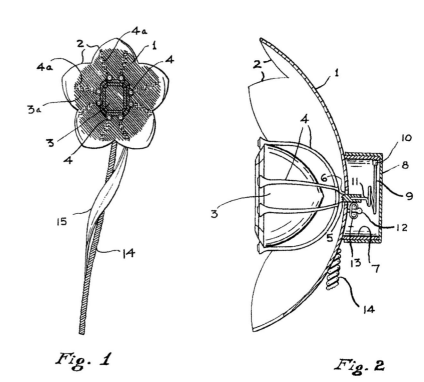

*Fig. 1*                                    *Fig. 2*

PCar39. "Reflecting Star," Cartier 1940****
Manufacturer Cartier, Inc., New York.
Designer Edmond Foret.
Patent n° 2,220,442 Edmond Foret, New
York, 5th November, 1940, filed June 29th,
1940, assignor to Cartier, Inc., New York, a
corporation of New York.

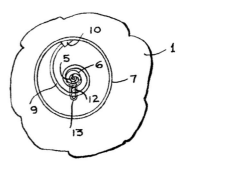

*Fig. 3*

Gold-plated metal pin clip of a concave star with a truncated cone at the center,
enveloped in the American star-spangled banner with white, red and blue enamel. The
concave surface of the star reflects the image of the flag with a mirror effect. At the top
is a circular gold-plated metal plaque with the American eagle in relief and the words:
"Friends of New York State Soldiers And Sailors". Diameter: 4.4cm, depth: 1.5cm.
   Marked CARTIER Us. Pat. 2-220-442.
   The pin is an modified version of Foret's patent of a flower with concave petals that
mirrored the image of a bud which had been applied to the center of the flower with
a spring, thereby creating both a mirror and a quivering effect. The flower had been
designed in two versions, with and without a stalk, and was meant to be a precious
jewel. In the modified version, the flower became a star and the truncated cone was
immovable. In 1940 Cartier, Inc., New York, made some non-precious patriotic jewels,
the proceeds from which were totally or partially contributed to various funds for the
financing of the war effort, especially of the European allies. One of these brooches
(*WWD, 28th June 1940*) is the "Coq Gaulois," the French cock, made of gold-plated
metal with white, red and blue enamel, sold by the American Committee for French
War Relief at $5.

PR40. "Atomic Bomb," Réja 1946****
   Manufacturer Réja Inc.
   Designer Solomon Finkelstein.
   Not patented.
      Gold-plated sterling brooch and earrings, rhodium-plated sterling on back, large
   drop-shape blue crystals and rhinestones with pendant. The brooch depicts the atomic
   bomb with shell-splinters that encircle the drop-crystal, symbolizing the explosion. The
   earrings reproduce the design of the pendant in miniature. Brooch: 5x5cm; earrings:
      2.5cm.
         Brooch marked Réja Sterling, earrings marked Réja Sterling Pat. Pend.
         The mark Pat. Pend. on the clip of the earrings refers to the patent of the
      clip mechanism and not to the design which is not patented.
            It was one of the most interesting novelties of the Spring 1946 collec-
         tion presented by *WWD, 11th January 1946*, with the name of "Atomic
      Bomb" given by Réja itself.
            The first atomic bomb was experimented on 16th July 1945 at the
      Alamogordo air base, New Mexico, (Trinity Test). On the 6th and 9th August
      1945 two atomic bombs called "Little Boy" and "Fat Man" were dropped.
   The first on Hiroshima from the bomber "Enola Gay," and the second on
   Nagasaki, dropped from the bomber "Bock's Car". Japan was forced by these
   events to surrender unconditionally (this was announced on 10th August and officially
came into force on 1st September 1945).

# BIBLIOGRAPHY

**NEWSPAPERS AND MAGAZINES**

*American Magazine*, passim.
*Fortune*, passim.
*Glamour*, 1935-1950.
Harpers' Bazaar, 1935-1950 & passim.
*Jewelers' Circular Keystone*, 1934-1950.
*Ladies' Home Journal*, 1935-1950.
*Life*, passim.
*Mademoiselle*, 1935-1950.
*Modern Plastic*, passim.
*The Saturday Evening Post*, passim.
*Town & Country*, 1935-1950.
*VF&CJ* (*Vintage, Fashion & Costume Jewelry*), passim.
*Vogue*, 1935-1950 & passim.
*Women's Wear Daily* (*WWD*), 1925-1975.

**BOOKS**

*A onor del falso,* cat. mostra, De Luca, Roma, 1993.
Aikins, Ronna Lee. *20th Century Costume Jewelry 1900-1980: Identification & Value Guide.* Collector Books, Paducah (Ky), 2004.
_____. *Brilliant Rhinestones Vintage and Contemporary.* Collector Books, Paducah (Ky), 2002.
Baker, Lillian. *Fifty Years of Collectible Fashion Jewelry, 1925-1975.* Collector Books, Paducah (Ky), 1986.
_____. *Twentieth Century Fashionable Plastic Jewelry.* Collector Books, Paducah (Ky), 1992.
Ball, Joanne Dubbs. *Costume Jewelers – The Golden Age of Design,* II ed. Schiffer Publishing Ltd., Atglen (Pa), 1997 (III ed. 2000).
_____. *Jewelry of the Stars – Creations of Joseff of Hollywood.* Schiffer Publishing Ltd., Westchester (Pa), 1991.
Ball, Joanne Dubbs & Dorothy Hehl Toren. *Masterpieces of Costume Jewelry.* Schiffer Publishing Ltd., Atglen (Pa), 1996.
Battle, Dee, & Alayne Lesser. *The Best of Bakelite.* Schiffer Publishing Ltd., Atglen (Pa), 1996.
Becker, Vivienne. *Fabulous Fakes.* Grafton Books, London, 1988; Amer. ed.: *Fabulous Costume Jewelry.* Schiffer Publishing Ltd., Atglen (Pa), 1993.
Behr, Caroline, & Tracy Tolkien. *Miller's Costume Jewelry: A Collector's Guide.* Mitchell Beazley, London, 2001.
Bennet., David, & Daniela Mascetti. *Understanding Jewellery.* Antique Collector's Club Ltd., 1989; Ital. ed.: *I Gioielli.* Fabbri, Milano, 1991.
Brown, Marcia. *Unsigned Beauties of Costume Jewelry.* Collector Books, Paducah (Ky), 2000.

_____. *Diamond Anniversary – Gene Verri's story.* Vintage, Fashion & Costume Jewelry, Glen Oaks (NY), Vol. 11 N° 1, 2001.
_____. *Signed Beauties of Costume Jewelry,* Vol. I, 2002; Vol. II, 2004. Collector Books, Paducah (Ky).
_____. *Coro Jewelry.* Collector Books, Paducah (Ky), 2005.
Brunialti, Roberto, & Carla Ginelli Brunialti. *American Costume Jewelry 1935-1950.* Mazzotta, Milano, 1997.
_____. *Tribute to America.* Edita, Milano, 2002.
Burkholz, Matthew L., & Linda Lichtenberg Kaplan. *Copper Art Jewelry.* Schiffer Publishing Ltd., West Chester (Pa), 1992 (II ed. 1997).
Cannizzaro, Maria Teresa. *Brillanti Illusioni.* Dives edizioni, Genova, 2002.
_____. *Bijoux Americani.* Federico Motta editore, Milano 2003.
Carrol, Julia C. *Collecting Costume Jewelry 101.* Collector Books, Paducah (Ky), 2004. II ed. 2007
_____. *Collecting Costume Jewelry 202.* Collector Books, Paducah (Ky), 2006
Cerval, Marguerite de, ed. *Dictionnaire international du Bijou.* Editions du Regard, Paris, 1998.
Cohen, Marion. *Costume Jewelry Variations.* Krause Publications, Iola (Wi), 2003.
Davidov, Corinne, & Ginny Redington Dawes. *The Bakelite Jewelry Book.* Abbeville Press Inc., New York, 1988; Ital. ed.: *Bijoux di un'Epoca – Bachelite & C.* Idea Libri, Milano, 1989.
Dolan, Maryanne. *Collecting Rhinestone & Colored Jewelry,* III ed. Books Americana Inc., Florence (Al), 1993, IV ed. 1998, Krause Publications, Paducah (Ky).
Edeen, Karen, L. *Vintage Costume Jewelry for Investment and Casual Wear.* Collector Books, Paducah (Ky), 2002.
Ettinger, Roseann. *Popular Jewelry, 1840-1940.* Schiffer Publishing Ltd., Westchester (Pa), 1990 (rev. ed. 2000).
_____. *Forties & Fifties Popular Jewelry.* Schiffer Publishing Ltd., Atglen (Pa), 1994 (III ed. 2003).
_____. *20th Century Plastic Jewelry.* Schiffer Publishing Ltd, Atglen (Pa), 2007
Farneti Cera, Deanna, (editor). *Gioie di Hollywood.* Venice Design Art Gallery, Venezia, 1987.
_____, (editor). *I Gioielli della Fantasia.* Idea Books, Milano, 1991; amer. ed.: *Jewels of Fantasy,* Abrams, New York, 1992.
_____. *Bijoux.* A. Mondadori, Milano, 1995; amer. ed.: *Amazing Gems,* Abrams, New York, 1996.
_____. *I Gioielli di Miriam Haskell,* Idea Books, Milano, 1997; amer. ed. *The Jewels of Miriam Haskell.* Antique Collector's Club, Easthampton (Ma) 1997.

Flood Kathy. *Warmans' Costume Jewelry Figurals*. Krause Publications, Iola (Wi), 2006.

Gabardi, Melissa. *Les Bijoux de l'Art Déco aux années '40*. Les Editions de l'Amateur, Paris, 1986.

———. *Gioielli anni '40*, III ed. Giorgio Mondadori & Associati, Milano, 1988.

———. *Gioielli anni '50*. Giorgio Mondadori & Associati, Milano, 1986.

Gordon, Angie. *Twentieth Century Costume Jewelry*. Adasia International, Hong Kong, 1990.

Gordon, Cathy, & Sheila Pamfiloff. *Miriam Haskell Jewelry*. Schiffer Publishing, Atglen (PA), 2004.

Greindl, Gabriele. *Strass*. Wilhelm Heyne, Muenchen, 1990; amer. ed.: *Gems of Costume Jewelry*, Abbeville Press Inc., New York, 1990.

Henzel, S. Sylvia. *Collectible Costume Jewelry*, II ed. Wallace – Homestead Book Company, Radnor (Pa), 1990 (III ed. 2003).

Kelley, Lyngerda, & Nancy N. Schiffer. *Costume Jewelry – The Great Pretenders*, III ed. Schiffer Publishing Ltd., Atglen (Pa), 1998 (IV ed. 2003).

———. *Plastic Jewelry*, Schiffer Publishing Ltd., West Chester (Pa), 1987 (III ed. 2000).

Leshner, Leigh. *Collecting Art Plastic Jewelry*. Krause Publications. Iola (Wi), 2005.

———. *Rhinestone Jewelry: A Price and Identification Guide*. Krause Publications, Iola (Wi), 2003

———. *Costume Jewelry, A Price and Identification Guide*. Krause Publications, Iola (Wi), 2004.

*Luxe et fantaisie Bijoux de la collection Barbara Berger*, Exhib. Cat. Norma Editions, Paris, 2003.

Lynnlee, J. L. *All That Glitters*. Schiffer Publishing Ltd., West Chester (Pa), 1986.

Mariotti, Gabriella. *All My Baskets*. Franco Maria Ricci, Milano, 1996.

Mauriés, Patrick. *Jewelry by Chanel*. Thames and Hudson Ltd., London, 1993.

McCall, Georgiana. *Hattie Carnegie Jewelry.*, Schiffer Publishing Ltd. Atglen (Pa), 2005.

Miller, Judith. *Costume Jewelry*. DK Publishing (Dorling Kindersley Ltd.), London, 2003.

———. *Costume Jewelry (Pocket Collectibles)*. DK Publishing (Dorling Kindersley Ltd.), London 2007.

Miller, Florence, & Patrick Segal. *Costume Jewelry for Haute Couture*. Vendome Press, New York, 2006

Miners, Steven, & Tracy Tolkien. *Costume Jewelry: How to Compare & Value*. Mitchell Beazley, London, 2003.

Moro, Ginger. *European Designer Jewelry*. Schiffer Publishing Ltd., Atglen (Pa), 1995.

Mulvagh, Jane. *Costume Jewelry in Vogue*. Thames and Hudson Ltd., London, 1988.

Pitman Ann M. *Inside the Jewelry Box A Collector's Guide to Costume Jewelry Identification and Values*. Collector Books, Paducah (Ky), 2004.

———. *Inside the Jewelry Box Vol. 2*. Collector Books, Paducah (Ky), 2007.

Rainwater, Dorothy Thornton. *American Jewelry Manufacturers*. Schiffer Publishing Ltd., West Chester (Pa), 1988.

Rezazadeh, Fred. *Costume Jewelry*. Collector Books, Paducah (Ky), 1998.

Rizzoli Eleuteri, Lodovica, (editor). *Gioielli del Novecento*. Electa, Milano, 1992.

Romero, Christie. *Warman's Jewelry*. Wallace – Homestead Book Company, Radnor (Pa), 1995 (II ed. 1998).

———. *Warman's Jewelry*, III ed. Krause Publications, Iola (Wi), 2002

Rudoe, Judy. *Cartier 1900-1939*. British Museum Press, London, 1997.

Russel, Lynn Ann, & Sandy Fichtner. *Rainbow of Rhinestone Jewelry*. Schiffer Publishing Ltd., Atglen (Pa), 1996.

Sallee, Lynn. *Old Costume Jewelry 1870-1945*. Books Americana, Ltd., Florence (Al), 1979.

Salsbury, Dave & Lee. *ABCs of Costume Jewelry*. Schiffer Publishing Ltd., Atglen (Pa) 2003.

Shields, Jody. *All That Glitters*. Rizzoli International Publications Inc., New York, 1987.

Schiffer, Nancy N., *The Best of Costume Jewelry*, III ed. Schiffer Publishing Ltd., Atglen (Pa), 1999.

———. *Costume Jewelry – The Fun of Collecting*, III ed. Schiffer Publishing Ltd., Atglen (Pa), 2001.

———. *Fun Jewelry*. Schiffer Publishing Ltd., Westchester (Pa), 1991 (III ed. 2003).

———. *Rhinestones!* Schiffer Publishing Ltd., Atglen (Pa), 1993 (IV ed. 2003).

Simonds, Cherri. *Collectible Costume Jewelry*. Collector Books, Paducah (Ky), 1997.

Simons Miller, Harrice. *Costume Jewelry*, I ed.. House of Collectibles, New York, 1990.

———. *Costume Jewelry*, II ed. Avon Books, New York, 1994.

———. *Official Price Guide to Costume Jewelry*, III ed. House of Collectibles, New York, 2002.

Snider, Nick. *Sweetheart Jewelry and Collectibles*. Schiffer Publishing Ltd., Atglen (Pa), 1995.

Sommer, Elyse. *Contemp Costume Jewelry*. Random House Value Publishing, New York, 1988.

Stringfield, Dotty. *Three Neapolitan Princes and the Legacy of Pennino*, Vintage, Fashion & Costume Jewelry, Glen Oaks (NY), Vol. 16, N° 1, 2006

Tanenbaum, Carole. *Fabulous Fakes A Passion for Vintage*. Artisan, New York, 2006.

Tolkien, Tracy, & Henrietta Wilkinson. *A Collector's Guide to Costume Jewelry*. Thames and Hudson, London, 1997.

Tollemache, Nick & Linde. *The Designs of Ruth Kamke*. Vintage, Fashion & Costume Jewelry, Glen Oaks (NY), Vol. 10, N° 1, 2000.

———. *The Costume Jewelry of Marcel and Sandra Boucher*. Vintage, Fashion & Costume Jewelry, Glen Oaks (NY), Vol. 9 N° 2, 2000

Van Hoover, Cheri. *Walter Lampl: Unusual ... As Usual*. Vintage, Fashion & Costume Jewelry, Glen Oaks (NY), Vol. 14, N° 1, 2004.

Villoresi, Simonetta. *Bagliori & Colori*. Loggia de' Lanzi Srl., Firenze, 1994.

Whitson, Sandra J., & Nancy N. Schiffer. *Star Spangled Jewelry*. Schiffer Publishing Ltd., Atglen (Pa), 2007.

# INDEX OF NAMES AND COMPANIES